WIGAN PIER
REVISITED

Poverty and Politics in the Eighties

Beatrix Campbell

Published by Virago Press Limited 1984
41 William IV Street, London WC2N 4DB

Reprinted 1984, 1985

British Library Cataloguing in Publication Data

Campbell, Beatrix
    Wigan Pier revisited
    1. Great Britain – Social conditions –
    20th century
    I. Title
    942.8′085′8   HN385

ISBN 0-86068-417-2

Typeset by Leaper & Gard Ltd, Bristol
Printed in Great Britain by The Anchor Press,
Tiptree, Essex

To Catharina Johanna Lorier Barnes
and James William Barnes
who set me on the road

Beatrix Campbell was born in the winter of 1947, the oldest of two children. Her mother came from Holland, and worked as a nurse in a psychiatric hospital, where she was a trade unionist for over 20 years. Her father, a Cumbrian, worked as a manual labourer most of his life before qualifying at night-school as an engineer and becoming a teacher. He has had a lifelong commitment to revolutionary politics. When Beatrix Campbell was fourteen she joined the CND Aldermaston march and became a communist. After leaving school she sought her fortune in London. She worked for ten years on the Morning Star and from 1979 was a news reporter on the London magazine Time Out, leaving at the end of a long occupation and strike in 1981 to defend equal pay for all and workers' right to consultation over investment. She then joined the majority of the Time Out staff in setting up the successful, co-operatively-owned magazine City Limits, where she still works, as a reporter. After an initial resistance to women's liberation, it became from 1970 one of the organising principles of her life. During the last ten years she has worked for socialist-feminist writing and speaking about sexual politics and a feminist approach to trade unionism and economic strategy. She was a founder member of the women's liberation journal Red Rag, set up in 1971, and has contributed to several feminist and socialist anthologies, and, with Anna Coote, she authored the bestselling book Sweet Freedom. She lives in London.

Cover:

New Romantics turn out for the Futurist night at Wigan's Pier Nightclub, winter 1983: Sue Clarke, 18, unemployed; Karen Sharples, 18, unemployed; Diane Grundy, 19, unemployed; Maria Harte, 18, bank worker; Karen Ashurst, 18, student.

Photographed by Gloria Chalmers.

Contents

List of Illustrations

Some of the 200 trade unionists who marched through Hammersmith, London, to protest at health service cuts, September 1979 (by kind permission of the *Morning Star*).

Acknowledgements

During the months I spent away from home, I was looked after by these people who gave me their homes and their help: Helen Todd, her son John and Carol Mason; Tony McNally, Ruth Longoni and their daughter Rebecca, Susan Green and her children Gareth, Justin and Rachel; Kath Kennedy and her daughter Heather, and Val Walters; Pat and Mike Devine.

Hundreds of people helped make connections and gave me their time and their talk. Here are some of them: Alexis Maddison, Mary Miller, Kath Monkhouse, Pervez Akhtar, Abdul Latif, Wayne Jessop, Paul Hartley, Mary Appleton, Abdul Tariq, Maggie Mound, Jennie Owen, Tony Carty, Peter Callaghan, Ronnie Queen, Jennie Scott, Rob Clay, Dick Copeland, Ken Ternant, Immelda Jones, Lesley, Iris, Caroline and Carl, Colin Anderson, Hilary Armstrong, Ivy Spry, Taxi Bhakta, Meg Robertson, Harriet Vyse, Doris Small, Connie Nelson, Dave Hopper, Eddie McCluskie, Dave Edwards, Tamar Edwards, Val Millman, Rona Hazell, Simon Frith, Gill Frith, George Hodgkinson, Bill Warman, Lorna Bridges, Shamar Khan, John Fisher, Lloyd Joseph, Jackson Jones, Harry Mellon, Leslie Barefoot, Ann Green, Margery, Margaret, Angela Konyk, Dorothy Booker, Brenda Wilson, Helen Charlesworth, Jean Edge, Dot Stephenson, Lena Jones, Jean Blackburn, Mark Hebert, Mandy Bryce, Karen Allan, Maureen Buck, Lillian James, Hyacinth George, Harry Hyde, Enid Hyde, Jean Miller, Frank Watters, Bob Smith, Colin Hill, Alan Thomas, Peter Mays, Nell Disley, Bill Disley, Amanda Patterson, Keith

Heseltine, Dennis Brears, Alan Kaye, Paul Colk, Ishtiaq Abbasi, Margaret Howard and her friends Harry and Lawrence, Angela Greenwood, Julie Breslin, Joe Breslin, Gwen Topless, Mikhaela Savage, Valerie Lawrence, Janice Thackeray, Caroline Swain, Alicia Winston, Doris Askham, Ken Curran, Joyce Strawford, Brenda Haywood, Ruth Steinberg, Ilyas Khan, Barry Carpenter, Keith Brooks, Pat Ryan, Kate Richards, Cathy Burke, John Hosey, Emily Wallace, Wendy Rollins, Terry Rollins, Sid Turney, Kamla Granger, Harbhajaan Kaar, Mr and Mrs Kingham, James Hinton, Philip McGuinness, Derek Meecham, Barry, Nikki and their friends Louise, Andy, Lill, Jim, John Meecham, Peggy Meecham, Bill Fernie, Abdul Shamir, Edith Vincent, Geralyn McGarry, Angela Cadaxa, Margaret Elliott, Ann Pratt, Harry Mitchell, John Barnes, Linda Knox, Ronald Pratt, Judith Quiggin, Sue Watts, Violet Tosh, Lizzie and Alan, Dorothy and Richard, Pat Downs, Ken Granger, Carol Hayden, Martha Walker, Anna Bhakshi, Pete McLaren, Polly Smith, Veronica McGarry, Jim McGarry, Panna Joban Putra, Lorraine O'Reilly, Pam Horner, Lesley Jonas, Fred Micklethwaite, Albert Ali, Maggie Rosher, Euphemia Smith, Gloria Marley, Joe Stephenson, Reg Walker, Cliff Wright, Jude Stoddart, John Bennington, Oliver Hadfield, Jean McCrindle, Frank Johnson, Betty Eaton, Ann Murphy and Carol, Sue Caveney, Steve Munby, Catherine Meredith, Tracy Hughes, Andy Atom, Jimmy Brown, Lisa O'Neill, Harry Ascroft, Annie Broxson, Alan Foster, Irene Foster, Marie Pembleton, Noreen Johnson, Kathleen Farnell, Agnes Lawton, Brian Lawton, Lawrence O'Brien, Derek Glynn, Julie Hart, Phyllis Hammond, Billy Dipper, Jack Orwin, John Robertson, Margaret Banks, Margaret Metcalfe, Dorothy, Elizabeth Golightly, Jenny Smart, Mary Burton, Denise Ward, Isabel Ward, Phoebe Pickett, Peter Kershaw, Ronnie Stafford, Debbie Embleton, Tracy Embleton, Leslie Robinson, Judy O'Neill, Jean Taylor, Tracy Harding, Joe Connor, Bert Robertson, Patrick Dodds, George Jackson, Gordon Ashbury, Aileen and Jim, Neil Parry, Les Carothers, Brian Atack, Maria Mitchell,

Pam Herbert, Sharon Delaney, Jane Hubbard, Susan Smith, Timothy Hopper, Barbara Hopper, Ian Smith, Winston Winter, Joban Ali, Frank Newbold, John Morrison, Lloyd Merriman, Webster Freeman, Sam Mason, Brian Higgit, Ken Higgit, Heather Jackson, Salem George, Mike Peel, Elena Leiven, Jean Broxson, Ian James, Joan Ramsbotham, Chrissie Farley, Nick Varney, John Lemon, Jane Woddis, Mr Gilmartin, Kay Hosey, Chloe Gerhardt, Bill Moore, Frances Moore, Colin Brogan, John Tolshard, Peggy Khan, Petal Brown, Trisha Davis, Lynne Amory, Elisabeth Gharial, Hilary Haigh, George Crowther, Angela Lloyd, Nell Myers.

I am grateful to the Estate of the late Sonia Brownell Orwell and Martin Secker & Warburg for permission to quote the extracts from *The Road to Wigan Pier.*

All or some parts of the draft manuscript were discussed by my friends Frankie Rickford and Rosalind Delmar, Virago's Ursula Owen, and Julia Vellacott (who was much more than an editor), and finally Margaret Bluman, who read and re-read *Wigan Pier Revisited* as it was written and re-written, who serviced me, took care of me and made my life lovely during the hard labour.

Setting Off

The road from Mandalay to Wigan Pier is a long one and the reasons for taking it are not immediately clear ... I wanted to see what mass unemployment is like at its worst, partly in order to see the most typical section of the English working class at close quarters. This was necessary to me as part of my approach to socialism, for before you can be sure whether you are genuinely in favour of socialism, you have got to decide whether things at present are tolerable or not tolerable, and you have got to take up a definite attitude on the terribly difficult question of class.... All my notions – notions of good or evil, of pleasant and unpleasant, of funny and serious, of ugly and beautiful are essentially *middle class* notions; my taste in books and food and clothes, my sense of honour, my table manners, my turns of speech, my accent, even the characteristic movements of my body, are the products of a special kind of upbringing and a special niche half way up the social hierarchy ... to get outside the class racket I have got to suppress not merely my private snobbishness, but most of my other tastes and prejudices as well. I have got to alter myself so completely that at the end I should hardly be recognisable as the same person.

George Orwell *The Road to Wigan Pier*

Nearly fifty years ago a posh, lanky young man packed his bags and made off into the undergrowth of England. Like a mountaineer conquering his own nightmare, he embarked on a two-month personal encounter with the unknown – the working class, who populated his childhood memories as a spectre of fear and loathing. He made a sentimental journey – it was a conjugation of the personal and the political – amidst the supposedly silent majority, the people excluded from politics who appeared as vagrants on the doorstep of democracy.

The man was George Orwell and he called his journey *The Road to Wigan Pier*. He'd done something like it before, he'd tried to purge himself of privilege by becoming a tramp, descending among the down-and-outs of London and Paris. This time he didn't pretend to be other than he was, a writer in exile from his own class, setting out to see with his own eyes the state of emergency among the Northern unemployed.

The journey made the prodigal a pilgrim. He never became one of the people, but he measured the material conditions of their existence and tried to take their side. And if he did not give the people, the sherpas who guided him through the terrain of industrial England, their own voice, the journey gave him a voice of his own.

As the thirties was our last great depression it commands comparison with the great depression of the eighties. Now, as then, the compass of consensus quivers and makes a dash for the Right. Economic and political crisis, the attacks on the working class and its expulsion from the political stage, incites inquiry. Its absence from politics excites ruling-class fears of riotous rebellion and confounds its allies' belief that suffering is the agent of revolution. Then, as now, the obvious lesson is that socialist will in England is ignited not by misery but by buoyancy, not pessimism but optimism. For sure, the eighties has already had its riots and can expect more, it has seen insurgent movements for progressive and peaceful life on earth, symbolised by the first women's embrace of the Greenham Common base in December 1982 which shifted popular consensus against the new generation of nuclear weapons. But neither has found an authentic expression in the institutions of representative democracy. The eighties remains an enigma – already we know more about the rise of the radical new Right than we do about the demise of the old Left.

The last great depression took Orwell out on to the road, on a quest for the meanings of mass poverty. He also used his chronicle for an assault on both the Right and the Left: *Wigan Pier* was as much a political tract as a travelogue, it was an indictment of the Right and an ultimatum to the Left. Then, as now, the paralysis of progressive institutional politics found its echo in the threat of world war – this time would be the last time. The crisis of the eighties occasions a return visit.

So in July 1982 I set off on a similar journey. Throughout Orwell's *Wigan Pier* you have a strong sense of him tramping around on foot. I took my bicycle on the train, with two packs slung on the back and a typewriter. I used wheels where Orwell went on foot. For six months until the end of 1982 I travelled in the Midlands, the North-East, South Yorkshire and Lancashire, staying in working-class homes in Coventry, Sunderland, Barnsley and Wigan.

The genre of the journey is rooted in the quest for the essence of England and Englishness. My journey was both inside and outside that tradition, because I learned that the quest for an essence dissolves the dynamic differences which describe the working class itself (aside from class differences which are one of the most apparent characteristics of England) – poor and unskilled from skilled, men from women, young from old, waged from wageless, organised from unorganised, black from white. Now more than ever England is a reluctantly cosmopolitan society, and it comes easy in England to subordinate the different experiences of sexes and nationalities to a single archetype. But that habit falsifies a description of England, which is multi-cultural, multi-racial and multi-coloured. This book is not an analysis of that anatomy. It is only a description of some working-class experiences of poverty and politics in cities visited by George Orwell in the 1930s. While following his route I have added two other cities, Sunderland and Coventry. Sunderland is in the Northern region which has endured industrial decline for

much of the twentieth century. Coventry is in the Midlands,
England's industrial eldorado. Coventry is a new town, with
the proverbial shopping precinct and housing estates on the
periphery which are rescued from an atmosphere of
impermanence only by their inhabitants' gardens. It is a car
town and it is a city of immigrants, white, brown and black:
Scots and Irish have staffed its militant shop stewards' movement, and the races came together in the city's wondrous
two-tone band, the Selector. I wanted to go to Sunderland
because it is in my own region, the far north. It is an old shipbuilding town, it once produced a massive proportion of
British vessels, but it has been in decline for decades. It was
only recently a town that offered waged work for women,
though much of that has disappeared in the past few years,
and it was never a town that invited black workers. It's a
white place, like Wigan which only seems to have a Black
population on Tuesday nights when the music from the
Wigan Pier nightclub's jazz-funk DJ draws in young Blacks
from as far as the Midlands to body-pop. Wigan was once a
coal and cotton town, now those industries are dead and it's
much like anywhere else, with a bit of light engineering and
service industries. Barnsley was a coal town and Sheffield a
steel town, like Rotherham. But South Yorkshire's old industrial staples are deserting it. Rotherham has an Asian
presence, but most of the places I visited are the old, white,
axis of the English working class, immunised from the input
of England's new nationalities. If I had followed a different
route through Bradford or Brixton the complexion of this
story would have transformed some of its objectives: whiteness and blackness would have encountered each other
dramatically.

Although this return to Wigan Pier is a northern journey,
it is not an analysis of the regional dimension of England's
decline – although clearly the feel of the crisis in Sunderland
bears no comparison with Surrey. Throughout my journey I
found myself saying, 'they're different countries, North and
South'. Now I think that was wrong and that the odd and
interesting thing is precisely the opposite: Sunderland and

Surrey are different and they are both England. Similarly, I have not specified the Englishness or whiteness of people in this book, nor the blackness of others. Usually only blackness is named, which constitutes the white majority as the norm. So I have, for the most part, named neither although wherever I was I sought a Black or Asian presence. The fact is that Orwell's route takes us through a largely white part of England.

The first question that arose in my mind was: what have I to do with Orwell? The answer: only a point of departure. Though nearly fifty years later I have followed a similar route to Orwell's, his book is all that we share. He was an upper-class old Etonian, a southern ex-colonial. I'm from the North, from the working class. Like him, I'm white, I'm a jobbing journalist; unlike him I'm a feminist. I grew up among the kind of communists and socialists who guided him into the working-class communities and who staff some of their struggles. Politics is to me what privilege was to him.

My journey into the hinterland of industrial England led me on a trek across familiar territory among familiar people. Nonetheless, as for Orwell, it was an adventure. For twenty years my life has been lived within the Left, and the companionship and creativity of many of the people I have met have changed me. Just as his political commitments exiled him from his own class, so my politics involve an awkward relationship with my own class. Why? For a start, it is a subordinate class, and being a socialist means surrendering a culture of subordination for self-determination. It is a relationship of commitment and estrangements which haunts many activists, not only in the cosmopolitan community of socialists in London, but within the Northern working class itself. And being a feminist puts a woman both inside and outside the mainstream of working-class politics, which are stewed in sexual prejudice and privilege. I began as the kind of feminist who said, 'It's not men, it's the system,' but this journey convinced me that men and masculinity, in their everyday, individual manifestations, constitute a systematic bloc of resistance to the women of their own community and

class. Both individual men and the political movements men
have made within the working class are culpable.

So, while committing me to my own class, my politics also
has its own critique of working-class life and institutions. But
unlike Orwell, my journey didn't make me repudiate my own
class – it did the opposite, it recuperated my class belonging.
And for that I'm grateful to those who peopled my journey.
The men and women I met often spoke of regret and loss –
not a nostalgia for the past, those glazed memories that
falsify the hard history of the working people by claiming
that the past was better. It wasn't really that. It was an
unnamed, unacknowledged loss of something that never was,
a kind of melancholy, a mourning for unspecified neglect, the
neglect of a socialism spoiled by superstition, subordination
and sexism. Yet they also speak of resilience and creative
intervention in life, particularly the women. Orwell wrote his
experiences of the working class by reference only to men.
Men still do this – they talk of men's struggles, movements
and characteristics as if they were writing about the whole
class. As a feminist I didn't invert their bad habits by only
talking to women – this book is about women *and* men,
though it takes the standpoint of women as its reference
point.

Orwell begins his book in the long and honourable
tradition of popular journalism – you don't stalk your
readers, you shock them. He delivers the wretched data of
life in an itinerants' lodging house. It's the worst you can
imagine, down and out in Wigan. If the lodging house was the
bottom line of men's poverty then, what is women's today?
No doubt an account of a hostel for the homeless would be
audacious and arresting, but would it be an authentic
scenario of life lived on the edge of *ordinary* extremity? What
makes *ordinary* women homeless? What typifies that extremity in our time? To answer this question I followed
Orwell's first metaphor for working-class poverty and asked
the question: what does intermittent itinerancy tell us about
the conditions that produce the poverty of women? So my
road back to Wigan Pier started in a refuge for battered

women, mostly mothers. In the seventies the women's movement exposed the prevalence of violence against women and
provided safe passage in the network of refuges which exist
in about a hundred cities. They exemplify a new tradition
among women which defies the conventional wisdom that
community spirit is dead and that the women's liberation
movement is middle class and marginal. The refuges
symbolise the renewal of militant self-help by working with
women in crisis at the point where their sex and class
oppression meet.

Those first few days of my adventure were very sad, partly
because of the temptation to identify with the pain present in
the refuge. Like the other women, I'd recently left my own
home because I couldn't carry on there any longer and I'd
been given safe spaces by friends with room to spare. It was
an act of creative destruction, but in those first few days at
the refuge what had seemed positive began to seem rootless
and resourceless. I felt poor, wandering around lavish
shopping precincts, counting pennies in supermarkets,
always feeling hungry, saving change for telephone calls,
counting my losses. In embarking on this journey, I'd put
myself into store again and set off; like the other women I
needed safety, I needed to be taken care of, to take care of
myself and now to take care of this journey. But what had
slipped from sight was that these women weren't victims,
they were survivors. Their stories weren't ones of passive
pain, but tales of active resistance – having somewhere to
run to, they'd got a grip of their own lives. And their resilience changed the tone of my whole project.

The women I met in the refuge, and others I met in the
first few weeks of my journey, stated their own investment in
this book: they didn't want to be objects observed, they
wanted to be its subjects. Late one night, talking in one of
their homes, one of them said, 'What's this book about,
anyway?' I said it was about how working-class women and
men live the recession. 'Is it going to be *for* us as well as
about us?' she asked. Her question remained with me
throughout the rest of the journey. For six months I lived in

the homes of working-class women, men and children. I spent the days and nights talking with tenants, trade unionists, blacks and whites, punks and skinheads, single parents and old-age pensioners, their neighbours, workmates and relatives – anybody I could lay my hands on. I'd return home and do all the usual things that keep your sense of yourself – eat, play around with children, do my washing, telephone my nearest and dearest, talk late into the night with my hosts, have fantasies, pleasure myself. And throughout the journey, the question asked by that woman in the beginning anchored the emphasis of this book, it shook a fist at the ghosts over my shoulder (because like most people I give to others the power to intimidate and censor from afar) and it forced me to make the chronicle accountable to its subjects.

On the Dole

Our unemployment allowances miserable though they are, are framed to suit a population with very high standards and not much notion of economy. If the unemployed learned to be better managers ... I fancy it would not be long before the dole was docked correspondingly.

George Orwell, *The Road to Wigan Pier*

Could you live on £1,300 a year?* It's less than the benefit you'd receive if you were an invalid or an old-age pensioner and you'd get more if you were a widow or a student.

Most of us probably think that the dole is what you live on when you're unemployed, a statutory right which was brought in to bury the hated means test of the 1930s. However, when the modern national insurance system was introduced in 1948 unemployment benefit was still not expected to be sufficient to maintain a wageless man with a wife and children; it was an arbitrary figure which could be topped up. Unemployment benefit is now £25 a week. £1,300 a year, for a single person. According to the government, it's a figure which isn't expected to bear any relation to the minimum cost of living. Not surprisingly, most of the unemployed don't live on it because they can't. With mass unemployment, means-tested supplementary benefit is the new mass benefit for the unemployed. When Peter Townsend

---

* The figures quoted here and throughout are for 1982-83.

and his army of researchers monitored low incomes in the sixties and seventies for their massive study, *Poverty in the United Kingdom* (Penguin, 1982), they found that about a quarter of the unemployed were drawing supplementary benefit. The proportion has now soared to two-thirds – DHSS figures for 1982 show that only a minority, 713,700, exist on the £25 a week unemployment benefit alone – 2,612,000 'top up' with supplementary benefit, and another 1,428,500 depend on supplementary benefit alone. (These include school leavers who've never had the chance to make National Insurance contributions toward unemployment benefit and the long-term unemployed whose unemployment benefit is exhausted after one year. It doesn't include the unregistered and unmeasured unemployed – women with men who have to maintain them or claim for them, and those whose dole is exhausted but who are disqualified from supplementary benefit because they live with wage-earners.)

There are no criteria specifying the minimum conditions of existence supposed to be covered by unemployment benefit, but parliamentary regulations define the basic resources of daily life to which people on supplementary benefit should be entitled:

Food, household fuel, the purchase, cleaning, repair and replacement of clothing and footwear, normal travel costs, weekly laundry costs, miscellaneous household articles, cleaning materials window-cleaning and replacement of small household goods (for example, crockery, cooking utensils, light bulbs), and leisure and amenity items such as television licences and rental, confectionary and tobacco.

I've never yet met a claimant who could afford a television licence. The Supplementary Benefit Commission also says claimants should be entitled to an income that 'enables them to participate in the life of the community'. They mean that as well as being fed and warm, claimants should be able to buy newspapers, visit relatives, retain membership of trade unions and churches, and be able to live in a way that 'ensures, so far as possible, that public officials, doctors, teachers, landlords and others treat them with courtesy due to every other member of the community'. These conditions of participation are impossible for anyone living on supplementary benefit.

Here are some of the weekly incomes and budgets of some of the people I met living on social security:

One man and woman in their early twenties living in Coventry with one child, mostly unemployed since leaving school, have a total income of £63, including £5.25 child benefit. Weekly bills total:

rent	£27.36
loan payment	£3.00
sheets and blankets club	£5.00
TV hire purchase	£2.00
electricity	£4.00
gas	£3.00
bike payments	£2.00
	£46.36

Their food bill averages £15 a week. Their average diet is toast and porridge for breakfast, nothing at mid-day (the child has school dinners), sandwiches or beans on toast at tea-time, cooked meals only at weekends, usually sausages or chicken and vegetables. Sometimes the woman gets vegetables from her father's garden. This is what she spent on her last three pairs of shoes: £3.99 in 1977, £9 in 1980 (when she was working) and £4.99 in 1982. She has never possessed boots or winter shoes: 'I can't afford closed-in shoes, so I always wear sandals and in the winter I just put on two pairs of socks.' She never buys a paper and never goes out for the evening.

A redundant fitter from the Coventry car industry in his mid-forties lives alone and receives £61.02 a fortnight. His regular commitments – rent, electricity, etc. – are £38.08 and 50p insurance. That leaves him £22.44 a fortnight for everything else. When I met him he'd just done his shopping for two weeks. It included forty cigarettes, a white sliced loaf, tea bags, two lamb chops, half a pound of liver, pork for Sunday dinner, two tins of peas, two pints of sterilised milk – 'Not because I like it, but because it lasts longer,' he said. He slapped a £10 note on the table: 'That's all that's left to last me the rest of the fortnight.' He can't pay the television licence and tosses up every week between washing powder, toothpaste or soap: 'I can only afford one at a time – personal hygiene is an expensive item.' He only ever puts the gas on half-way to the first mark on the knob and in the winter keeps the central heating down to sixty degrees: 'I sit with the blanket round me.' He can't afford hot water, except for twice a week when he puts on his immersion heater for a bath. His shoes are one size too big, cast-offs from a friend.

A woman I spoke to in Coventry lives with her two children and husband, had worked as a cashier, a canteen assistant, a barmaid and a bingo cashier until she was sacked for organising a union. They get £54 social security, plus £10.50 child benefit. This is her weekly expenditure:

rent	£21.78
electricity (plus arrears)	£12.50
gas	£1.00
club	£6.00
sheet man	£1.00
boots club	£1.00
	£43.28

This left about £17 to feed the four of them for a week. They spent £16.80 and had 20p left.

A Coventry couple with two children: she has never had a paid job, he worked until recently in a Birmingham car factory where his last take-home pay was £65. Their income from social security is £66 and of this £40.20 – £23 rent, £12 electricity and £5.20 gas – is taken off at source by the DHSS (Department of Health and Social Security). This includes contributions towards arrears – heating bills are high on their hard-to-heat council estate. This leaves £25.30 a week. The week I met them they had £2 left after shopping for food. A good day's diet is spaghetti bolognaise for tea. Bad days are beans on toast, biscuits, or 'some days we just don't eat'. Birthdays are their only nights out, remembered as they repay the debt incurred and relish the memory of being full up. Their neighbours are all on the dole and they all talk about food: 'I'll say to them you can't be starving on Wednesday because it's not Friday – giro day,' says their next-door neighbour. They save their child benefit and draw it monthly to help buy big items, like new jeans bought after the DHSS turned down his application for a clothing grant, and to pay for driving lessons – he's hoping to get a job as a driver.

Heating is regarded as a basic amenity. In the 1970s the fuel boards were pressured by the Labour government not to disconnect households with children providing they would co-operate in paying off their arrears. This was formalised in the Codes of Practice introduced in 1976.

A spate of fires in disconnected homes, culminating in the deaths of children in Sunderland, prompted Southwick Neighbourhood Action Project to carry out a survey of disconnections on an interwar estate of semi-detached houses recently modernised with gas fires, back boilers and central heating. Seventy per cent of the people living on the estate had no wage and depended on state benefits. There were few electricity disconnections, not surprising since heat and hot water were provided by gas, but nearly a fifth of the households surveyed had had their gas cut off. Among households with children under sixteen the figure rose to 20 per cent: Twelve per cent of households with children under five had been disconnected, but this rose to 43 per cent among households with children between twelve and sixteen. Nationally, electricity disconnections total over 91,000 and gas nearly 30,000 and according to Richard Berthoud's comprehensive study, *Fuel Debts and Hardship*, published by the Policy Studies Institute in 1981, about a third of dis-

connected customers have pre-school children. A woman
living with three little girls, the youngest still only a baby, on
Coventry's hard-to-heat Woodend estate had no electric light
for eleven months. 'At least it got me reading,' she said.
There was an armful of Mills and Boon love stories on the
mantelpiece bearing witness to nearly a year of quiet, no
television or radio, only romances by candlelight.

Tenants on the Platt Bridge estate in Wigan were paying
staggering heating bills for one- and two-bedroom maisonettes, culminating in bills of between £200 and £250 per
quarter in 1982. 'It took us a couple of years to persuade the
council that it was their fault not ours. They thought we
misused the system when actually it was expensive in the
first place and faulty,' said a middle-aged woman who lives
on the estate. She never uses the central heating system, only
turns on a single bar of her electric fire for about half an hour
and then off again for another half hour or so. I met many
tenants on similar estates who do the same thing – their
heating amounts to 'taking the nip out of the air' and putting
on cardigans to go into the bathroom or kitchen.

Poverty changes the meaning of key words – one person's
credit becomes another person's debt. Basic provision of
shelter, heat and light often consume more than half the total
income of unemployed claimants. This means that although
the supplementary benefit regulations say that claimants are
entitled to shelter and warmth, their benefits rarely measure
up to it. An unemployed Coventry couple, a clerk and a
carpenter with two children, live on £64.50 including child
benefit. Rent, electricity and gas take more than half –
£35.28. They had to take out a loan to pay their last fuel bill.
That's typical – a survey by the Child Poverty Action Group
and the Family Service Unit in 1981 found that 80 per cent
of people on state benefits borrow money to pay their housing
or fuel bills.

Many of the people I met also rely on loan companies and
clubs who scour the poorest housing estates to find their
neediest clients. They buy bedding, household equipment,
clothes, shoes – and money. 'The club men have a field day,'

said one of their clients in Coventry.

One came round and sold me sheets and then he offered me a loan. You think to yourself, yes I could get the kids shoes or pay the gas bill. The card you get from the man says that if you get into arrears you have to pay extra interest, but it doesn't say how much. So you end up paying double what you borrowed originally – it's happened to me. A bill comes in and along comes sugar daddy with a loan, you can't resist it. And you end up buying food with it.

Mass unemployment once again makes the means test a mass phenomenon. Despite the entitlements spelled out in the supplementary benefit regulations, many of them are subject to discretion. 'I applied for school uniform grants for the kids,' said an unemployed woman in Barnsley with three children. 'This bloke said, "Well, it depends on discretion, you're not entitled, you know, and it's not in my hands, my superior has to decide." So I said, "discretion! I am entitled!" But I didn't want to get too argumentative because it might have alienated him and I need his support.' A twenty-one-year-old mother of two small children in Coventry said, 'I told social security that the children's shoes were too small, but they wouldn't give us a grant. All I've got for myself is flip-flops. The DHSS suggested I save 25p a week for new shoes.' She has an outstanding fuel debt of £200. She lives on a council estate packed with redundant car workers and her husband is himself one of them. He was given his last – and only – pair of trousers on his birthday nearly a year earlier by his father. When they acquired holes he applied for a clothing grant. 'They told me that the trousers would need to be stolen from me to qualify. But they couldn't be because I never take them off.' Did they ever go to jumble sales? 'No.' I asked why not? 'Don't want to.' Why not? 'Can you imagine what people round here cast off?'

A young mother living in a damp flat with unheated bedrooms where the mould appears in charcoal blots across the wall, has a child who has suffered several bouts of pneumonia and now has chest convulsions. She wanted to keep her telephone for emergencies, but 'the DHSS said it was a luxury'. Another unemployed woman with an epileptic six-year-old couldn't pay her £33 telephone bill. 'I wanted to keep it because I didn't want to leave him while I went out to use the phone – assuming there's one round here that works, which I doubt,' she said. But the phone was cut off, the DHSS didn't regard it as a necessity. Welfare workers complain that discretion increasingly means 'No'. An advice centre in Sheffield which helps claimants apply for special needs entitlements, like bedding, said, 'We apply but we often have to take the DHSS to a tribunal to get them. We don't bother any more if we've not got a good chance of winning. It's important to take a case just to try, but we've never won such a case yet. Discretion has nothing to do with it any more.'

But what is happening now is worse than discretionary whim, it is an echo of the power of the means-test 'nark' of the 1930s who could make people sell their goods and chattels before qualifying for relief. Households in the Coventry area report that they are being subjected to intimidation reminiscent of this time. When a woman in her early thirties moved into her council flat she was still working, so she bought a fitted carpet and a freezer. Now she's unemployed and her husband has tuberculosis and they live on supplementary benefit with their two children. When they applied for help with arrears, 'The DHSS told me to sell some of the furniture or the telly. They said sell the freezer and you don't need a fitted carpet.' Another couple living on total state benefits of £64 had acquired everything they own at least second-hand except for a coffee table, bedding and clothes bought through a tally man. Social security officials suggested that they sell some of their furniture and the television before receiving help. This contradicts the spirit of the supplementary benefit regulations and suggests that the means test is being enforced with new vigour.

Weekly budgets don't tell life stories. If you had to live on £25 a week you could, for a while. But sooner or later it turns into a crisis of resources – practical, personal and political.

When you've lived on subsistence for two years what do you do when your shoes wear out, when you get a £100 fuel bill, when the washing machine breaks down, when a pair of children's shoes cost you more than you'd spend on your own? Poverty makes economy impossible, not because the poor are improvident but because economy is always a matter of scale – bulk buying demands bulk incomes. The poor don't possess *The Pauper's Cook Book* or *Good Food on a Budget* or magazine pull-outs of cheap casseroles – for a start, a 'pauper's' cuisine is always more expensive than beans on toast and if you're a pauper you can't buy books and magazines anyhow. You can't have an overdraft and you may not even have a bank account.

Weekly budgets also don't describe what *isn't* bought – a television licence, a holiday, a night out, trips to the swimming baths, roller skates, the *Radio Times*, a pound of plums. Common fantasy that a spell on the dole is the change that's as good as a rest assumes that the pastimes of the poor are the weekend pleasures of the employed – drinking, fishing, playing with cars, playing pool, playing bingo, going to the cinema. But none of this is possible on the dole; even going to the park carries the risk of unexpected expenditures – ice creams and bus fares back. The resources for participation in the life of the community – promised as an entitlement by the Supplementary Benefit Commission – disintegrate. An unemployed couple I met in Coventry cannot visit their parents on the other side of town – at £2.88 the cost is prohibitive. A whole family employed in the Midlands engineering industry have been living on supplementary benefit for two years: the grandparents in their mid-40s, two married sons with children and a teenager living at home. The only people they ever see are each other. People can't keep telephones, they can't indulge in the little white collar thefts of stamps, stationery and phone calls from work, they can't buy newspapers or maintain friendships. My dad tells me he met a friend of his aged 59, unemployed, who'd sold his house, car, video and now his wife is in hospital after taking an overdose. They can't claim compensation from the government for that. Life on the dole becomes a very little life.

Like pleasure, politics costs money. The poor are collectively starved of political resources and support. The cult of self-help, usually visited upon the poor, actually belongs not to the poor but to participants *in* society, the respectable, self-helping, self-respecting institutions of *organised* communities and classes. The very fact of unemployment cuts the wageless off from the resources of the waged working class and its labour movement. They aren't just individually unequal, therefore, they have unequal access to the resources of organisation. Political organisations have secretaries and stationery, offices and officials, telephones, minutes, records, xerox machines, bulletins, handbooks, pension funds and subscriptions – all of which amount to the means of making decisions and developing self-determination. Time the unemployed have got, money they haven't. But to be a political person, to intervene in life, you need to have these minimum resources – telephones, stamps, stationery, posters and printing presses – and the price of a bus fare and a pint after a meeting. An unemployed engineer in Coventry, who joined the Labour Party after being made redundant, walks to all his meetings and reckons he wears out his shoes three times faster than when he was working. He goes to the meetings but he can't stay behind afterwards for the real meeting – in the pub.

Everyone but the columnists of the *Daily Mail* and the *Daily Express* knows that the dole isn't enough to live on and asks the rhetorical question, 'How do people manage?' The answer is that they can't. But that knowledge has been buried in the war of words which has accompanied mass unemployment. In the 1930s the words 'means test' was a curse, fuelling the resistance against it both among the unemployed and some of its administrators. Its renaissance with the new wave of unemployment has been echoed by a new contest of concepts. And this time the poor are losing – the notion of 'scrounger' has been mobilised as a new scourge against them, not only successfully legitimating the dole as the lowest of low benefits, but also its actual *reduction* (through the abolition of earnings-related benefit in 1981) and the enforced dependence on the means-tested supplementary benefit. And now the Thatcher government threatens *further* reductions. Just as the government of the 1930s defended cuts in relief and the expulsion of categories of claimants on grounds of costs to the country, so the Thatcher regime has conquered popular concern with poverty by a populist counterattack. The scourge of scroungerism has converted the unemployed into the poor, the poor into the undeserving poor and sympathy into suspicion. The demands of the unemployed workers' movement of the 1930s had an unexpected radicalism, not because people then were more 'political', but because the unemployed were able to make their *own* measure of an income. Now it seems unthinkable to ask the question: *why* are the unemployed so poor? *Why* are the unemployed poorer than students, or the sick, or widows or old-age pensioners?

Because the unemployed don't have their own political resources, there is no popular campaigning focus for the minimum income needed for participation in the life of a community. There is a wilful scorn for the problem on the Right, and a wilful fantasy on the Left that the worse it gets the better it gets – the people will rise in spontaneous combustion the more intense is their misery. You hear it all the time, as Thatcherism makes its long march against the historical inevitability of socialism. The labour movement bewitched by the enemy, bothered and bewildered by the 'passivity' of the people, waits like Micawber for something to turn up.

The Witchhunt

The Means Test is very strictly enforced, and you are liable to
be refused relief at the slightest hint that you are getting money
from another source.

George Orwell, *The Road to Wigan Pier*

The weary DHSS staff of respectable old Oxford were
relieved of certain unpleasant duties in the early autumn of
1982 when a 200-strong squad of police mopped up
unsuspecting itinerants said to have defrauded the welfare
state by allegedly drawing social security for rent when they
were sleeping rough. This was a supposed £1½ million
racket. It was the consummation of a campaign waged for
five or six years to change the acceptable face of the
unemployed into the unacceptable face of the scrounger. All
the better that the operation rehabilitated the credibility of
the police who'd been having a bad press in the early years of
the decade. Here was the strong arm of the law moving in
where the seemingly soft-hearted and soft-headed welfare
state feared to tread, the unwitting accomplice in benefit
banditry.

The campaign against scroungers began in the mid-seventies when the Labour government inaugurated the recession
with public spending cuts and implicated the poor in the
nation's plight by refusing to immunise them against the
economic squeeze. This rendered all claimants potential
suspects. Special squads were set up in 1976 against what
the *Daily Mirror* called 'Britain's army of dole queue

swindlers'. The *Daily Telegraph* joined in, fulminating against the welfare state's profligate fanatics, spendthrifts of the taxpayer's money. The campaign in the popular press mobilised a backlash against the very idea of the welfare state itself. Any evidence of the growing army of unemployed being anything other than paupers – smoking cigarettes, having holidays, playing bingo, having children – was regarded as, if not illegal, then certainly improper.

Scroungerphobia was monitored by two researchers, Peter Golding and Sue Middleton, who reproduced in *New Society* one of the *Daily Mail*'s diatribes against 'Scroungers by the Sea' in 1977: 'The seaside social security offices are thick with subsidised cigarette smoke, the smell of alcohol paid for by the state and the smugly tanned faces of leeches feeding off the hard-working, ordinary, silent majority.' Golding and Middleton argued that the 'focusing of moral outrage on items like this does as much to create concern as to reflect it.' A plague was diagnosed, the symptom was the scrounger, the cause was the state's slush fund and the victim was the people. At a stroke, claimant became synonymous with criminal. The campaign crossed class boundaries and created an apparent unity of interest between taxpayers and workers held to ransom by skivers supported by a soft state. The Labour Party itself, in sponsoring vigilante sleuths within the social security system, was implicated in this political realignment of wage-earners against the wageless. Scroungers, like Reds, became the enemy within, rootless, lawless and workless, a ragged spectre scavenging among the respectable citizenry.

Even before the witchhunt began, one million eligible claimants were estimated to have failed to collect £240 million in supplementary benefits to which they were entitled. By the end of the decade, unclaimed supplementary benefit reached £410 million. Of the 4,190,000 households entitled to rent rebates only 2,930,000 received them.

There are special targets of scroungerphobia – homeless men and single mothers. Both are under the greatest attack from a government committed to drawing back from the welfare state. This it does by minimising public provision of childcare, child benefit, housing and jobs and maximising the private responsibility of men for dependent women and children. These two categories, single mothers and homeless men, disturb accepted notions of normal male and female roles. Unemployment leaves many men without the means of providing for women and children, and increasing divorce and separation is symptomatic of a growing instability in sexual relationships between men and women. More and more women are going it alone, and men are rendered homeless by housing allocation policies which do not account for the needs of the single and childless. It is single mothers and homeless men who are subject to the most intense state scrutiny because they are both in greatest need of state support and represent the greatest challenge to 'normal' masculinity and femininity within the family. 'Responsible' men are men with responsibilities, homes, children and wives, and that moral code is written into social security regulations to enforce responsibility for women and children as the economic essence of masculinity. The very idea of dependency is incompatible with masculinity. Former Social Security Secretary Patrick Jenkin alluded to this when he cut the benefit to which homeless men were entitled on the grounds that people would be aggrieved by these itinerants getting 'more actual cash in hand by being homeless (sometimes by choice) than by contributing toward the cost of a household and accepting the attendant responsibilities.'*

The Oxford saga began when a local reporter investigating landlords who appeared to be cheating the DHSS was taken off the case. The next thing he knew, the Thames Valley Police were calling the landlords as *prosecution* witnesses in 'Operation Major' – dubbed 'The Sting' by a tabloid news-

---

* Quoted in Ros Franey's excellent investigation of the Oxford affair, *Poor Law*, published in 1983 by CHAR, the single homeless campaign together with the Child Poverty Action Group, Claimants' Defence Committee, National Association of Probation Officers and the National Council for Civil Liberties.

paper – after the police had arrested hundreds of their tenants (all claimants) for allegedly defrauding the DHSS, by supposedly drawing social security to pay their rent when they were actually not paying any.

It seems that the Oxford DHSS management collaborated with the police. Their own staff had become acutely discontented – they were understaffed and overworked, and after the hype was all over Oxford DHSS was closed down by a strike lasting two months against understaffing. The DHSS had known the landlords were overcrowding their hostels, sometimes cramming four or six men in a room, and some were even lodged in an asbestos shed. Conditions were gross. A local charity worker visited one of the hostels and found four old men sleeping in a basement 'using a large baked bean tin as a chamber pot'. Residents complained that sometimes they'd come home to find someone else sleeping in their bed. One of the landlords was reckoned to make £400,000 a year from the DHSS. It appeared that they encouraged the men not to live there, but to claim social security as if they were. The landlords took a cut of their social security in exchange for verifying their tenancy. The incentive for the men was that as homeless itinerants their social security would be under £20 a week. Under this transaction they collected both rent and other money. Sleeping rough in the open air that summer seemed no worse than sleeping rough inside. Few people seemed to care about the conditions of the hostels or the chronic shortage of appropriate accommodation which rendered these men vagrants. The victims could be blamed and punished with impunity. After all, they weren't proper men attending to their responsibilities. That made them eminently punishable. They were outlaws. Men in other hostels around England watched the witchhunt with resignation. One, living in Newcastle on Tyne's Salvation Army Men's palace, told me that homeless men lost basic citizen's rights because 'laws apply *to* them but never *for* them'.

The moral panic generated by scroungerphobia represents homeless men as feckless fugitives from their proper role.

But the overwhelming majority of the palace's clients when I was in the North-East were local men, and nearly half – the biggest single category – were there because their own homes had been disbanded.* Housing allocation policies have no place for men once a family has broken up, so hostels for the homeless become their place of first and last resort. Far from helping the men help themselves to their rights, neither the Salvation Army nor the housing agencies told them they had any. And when they attempted to claim them, they were offered the ultimate solution – the street. Nearly ninety homeless men staying at Newcastle's palace signed a petition protesting against the food. According to one of the inmates, 'You know what they said? "There's the door" ...' The rules and regulations of the hostels make sure they never feel they actually *live* there. In the absence of any alternative network of support provided by the politics they participated in as employed men, the labour movement, they are thrown on a charitable sector dominated by a punitive and puritanical morality. As a result, they feel themselves not only homeless but in a total existential crisis – ending up on the dossers' circuit removes the last residues of respectability. A middle-aged building worker who arrived at the palace – his first time in such a place – after his marriage had broken up, said, 'I was a little bit disgusted, they don't treat you as if you were just unemployed, they treat you like a person who has just crawled out of the gutter.' He is unemployed because he is ill, he gets £40.95 sickness benefit and the hostel takes £30 for bed and breakfast. He spends his days on the street, in cafés or on buses. A former Post Office engineer returned to the South after his marriage broke up. He was unable to find work and went back to the North to be near his little boy. After breakfast at the palace all the inmates are thrown out, whatever the weather, and the only place he can take his child is outside: 'Usually I take my little boy at weekends to

---

* *No Salvation for the Single Homeless*, published by Single Homeless on Tyneside, 1981.

the fair at Whitley Bay, or I take him on the metro and we sit at the front – he loves trains. Or we play in the park all day. I haven't anywhere else to take him.'

At night, the temporary territory is hardly their own: 'You get your own room in the Salvation Army, and technically you've got a lock,' said a man in his early forties who was sent there after losing his job and marriage. 'I learnt to live with other people when I was in the Services, but when you've paid for your own room and it isn't your domain you feel insecure. They can just walk in.' Another unemployed divorcee said he'd been sitting in his room late one night talking with a fellow inmate:

There's a rule about bed time, 11.30 p.m. One bloke burst in and told us to go to bed. We refused. Then we were asked to leave. So I decided to do a bit of checking. We discovered from a Department of Environment Circular that a House of Commons Committee was disgusted at our lack of rights in hostels. I was convinced that the law would back us, so I found someone at a local law centre and she confirmed it, so we went back. We took a couple of cops with us to prevent a breach of the peace and I heard one of them saying it was pointless putting rules and regulations on the wall because most of us couldn't read! At the hostel they were furious with us for bringing the police, they just wanted us out, literally, and we were out! Because we were on a voucher system from the DHSS that pays your rent we had no choice about where we were sent. So we were sent to another hostel. It was a large warehouse that had been converted by the addition of beds into a dormitory. I had a very lively night – I woke up and the sheet was crawling, literally crawling with lice.

The assumption is that men live in their father's family until they have families of their own. When that breaks down, they're sent to what used to be the poorhouse. It still is.

It is also women who are the targets of the state's sex stormtroopers, the Special Claims Control squads set up in the 1970s. These are flying squads who descend on social security offices to make random raids on both men and women. The men they're looking for are those with skills saleable on the black economy – plumbers, mechanics, electricians, etc. The women are single parents: they are easy quarry. The squads arrive, often unwelcomed by DHSS staff, scour the files and pull in the mothers in order to ensure they're not cohabiting. Social security staff, welfare rights workers and men and women in several cities have picketed the interlopers on arrival. One of them saw a list of their original haul when they visited Coventry. 'They were all files of single parents,' she said. The campaign works indirectly by rumour to frighten people, and whatever they can or can't prove the threat is carried by word of mouth and claimants run for cover. A Sunderland woman in her twenties who had a lover for several years who spent some but not all of his time in her home, said, 'We decided to start claiming together because there were a lot of snoopers around, and people I knew had got done. But we were £10 shorter as a result.' The Special Claims Control squads also harass women directly by threats that their benefit will be stopped and with soft talk about men sponging off women. 'Bring him down to see us,' they say, 'and we'll tell him how he can and *ought* to claim for you.' They do this despite evidence of noncohabitation, or by forcing couples to cohabit. Here is the story of one of them, a women in her forties, the mother of three children:

I had my eldest child when I was twenty. I was working in a car factory at the time. I loved that job and the money was good, oh god yes! I was living with my mam in a council house. Then I went to work in another factory as a machinist and I moved into a room with the child. That was the hardest time. My mother was a pensioner. I was on the dole then, getting £5.50 a week and the rent was £2.50. God knows, I ate nothing half the time. I was there six weeks without heating, and every day I walked to my mother's, which was quite a distance. Then I got another job, the same kind as a machinist, and I put the baby in a nursery. I kept on at the council, but it wasn't easy to get a council flat in those days. Eventually I got an old house, I had another baby, I was still working and put the kids in a nursery. The father moved in and I got a full-time job in another engineering company. But it wasn't the same when they went to school. When they were at the nursery I could take them at 7 a.m. and pick them up at 6 p.m. But when they were at school they were just in and out, and home at 3.30 p.m. So I couldn't work, and he got the money from the social security. It was terrible, I'd always been independent, or when I wasn't for a while I got my own social security money. But I never knew from one week to the next if there would be any money. We got transferred to another old council house, it was very damp, but it was a new start, and I decided that if he wanted some responsibility, OK the tenancy could be in his name. But we didn't get on so he wanted a place of his own. I had to sign a paper saying I'd be responsible for the arrears. To get rid of him, I did. I don't know how I did it, but, do you know, I did. I was determined, so I agreed to pay it back every week. Even though he'd gone, I saw him a bit, he'd visit me and the kids whenever it suited him. I'd also got an injunction against him because he became violent, and that was all right for a bit.

By then I was on the dole. He'd come and visit, but I wasn't having any trouble with him and life was pleasanter. Till the knock on the door – two investigators said they'd been watching my house and he was living with me. I admitted he visited me but that I'd had a history of violence with him, and anyway I'd got an injunction. I told them the truth – he visits me, but he doesn't live here. I gave them the address where he was living. They said me and him had to go to the social security the next morning, and if he didn't he'd be picked up. I spent the day frantically trying to find him. They said if we didn't consent for him to claim for the two of us, they'd summons me and him for aiding and abetting. Well, I found him and we went to the 'liable relatives' section of the DHSS. They did a crafty one – one came out and a woman came in, very nice, telling him he had to face up to his responsibilities, she said she'd help us, they'd get him a job, they'd pay his rent and he had to move in with me for a month's trial. I just kept saying to her it couldn't work. I said I've had nearly ten years of this and it can't work. I said I know what my life is like with him, I had an injunction, plus I had my own money and I was managing better. They wouldn't take any notice. They only had one objective – to save a few bob for the government. So we left there that Wednesday morning and they said they'd give us until the Friday to think about it.

But we still got the threat: I'd be summonsed, and no way did I want to go to court. It was a terrible position to be in. But they left us no choice. They came on the Friday and we signed the damned papers, didn't we, and they took away my social security book. I knew. It took only until the next Wednesday when he beat me. The first thing I did was get on the phone to her. So she came out and read the riot act to him. 'Face up to your responsibilities,' and all this. I said, 'You've given him a bloody licence to do it.' These new laws mean the police can't chuck him out. They can't. During that time I had them out three times because I thought I'd make them see. He started then with the money, because he had the giro, so I was getting into a mess again, wasn't I. So for a couple of weeks we were paid separately. She said to me, 'Can't you get away for a few days?' My sister and me are very close, so this woman gave me a giro to go to my sister's – they took me to the station and put me on the train. The giro was £20.60, the fare was £12 and I stayed about six days. I came back – god, I'll never forget it, the house was a pig hole. I was only back a couple of days and it started again. I picks up the phone and dialled a special number for the fraud squad. I was just politely told they'd left the area – 'This number is no longer available as the special investigation team has left the area.' I was lumbered. This just went on – the arguments, no money. Life got that bad that I just used to sleep with the kids.

One night he came back, ripped the bedclothes off and one of my kids managed to get out somehow and call the police. They came and saw the state of me – black eyes, my nose bleeding. They took us to the police station and then to a battered women's house at about 2 a.m. The person on call made us a cup of tea – battered wives' homes are the greatest! Even though we were only in one room, me and the kids, and one of the boys was thirteen then. Anyway, they were marvellous, they couldn't do enough for you. They helped sort out the money. I'd left with nothing because he was still in the house and I was terrified to go back. They helped fix us up with clothes, then with a solicitor for an injunction. No way was I going back to that house. About six months earlier I'd put my name down on the lists of three housing associations, because I was sick of the council houses they were giving me. So the letting officer from one of them said they'd got a house for me. The DHSS made me go to see them every day – I had a broken bone in my ankle but they still made me go every day!

So, I'd got this house and two or three of us from the refuge went up to the old house and packed everything ready to move. The DHSS were playing me up over the removal grant, so one of my sons went up to the house to see if there were any letters – everything had been smashed, crocks were smashed and the beds were slashed. I phoned the police and they arrested him, then they took me up there. I couldn't believe it. I hadn't got a cup. So then I had to put in for another grant because he'd smashed every damn thing. They agreed to allow one of the workers in the battered wives' home to go up there, when she arrived the house was in two feet of water – the pipes had burst. We lost nearly everything, because it had all been packed in plastic bags and it had got mildewed. That was another shock. So she got straight onto the DHSS and I got a grant for three single beds and bedding. One of this and one of that, four cups, plates, knives and forks. My three-piece was wringing wet, but eventually I dried it out, and the rest I just bagged together. My house wasn't posh, but it was clean and it was mine. It was what I'd worked for for twenty years. Nobody from the social went to see it – that grieved me more than anything.

I think the system is wicked. I sit and think how I've struggled to get a home together, and within a couple of minutes it's all smashed up. It hit me when I phoned up and they said those two had gone. So nice. They should have been brought back to see what they do in saving more for the government, and all the extra work they've caused.

I listened to her story. She lost everything she had. It was probably stupid asking her what she felt about it. When I did, she reflected. She heard the question and didn't answer for quite a while, just looked at me. No words.

Under the old DHSS cohabitation ruling, beleaguered by years of criticism from welfare workers and the women's movement, women who had male friends, family or lovers around ran the risk of losing their benefit on the grounds that these men were or should be maintaining them. Snoopers were obsessed with finding evidence of sex – slippers under the bed, clothes in the cupboard, pipe on the mantelpiece. Sex meant money. But now welfare workers believe 'they aren't bothered about your sex life. They don't care if you are sleeping together. They're pursuing a different tack – they are less concerned with what *is* the economic connection than what *ought* to be'. Thousands of women refuse to accept that celibacy is the price of self-sufficiency, and economic dependence the price of sex, but state social policy trails behind this cultural revolution. It fails to provide the infra-structure for mothers' independence – shelter, childcare and jobs. And what affronts the system most of all is the idea that the state could help to *support* women's independence.

The Landscape

As you walk through the industrial towns you lose yourself in
labyrinths of little brick houses blackened by smoke, festering in
planless chaos round miry alleys and little cindered yards
where there are stinking dustbins and lines of grimy washing
and half-ruinous w.c.s. ... at their very worst the Corporation
houses are better than the slums they replace. The mere possession of a bathroom and a bit of garden would outweigh almost
disadvantage.... If people are going to live in large towns at all
they must learn to live on top of one another. But the Northern
working people do not take kindly to living in flats....

George Orwell, *The Road to Wigan Pier*

The landscape George Orwell saw when he wandered round
the backyard of England is a scene that still inhabits people's
memory, though memory incites nostalgia about those 'cruel
habitations'. People associate them with community spirit
and sunshine, the days when 'we had nothing, but were
happy'.

But as Orwell recorded the state of interminable slums, he
also saw the landscape in transition. The labyrinth of little
streets was giving way to new suburbias stretching beyond
the old city boundaries. Some were corporation housing
estates, reservations for the rehabilitation of the working
class. Unlike the back-to-backs and the tenements built for
the poor in the nineteenth century, which treated the poor
like prostitutes – they'll always be with us, but at least keep

them off the streets – their function was to take the street-
wise communities off the streets and clean up the gregarious
clamour of the slum-dwellers. New public housing was one of
the strongest demands made by the working class on the
postwar political parties, whose viability depended on their
promise to provide it. The new mass housing was the corporation estate, which mimicked the form if not the content of
the middle-class suburbias, though on an unprecedented
scale. What we got – and what George Orwell was beginning
to see – were mass municipal prairies.

I'm a product of that process. In 1950, my family, four of
us, about to be five, living in one room, were rehoused on a
new estate in a Cumbrian town. We got a house with three
bedrooms, a bathroom, a separate sitting room and dining
room, a kitchen big enough for a table and chairs (saving
mothers from solitary domestic confinement), front and back
garden, a coal house, inside lavatory *and* outside lavatory
and wash house where people stored dolly tubs and mangles,
bikes and prams. And it was brand new. Estates like ours
were out on the urban edge, the new boundary between town
and country. Although we were city kids, we built dens in the
fields behind the estate and harvested bluebells and
brambles. Allotments kept people in winter vegetables and
summer salads.

When we moved we had one armchair and a sewing
machine. The kitchen had built-in cupboards and shelves –
my first memory is of sitting with my little sister in the most
commodious shoe cupboard. Happiness was an inside
lavatory and built-in cupboards. Unhappiness was our cold
bedrooms and condensation settling like dew. So, despite
seeming to have all that space, you didn't. Our new houses
were cold and uncomfortable. The rent, my dad reminds me,
took a quarter of his wages. Now, of course, we are told that
council tenants pay more, on average, than the average
mortgagee pays in repayments. Like everything else, things
were never as they seemed.

A year after we moved, there was a general election.
Labour recorded its highest vote ever but the Tories got in.

Their Housing Minister was Harold Macmillan. His main claim to fame was that, bowing to postwar pressure, things should never again be so bad. 'You've never had it so good.' He must also be remembered for his housing policy – he stole Labour's thunder and promised 300,000 new homes a year. But they had to be cheap. So they *were* cheap, and nasty, and we now have a housing crisis which will endure beyond this century. Already, the mass housing programmes of the fifties and sixties are the new slums, having to be rebuilt or pulled down.

People outside London have a strong sense of London being there being somewhere else, Tower Bridge and beefeaters and the Stock Exchange, and BBC voices bring it all into their living rooms. But London experiences the 'provinces' as if they were up the Amazon, up a mysterious not to say treacherous jungle path. The M1 has carved a path to the hinterland, yet still the cluster of towns around it seem autonomous from the centre. The very notion of the Socialist Republic of South Yorkshire speaks of a Northern conviction that the North is where class is, the real working class. But why is it that Northern towns, like anywhere else, have their monumental civic buildings, public libraries and baths, named after and often founded by the old city fathers, local entrepreneurs, the class enemy? Sheffield Polytechnic's student union is named after the South African black revolutionary Nelson Mandela, but still the streets and civic buildings aren't named after strikes, or tenants. It is extraordinary how a nation so characterised by class difference should still be so timid about immortalising its own class struggles in place names. There's a mill near what has come to be known as Wigan Pier. The old mill owner, who became a millionaire, once installed cannon borrowed from the local landowner at the gates, to ward off machine-breakers. There's no plaque there to remind the citizenry of the city's civil warriors. Housing estates are the modern monument of municipalism, more typically than the new civic centres and town halls, and yet they often look improvised or makeshift, as temporary as if they were plains of prefabs. Something as simple as whom you name buildings after plays its part in burying history. And now government-grant-aided industrial units are being built as the centres of our old industrial universe are being laid to waste. They are a stark contrast to the derelict steelyards of Sheffield, where there's nothing left but acres of scrap lying on flattened ground, or the old factories, which look either like the work-house or satanic hangars. It still shocks you to see them – that's where they put the people to work. If George Orwell were to return to Sheffield today he'd see the metamorphosis from spacious if spartan semi-detached suburbias to dense tower blocks. An epitaph to this era of modern housing stands on the crest of the city – where once there was a slope of slums, there now stands a barrage of flats for thousands. They were hailed in their day as 'bold' and one of the most 'uncompromising' developments of the fifties, which simply meant that they were deliberately ugly – the genre of 'brutalism'. The only concession to the consumers in this awful, artless building is an attempt to build community spirit into the structure, as if this, one of the few social assets of the working class, would otherwise be given no natural home. The architects built a system of simulated streets in the air and presumably the people are supposed to play their part in making it all a success by playing in those streets, which measure three metres wide. There is nothing in the 'street' other than front doors – no shops, pubs or laundries, cafés or telephone boxes, no places to gather. So the only point of being in the street is to come and go, which is precisely all that people do. The designers also wanted to provide privacy. They did this not by providing sheltered gardens or sound insulation, they just put no windows in the street. Blind alleys.

Such a contrast between those old, solid, yellow stone houses, which seem to last forever, and the corporation estates. Is anybody proud of this estate, except maybe some of the people who live there who've tried to humanise them with their own gardens? Because nobody is proud of them, the whole principle is undermined – even lefties are now

saying the people want to buy their own homes? Do they?
Most of the council estate dwellers I meet don't – they only
want a council house they could like and feel some control
over. I know what they mean – I've lived three quarters of
my life in council estates, that's where I feel at home. But
why didn't we get the best housing?

This brave new world of social engineering produces the
opposite of community contact. Social scientists doing
research at the estate in the seventies were told by one
tenant that it would have been 'difficult to be more isolated if
you had lived in Egypt'. The social scientists commented
that although this was going a bit far, social contact on the
estate was 'extremely low'. Estates like this were often sold to
the local authorities as packages – they weren't what they
wanted, just what they got. This estate is now one of the
most unpopular in the city. Similar disasters are scattered
piecemeal all over Britain, on bomb sites and over the slums
they were built to clear. There's another block in Coventry,
neither the best nor the worst of its type. It's easily missed
because its name has fallen off the entrance, leaving an
incomprehensible hieroglyph. But it still stands out, a lone
tower surrounded by sedate semis. The entrance is a brief
concrete patio with three smelly skips about four feet high
and full of rubbish. Corrugated shutters supposed to cover
the unsightly skips in their cubby hole probably haven't been
pulled down since the block was first occupied in the 1960s.
The path from the entrance is littered with remnants from
these skips – birdseed, yoghurt cartons, broken glass and old
crusts. Across the patio are a dozen doors, none intact. They
are ex-pram sheds, harbouring bean tins, bits of cookers and
carpet. The patio floor is swept but still stained with grease
and barnacles of chewing gum. A few steps past the skips
brings you to the lift, an aluminium cell sticky with spit and
sweets and smelling of disinfectant. I saw this block one
sunny August afternoon and although there was no one in
sight, there was a murmur of music and children's voices
through windows. Nobody ventured out into the weather,
except one woman watering some sweet peas on her balcony.

These homes were like an unsavoury silo, places to store people rather than house them.

Tower blocks have become the symbol for all our disaffection, monumental mistakes for which we can all justifiably blame the politicians and professionals. It wasn't as if they didn't know they were taking a risk – during the fifties and sixties debates raged in the press about highrise housing, with its defenders calling opposition simply prejudice. But the pressure was on, with state housing subsidies inciting the architects, builders and local councils to build ever upward and experiment with barely tested materials, to cram the maximum population onto the minimum land mass, so that during the twenty-year tower block boom nearly half a million high-rise homes were built.

All over England there are relics of this reckless eldorado. One block in the middle of the Northeast garden city, Washington New Town, now stands completely empty. These flats, the size of a Victorian mill, were evacuated only fifteen years after being built. People just won't live there. This sort of thing is found throughout the Northeast. What was once a landscape of banks of back-to-backs has become an asymmetrical mess of flats and maisonettes. There's the notorious low-rise Noble Court stranded beside a highway overlooking the Tyne with 'Get us out of this hell' written on the wall. There are the high-rise towers around the edge of Newcastle with a motorway fifty or a hundred yards from their windows. There's the city's sprawling badlands where all that distinguishes the housing from the old brick back-to-backs is that they're further away from everywhere.

Unlike the ghettoes we all know about, used to keep races apart, where only fools or angels venture to buy sex or sell salvation, these are just another corporation estate. Nobody visits except debt collectors, reluctant relatives and social workers. The most frequent visitor is the ice-cream van announcing itself several times a day with chords from 'It's Now or Never' or 'Happy Days Are Here Again'. One estate in Coventry has all the languor of the ghetto. Fifty per cent of the men are unemployed, and the percentage of women without a wage is of course even higher. Like many of the city's estates, it was built for car factory workers. The small square of shops reminds me a lot of Belfast's battle-scarred Divis Flats – the shop windows are permanently barricaded, many flats boarded up and the walls covered in spray can slogans. Only one spot is free from juvenile protest, it's a rustic mural across one wall with cows, country cottage and a garden gate. People said it was painted by 'the students' – they're among the few willing takers who get homes on hard-to-let estates – who sound like Siberian exiles doing good works among the peasants. A pack of dogs swarms out of the entrance hall of some flats. 'That's another thing! Dogs!' said somebody standing by the bus stop, as if the list were endless. The people here are marooned on these estates. They are very, very depressed and consequently quite immobilised.

Low-rise blocks of flats on the same estate squat on scabby scraps of grass, a minefield of dogshit and broken glass, unused even by the army of under-fives who live there. One patch is even rougher than the rest: the landscaped relic of a bulldozed block, which had to come down because sewage erupted into the sinks and lavatories.

There are no safe spaces around the flats, no fences or shrubs, sheds or seats, to shelter bikes, prams, washing, last year's bulbs, or children. No places to sit in the sun. Just nude space. Kids rush out, only to be followed by shouts of 'Wayne ... Lee ... Karen ... come in here ...'

The very complexion of some of our cities has changed. The regional shades of red brick and yellow stone which once coloured the cityscape have disappeared, replaced by the grey monotone of concrete. On the edge of Sheffield town centre the eye confronts some long walls the colour of a storm, so forbidding that not even the kids have made their mark. This is another monstrosity celebrated as a brilliant piece of architectural engineering. It looks like a bunker. Inside it is like a cave, cold and wet. It has never been water-tight so whenever it rains, water seeps out along the concrete panels, or drips into the middle of somebody's living room.

Insulation, incredibly enough in our climate, did not get housing subsidy and so is primitive or non-existent. Walls are the surface upon which external cold clashes with internal warmth, the result – condensation and cold walls. Where tenants in the worst flats have tried to paper the walls, the paper either falls off or clings to the surface with the mildew. One of the tenants I met looks through her window on to a neat square garden. But her weeping window sill sheds tears of condensation, scarring the wall down to the carpet which has curled and crumbled at the edge. Looking over to the block of flats opposite, I can see a window with a dark, damp patch underneath it as big as the window itself: it wasn't raining, but somehow it was wet. Condensation is an epidemic on this estate and usually the tenants are blamed, as though it were some kind of social disease, not a structural defect. One of the legends here is that a local authority inspector told a tenant that her furniture was too near the floor and thus rotting her carpet. It's said tenants cause condensation, by boiling kettles. And breathing, presumably.

If it isn't rising or descending damp, water finds its way in by stealth. Rain penetrates through the joints between concrete panels, it accumulates on balconies after rainfall, sits there and seeps through the structure. 'I was in bed and suddenly this water started, drip, drip, drip, on my face,' an elderly man told me. He was moved to the estate after his old home was 'redeveloped'. One of his neighbours finds water dripping from the balcony above along her ceiling and out near her electric fire.

In certain combinations, concrete, cold and water form a fatal triangle rendering thousands of dwellings unfit for human habitation according to postwar regulations. Sometimes the structural stability of the buildings themselves is undermined. During the prefabrication boom of the fifties and sixties some contractors used many times the permitted level of calcium chloride to help speedy setting in concrete – it also helped speedy corrosion. This has caused dilapidation on the Sheffield estate, constructed on the same system as a consortium of other Northern cities. After tenants' complaints, the "Nottingham local authority commissioned a structural survey which found that the estate was dangerous and in need of immediate support.

Sometimes you can see the results of this decay on the corporation landscape – scaffolding canopies thrown around the base of tower blocks to catch falling concrete, the cracked and corroded corners which drop off like snow, but unless you are looking for it you don't notice it. This protects the public gaze from the true story and means that for a decade the authorities have been able to work on the assumption that what the eye doesn't see the heart won't grieve over.

As long ago as 1968, central government knew that some prefabrication and high-rise buildings were an economic, engineering and social disaster. A National Building Agency report in 1968 noted that water penetration and condensation became quickly apparent after occupation, and registered design and structural faults. It was kept secret. Blocks kept on being built. Only after years of dogged activity by tenants backing up their own experiences with systematic surveys, did local authorities bring in the experts, and the tenants were right all along: they were living in leaking, sweating, unstable structures.

Now the local authorities are caught in a cleft stick, hostages to their own political process. Having ignored the wishes of their own constituents, they must finally heed them. But, having been seduced into housing packages by the government and the building industry, it is they who must foot the bill – the government won't help and many firms have either gone out of business or seek immunity behind a labyrinth of legal protection. The London Borough of Hillingdon reckons that the cost of repairing its homes built on the Bison Wallframe system will cost between £1 and £3 billion. The Colditz cave in Sheffield, described earlier, was built by Shepherd Construction. In 1983 they were the subject of a strike in Warrington on a £9.5 million government contract. The builders' union accused the firm of subcontracting wildly to lump labour. This Colditz estate is to be pulled down. Though the tenants didn't like living

there, they grew into a community in the course of their
campaigns: 'We're like old friends now, in and out of each
other's houses,' said one of their organisers. 'We don't want
to be separated from each other.' The demolition of some
irreparable towers on Merseyside and London have made
high-rise the focus of attention, eclipsing the equally
dramatic decline of suburbias. Since the fifties, the law has
ratified tenants' right to freedom from damp, but nearly 40
per cent of the tenants in Shepherd's Nottingham estate said
their health had been impaired by damp. A survey of some
Coventry council estates done by Shelter and Coventry
Community Workshop in the seventies showed that over 30
per cent of tenants reported furniture ruined by damp.

But the cost of rehabilitation is prohibitive in these
complex buildings, honeycombs beyond the reach of reason-
able repair. An idea of the costs involved were given in a
Coventry officials' confidential report to councillors and
fellow officials in the seventies. It said the only solution to
endemic condensation was full insulation and constant heat
– a 'provocatively contentious and quite unacceptable'
conclusion, confessed the report. And it isn't just the concrete. Most corporation dwellings are either inadequately or
extravagantly heated. Thousands are stuck with some of the
most expensive forms of electric central heating, and most
systems heat only one or two rooms. Architects, councillors
and contractors don't seem to think that the working class
need or want warm bedrooms.

We don't inhabit our homes as we used to. Our grandmothers grew up in the days when women rose at dawn, laid
the sticks and lit the fire. A fire and a woman were the
permanent feature of a household. Since the Second World
War only a minority of women work full-time in their own
homes. Most work for most of their lives *outside* the home.
But heating and housing technology were not brought to bear
on this, the single most significant change in the way we live.
Design and costs conspire to make many working-class
households huddle as they always have – all together in one
room.

In the late seventies and early eighties an era of public housing came to an end. The high-rise hype blew up in our faces, with the demolition of tower blocks in London and Merseyside appearing as slow-motion spectaculars on television, hundreds of homes up for less than a lifetime now squandered. But the high-rise epic eclipses another drama. A senior corporation planner in the Northeast, who spends most of his time not so much planning as picking up the pieces of careless politics, recalled the principle of high-rise:

They never asked the people what they wanted. I've been trying to get councillors to find out since then, but that's a very hard job. Really they don't want to know. They thought that all they had to do was accommodate people. Nobody ever asked whether people wanted play space, or this or that kind of housing. They'd built estates after the war with no amenities at all and they didn't learn from that either. They just didn't ask the people what they wanted.

The need to put roofs over heads is the excuse councillors always came up with when confronted with the consequences. It seems honourable enough until you think about it. But why did they ever think a roof on its own was enough? I spoke to a middle-aged woman in Sunderland who moved into her council house when it was new thirty years ago.

All there was on our estate was houses for families. There were no shops, no church, no pavements. The first things that were provided were pubs and working men's clubs. One of the biggest problems was always money. People had big families. And men were always resentful about their wives getting into anything. There was nothing for women and children and nowhere for women to go. It was a long time before I did anything or went anywhere, and then I got involved in the church. Do you know, when television came it was the biggest event in our lives, for women. Mind you, there was a lot of going in and out of each other's houses. I had a friend and we'd cook a meal and share it and bring the kids together. Or if you had knitting or sewing to do you'd take it round. The women used to get very depressed and there were always debts. And we had battered wives in those days, you know, on our street. Later on I worked on

the twilight shift in a components factory and as our kids grew up
people moved out and others moved in. But they seemed to have
less, don't misunderstand me, I'm not class conscious, but it was a
different class of person.

As the original inhabitants leave these barracks, the
estates become unwanted stock allocated to people in the
greatest need with the least choice – usually poor households
with small children. Several of the worst estates I saw, those
with fewest amenities, had double the average number of
children on other council estates. That's not because people
had bigger families, it's because they pack them with young,
poor parents, ghettos for women and children.

How do they get there and what is life like? 'I got the keys
and I just opened the door a wee bit, then I shut it. You
name it and it was there. Shit all over the floor and the
walls,' said a twenty-one-year-old machinist who'd been
banished to Coventry's notorious Woodend estate. It was
thrown up after the war to house the car workers. Nobody
wants to live there now.

It happened because me and my little boy were living with my
mam. I'd been working in a factory, but I had to give that up
because I couldn't afford a nursery. My mam moved away but the
landlord wouldn't let me stay on because I was on social security. So
I went to the council and they offered me here or a boarding house.
Here is where they put you when you've got nowhere else to go.
Anyway, I went back to the council – they said it wasn't too bad,
but I refused to take it. They gave me another flat somebody else
had turned down. So I took it. I had no cooker, no fire, no bed, no
furniture, all I had was blankets and sheets and clothes. The baby's
bedroom was damp and his bed got soggy. The council said it would
cost £10 to send somebody to look at the wall and then I'd have to
pay to have it repaired.

Since then she's got a new man and a new baby, five weeks
old, who lay in her father's arms clad in the all-white uniform
of the newborn. 'We didn't scrounge off the social security for
her, did we?' he said, looking at the child's mother. 'We've

bought everything new for her.' Virtually everything else they own is somebody else's discarded rubbish, a miscellany of ramshackle furniture. 'Watch that one,' they said as I sat down on one of the armchairs, 'the seat falls through.' Small squares of a once-fitted carpet were arranged across only half of the living-room floor. The estate is boycotted by hire firms, so they'd been forced to buy a television and washing machine new.

The council denies that this Coventry estate is a dumping ground for single parents, a denial which is contradicted by the evidence of the inhabitants. 'We got the keys to a flat here just before my baby was born,' said another woman in her early twenties, who married at sixteen because she was pregnant. 'But it was very damp and mildewed. Then it got flooded because people had ripped out the pipes next door, which was empty too.' She couldn't bear to move in because the flat was wet and it was winter, so she went to her mother's. Because she couldn't live in the flat, she didn't pay the rent, which meant arrears and no possibility of a transfer. Only when she and her husband separated did she become a potential tenant in her own right. So she was offered a second flat.

Before I moved in the ceiling got smashed in and the place was covered in water – it happens because the places are left empty. The council told me just to stay there the weekend. But I couldn't – when I arrived there was no door, the boards were still on the windows, there was no electricity and no cooking facilities, only cold black floors and dog shit. I couldn't have stayed there with the baby. The only alternative was the Salvation Army. So I went back to my mam's.

Her mother lives in a council house with four other adolescent children, so she slept with the baby in the sitting room. Then there was a third offer, where she now lives. It is a ground-floor flat, one wall is a window, which keeps the place cold and which looks out onto a bare field, with two scaffolding poles and a tarmac patch. That's where people are supposed to hang their washing, but they don't because they're afraid it will get stolen. Outside the window are a few sticks lying around on the grass. 'That used to be a fence, which was good because we could let the little boy play out there. But the council pulled it down because we're not supposed to have fences.' Everything is second hand, including her clothes. 'Watch that couch, its got a spike somewhere that sticks into you.' She found the green carpet in a neighbouring flat, after it had been left empty. Like her neighbours, she never goes out in the evenings, and rarely ventures off the estate which is on the edge of town. Going anywhere is too expensive.

I met a woman, called skinny Linda, who is very, very skinny. She is quite keen on a tenants' association. Anyway, she had a four-year-old boy called Keith, who she never let play outside unless she was watching, because there was no defensible space. He had a bike which she'd stopped letting him use because it had become dangerous. Anyway, one day he shouted to her that he was taking the bike out, she was in another room doing something, and minutes later he was dead. He got run over by an articulated lorry. She is 25. She used to live on another estate in Coventry, in a council house there, and was in arrears, like an awful lot of people. And so after a month or so's arrears accumulated she got the inevitable form – an eviction notice. It is standard procedure, and it doesn't usually mean you actually get evicted; it is a way of frightening people. But she quit, left home because she thought she had to.

In Sunderland everybody has heard of 'the courts', the place is talked about with that combination of ignorance, fascination and repulsion which people reserve for child-molesting, torture and exotic oppression somewhere else. Actually they're fifties maisonettes in the city's East End, there's nothing satanic about them, they're just like any block of flats you've ever seen, only worse. 'God, what's that?' I said to a companion while we were wandering around the city. 'It's the courts,' she said. They were shocking, though explaining why is difficult – just boring flats with debris lying around. It's what's missing that is telling. They looked uninhabited. There are no fences, trees, shrubs, window boxes, sheds, prams, bikes or washing lines. There is no evidence of human habitation, only the appearance of absence. Everything is bare, some windows are boarded up and some broken, all the signs of vacancy and abandonment. But people do live there, though when I moved in it became clear that a third of the flats were empty. The door at the entrance to our block had both windows smashed, and although the council was supposed to have fitted a safety lock on the door into the lobby, it hadn't. The stairs were brushed, but pocked with scraps of eggshell and solidified tissues. All the flats on the way up were empty and boarded up, though most of the boards had been prised open. Not even squatters camped in this place, so more likely they'd been broken by locals scavenging for carpets or pipes.

When I first arrived at the flat and knocked on the door there was no answer. I wandered back down the stairs, past the washing draped over the bannisters and out onto the broken glass of the yard. This was another of those naked spaces, so exposed it was useless – putting a chair out there to sit in the sun seemed unthinkable, there were none of the nooks and crannies or spaces that invited use. It would be like knitting in the middle of a giant car park. Even some washhouses had been razed to stumps, people *never* hung their washing out. Ball games were impossible: the yard had kitchen windows every few yards. The kitchens faced rubbish skips three or four yards away. Nothing grew, except weeds and slime choking all but two of the drains. 'Hey,' somebody shouted, and when I looked back, it was the tenant of the flat I'd just knocked at. 'Come on up,' she said. I just hadn't thought – the door was never opened to callers. Friends shouted through the letterbox. Everybody else was a foe. They'd be after money.

Go to almost any city and you find sink estates where you get the feeling that the council hates the place and the people too. After years of discourtesy, the feeling is often returned by the tenants. The poorest tenants are in the poorest accommodation, starved of resources for self-help and political help, because their leaders are also their landlords. A single parent living with her four children on this Sunderland estate had kept a large bedroom window covered with plastic sheeting for nearly a year; the council hadn't fixed it and she didn't have the wherewithall to do it herself. Only when the tenants brought the local newspaper down to see the dead rats and disrepair was the council moved to begin some repairs and rebuild the roof, but not before telling the press what it thought of its tenants. 'Coventry's tenants are the worst in the country,' blurted out a Coventry councillor, But when some of his colleagues on the council, together with fellow Labour Party activists, surveyed the extent to which repairs correctly reported had been made good by the council on several large estates, they found that 70 per cent had not been carried out. The survey also reported hundreds more repairs which had not been reported by the pessimistic tenants. The local Labour Party published a dossier of this record of disrepair and urged that other surveys be carried out 'and the results published in an agitational way, as part of the wider demand for decent housing, run for and by the working class'. The councillors involved were expelled from the ruling Labour Group on the council.

The repairs debacle has become a political battle symbolising the party's awkward relationship to its own supporters. It is not only a conflict between old and new generations of activists, it symbolises a deeper malaise between the only mass party the working class has ever had and its working-class electors, who are also its clients. The conflict also comes out of another division within the working class itself, between its respectable and upward-striving representatives and the poor, who have been dumped on the derelict estates. Increasingly the protagonists are women. That's because the energy for tenants' politics has always come from women, and now the emergence of women's ghettos puts poor women in the frontline with the local state.

I've been reading Richard Hoggart's *The Uses of Literacy* on this journey; he goes on about the working class not being able to think abstractly, generally, metaphysically or politically. It conjures an image of the working-class brain cauterised at birth. The people I'm meeting think; certainly they think locally and familially, but thoughts must operate within a world they can influence and know. Most people can only influence the local and the familial, so if people are parochial it's probably because they're relatively powerless elsewhere.

The poor have access to neither personal nor political resources. Subsistence incomes leave no surplus for self-help. How can a twenty-two-year-old mother with three small children, whose stock of crockery consists of three cups and four plates, find the economic or emotional hardware to plug up the six-inch hole around the pipe running from her sink to an outside drain, or similar holes round all the pipes in her kitchen? Where would a woman whose children possess not a single toy find the resources to restore plaster crumbling off the joists between the walls and the doors, to put five doors back on their corroded hinges and fix all the loose boards on the stairs? The children pull them out for strangers like me, just to show how loose they are. And what do we expect the tenants on another sink estate to do when their toilets overflow, spewing sewage from the pipes outside over their bathroom floors? Some tenants to whom this happens every few months said they'd been told that next time they'd have to sort it out themselves. None of these tenants have access to any tools or materials, and in some cases they've been told that they'll have to pay for the repair work. Others would if they could, because it's common knowledge that the work won't get done otherwise. 'Some of our employees hate tenants on the rough estates,' admitted a Sunderland council official, so workmen just won't go there.

Some of the worst estates aren't the oldest, they were built in the fifties rush. There's one in Sunderland with 2,500 dwellings; the older end is respectable, with tree-lined avenues and mature privets, and concessions to the eye in design details around the doors and windows. The newer end is rough, treeless and spartan. Legend has it that the 'great unwashed' don't put coal in the bath any more, they burn

the doors and gates for fuel. Citizens Band Radio calls it
Matchstick City and you can see why: boarded-up houses,
houses with wild shadows staining the walls where flames
have leapt to the roof. Cost-cutting experimental panels were
used in these dwellings, making them highly inflammable.

There is often a stark contrast between private space for
which tenants have responsibility for upkeep and the public
space which are the council's responsibility. Private space
where people have some resources, is smart and well cared
for, but the public spaces always seem to be mucky or
breaking down. It isn't because people don't care. It's just
that lifts only break down because people use them, rubbish
shutes only get blocked with rubbish and debris only
accumulates because public spaces aren't cleaned often
enough. Densely populated estates, centralised housing
management and scarce allocation of resources to public
space equals wastelands. What in any other circumstances
would be counted as normal wear and tear become weapons
used against the tenants. They get the blame for the decline
of their homes. And often as not, it's the children who get the
blame. Every wanton scar defacing the walls, every time the
lift breaks down or a pain of glass is broken, there's a ready-
made culprit: 'It's the kids again.' It may be that the kids are
moderate in their reprisals, they could do worse. Either way,
the tenants feel besieged by the authority on the one hand
and their reckless juniors on the other. But they feel the
authority deserves the blame, the children they sometimes
forgive.

If repairs symbolise the council's discourtesy, then arrears
symbolise another dimension of the breakdown of relations
between the authority and the residents. Arrears are pheno-
menal in most authorities, a function of both the impoverishment of tenants and of their rebellion. A woman on the dole
in a Sunderland sink estate tells me she has only voluntarily
paid rent for two weeks in three years. 'Why should I, if this
is where they put you? They can't put you anywhere worse
than this.' A combination of poverty and protest. But even
this punishes the protagonists. Arrears means no possibility

of a transfer: 'We're imprisoned here.'

Arrears were to have been resolved by the introduction of the 'unified housing benefit', according to which tenants on supplementary benefit were to be relieved of responsibility for paying their rent by having it siphoned off directly by the DHSS. Over 25,000 of Wigan's 36,000 council dwellings are on housing benefit. In 1983, more than 46,000 out of the total 114,000 homes – public and private – in Wigan were on housing benefit. Staggering. The aim was to help tenants not to get into arrears. However, like the paternalistic approach to the working class of the Peabody Trust and the Octavia Hill system of housing in the nineteenth century, which attempted to train tenants in the virtues of punctual payment and thrift by enforcing a ban on arrears, the housing benefit simply seeks to *make* people pay their rent by paying if for them. This removes the tenants' choice. Under the old system, which included rent in supplementary benefit so that tenants could pay it themselves, many tenants were able to shuffle their weekly budgets – this week buy some kids' shoes, next week the rent, this week the gas bill, next week the rent. But with their rent paid direct this became impossible. Subsistence incomes force the poor into improvidence – they're never able to save, or plan their purchases. What is more or less manageable on an average wage, like paying the TV licence or buying shoes, causes a major cash flow crisis when you're living on supplementary benefit. Furthermore, the housing benefit has removed one of the few rights of protest left to the poor tenant in terrible housing conditions — arrears. It has wiped out, at a stroke, their right to strike.

But amidst this tale of decline and dereliction, there are havens of optimism, half-way houses to heaven. There's a block of maisonettes in one of Coventry's most notorious 'rough' estates; it looks almost, but not quite, like the others around it, a grey wall of dwellings, unrelieved by the only thing which humanises most estates, whether council or private, greenery, gardens and window boxes. This block has the distinction of a tall, geranium-red door. As you walk through the door, however, you see something that exists nowhere else: a secret garden. There is an immaculately manicured lawn, a little pond surrounded by rushes, a high wall with young trees and creepers climbing up toward the wire netting at the top, beds of flowers, and, by some of the front doors, holes have been gouged out of the paving and clematis and creepers planted. When the Tories briefly took control of the council, they implemented current Conservative philosophy – to sell council homes and encourage what for them represents the truest democracy, a property-owning democracy, which is less about one-man-one-vote than every man a home-owner. They offered the maisonettes for sale at a peppercorn price, less than £2,000. They were bought mainly by Labour voters, single mothers and divorced men unable to buy accommodation at market value or to find accommodation through the housing list. They're still Labour voters. When they acquired their homes, they persuaded the council to section off some land at the back, and that became their secret garden. They contributed a small sum every week to buy the plants, build the pond and buy a lawn mower and two church benches, and they made their collective garden themselves. One of the group makes his own wine, and in the summer they sit out late into the night, drinking the wine and talking. The majority are now unemployed, resources are few, but they can manage 50p a head for the garden, and for many of them it provides the only pleasure they have in life.

Nothing, other than ownership and the secret garden, appears to distinguish them from the other tenants around them. But that is everything – the residents of the neighbouring blocks remain tenants, and they aren't allowed to build fences or gardens. Most of their neighbours have children, and because all the space around them is spare, it is space over which they have no control, and therefore can't use. The real distinction doesn't lie in the fact of ownership, but in control.

There is a desultory and demoralised tenants' association on the estate, burdened by the council's unresponsiveness and its own lack of any effective sanctions. 'What we could do with is a bit of success,' said a member of the tenants' association on a big Coventry estate. 'But god knows where you get that from. The effect is that anybody here with get-up and go gets up and goes.'

But there are success stories. There's a cluster of old streets in central Sheffield, small terraced houses and the grand old houses built by the industrial bourgeoisie in the nineteenth century, now largely in multi-occupation. When George Orwell went to Sheffield he visited the area and described the conditions of houses in Wallace Street. The old slums in Wallace Street have gone now, replaced nearby by a small, neat council estate of flats and maisonettes; across the main road there's a sixties estate of dour concrete so riddled with damp and concrete corrosion that it may be demolished by the time this book is published. The remaining web of streets was due for redevelopment – the standard solution to housing decay in the last couple of decades. But the residents resisted and formed themselves into a community association and negotiated with the council to save their homes. Access to urban grants and, ultimately, a sympathetic local authority, has allowed the residents to intervene in detail in the determination of the physical fabric of their lives. They've learned to read plans, negotiate with housing agencies and councillors, and ponder long and hard on whether they want a one-way street, trees, bollards, here, or there. If you have a road block here, what happens if you need to get an ambulance? they wonder, and then they work it out. A derelict piece of land nearby was due for development, but the residents decided to make it into a garden. They got the council to agree that if the authority would supply the shrubs, they would landscape the land. Through their association, the residents have achieved what few can even dream of: self-determination not so much by *individual* property ownership as their association's *collective* control of their immediate environment.

Wigan is interesting as a small northern town, sort of happy to be a little, quiet, workers' town. I like that. Though still it has all the marks of makeshift industrialisation and decline, with municipalism picking up the pieces, building endless estates of council houses. Municipal minimalism, or, as my dad puts it, barracks and buses. There's a housing estate built about forty years ago on a disused pit. One day, a tenant went out to work and found a hole in his garden; hours later it was even bigger, and within yet more hours it became a twenty-foot pit. The old shafts are subsiding, a honeycomb of holes are shifting and settling, the place feels like a slow, inverted volcano. When the council threatened to raise the rents some of the local men started arguing about it in a local pub. 'We started falling out over it, so we decided to form a tenants' movement,' one of the tenants told me. Word went round the local Labour Club that the tenants couldn't use its premises because they were communists. So they got the agreement of a local pub to use one of their rooms, and started campaigning for their own community association. One Labour councillor was sympathetic and brought his local ward committee down to see the tenants 'to check it wasn't political'. The organisation rapidly accumulated 1,000 members and began organising children's discos and bingo nights to raise money for the community association. 'Do you know, it was like a holiday camp when we organised the disco, 400 kids turned up.' They've also got a boxing club for about seventy boys. Now they've been given a derelict school building, gutted by fire, for their new community association. They have raffles on the go around all the local clubs – 'On pay day, which is giro day round here.' Together with the bingo, that's their main source of income, though now they're negotiating for government grants. They scrounge wiring, plasterboard, wood, all kinds of building materials from local firms and are rebuilding the charred structure.

The committee which runs this elaborate web of activity includes about eight or nine people, half men, half women. Most of them have never been involved in politics before, though all of them are Labour voters. Despite their contest with the Labour council, they retain their loyalty. 'Oh yes, definitely, we're all Labour round here.' 'Before, we were only a minority who complained, but with the association we won't stand for it any more. The Labour Club does nothing about it all. Yes, we definitely vote Labour, and if the councillors were doing their job we wouldn't have to do all this,' said one member of this committee. 'But we don't want the council in on it,' said another, 'they'd want something out of it, but we just enjoy doing it ourselves. We get more involved in things now. It's like life used to be, there's real community spirit.'

Sometimes, Labour politicians *have* sought their electors' views, but usually only to ratify completed plans. A veteran local government leader in Coventry who went into city politics from the car factories where he was a militant shop steward, remembers an attempt to communicate with electors after the Second World War:

We had a vision of a brave new Britain and a brave new Coventry. We'd been heavily blitzed and this gave us the opportunity to think big and boldly and to think philosophically. There was a Klondike atmosphere. We approached it with a will to get things done with socialist thinking. The central area development came relatively easily. We went to the government to mark 430 acres of prime property. But the government was overridden by the Treasury, we only got 270 acres.

And the central area plan was circumscribed by the rights of the city's main shops. 'But anyway we believed in buying land and that the municipality ought to have a share, that the community ought to have a share in the equity of real estate.' And then came the building of the mass housing estates. 'We wanted to try to involve the community in influencing town planners. So we had thirty-nine public meetings to take into account what ordinary men and women wanted.' Did they learn much from those meetings? 'No, they didn't tell us much; we told them. But it did cultivate good will.'

Compare that with the mushrooming of tenants' housing co-ops in Liverpool, in the face of Labour Party opposition. People living in slums due for redevelopment would normally expect to be rehoused on rambling estates around the periphery of the city. But people living in an old street of Victorian back-to-backs in the middle of Liverpool 8, riot territory, wanted to stay together and wanted to have some say in what they live in. If housing associations could organise co-ops, so could they. So they set about it, with the help of a co-op development agency, which provided them with management services. They learned to negotiate for grants, find a patch of land, buy it, hire their own architect, and then work on detailed plans for their own homes, the colour of bricks, the design of window frames, the landscaping of their estate. It's built now, and it's beautiful.

Tenants living in a ramshackle tenement in the middle of a cosmopolitan district of Liverpool 8 were, likewise, due for redevelopment. They, too, formed a housing co-op rather than be dispersed to the outer edges in identikit 'corpy' houses. They meet regularly in the newly built Chinese community centre. At the meeting I attend, the architect they hired brings his model of the site and their homes. A long discussion takes place about details of design. The tenants don't want to be hurried into any decisions, so they sit quietly and listen. 'Don't hassle us,' says a middle-aged white woman in the co-op. She is sitting next to her neighbour, a black woman who was born in the tenements and whose brother lived nearby. He, too, was a member of the co-op. 'This is the rest of our lives we're talking about, you know,' she says, to collective, silent assent. When the tea break comes everybody rushes to the model, holding their cups over the plan. A huddle gathers round one street where one house was several yards behind the line of the street. They call the architect over. 'Why's that house behind the others? Can't they all be together?' The architect explains his reasoning and says he thinks the tenant might enjoy the privacy. 'Privacy!' they laugh 'What do we want that for? We live with each other anyway!' The black woman scoffed confidentially and points to one of the younger women. 'I laid her mother out,' she says.

There are nearly twenty co-ops in the city now, all of them involving the tenants in deep and detailed commitment both to the planning and to each other. One co-op met several nights a week for three years. Now they're not just tenants, they're experts. Though most of the tenants are probably Labour voters, the local Liberals and Tories have supported the co-ops. For obvious reasons, the tenants absolve the local authority of responsibility. The Labour Party is opposed to them because they challenge the principles of state housing and of equal access to a democratic *minimum.* Labour authorities have a tendency to disarm tenants. They want them to be more responsible, more self-determining, to take matters into their own hands, and yet they oppose the only thing the tenants have of their own – organisation. That's because they see it as a threat to their political authority as the *only* representative of the people. In touring Northern England George Orwell saw the era of state housing moving into its expansionist phase and beginning to transform the urban landscape. The eighties is the end of that era, with the Labour Party hoist on its own identification with a housing form which was borrowed from ideological sources which were never formulated by and for the working class itself. So, it's stuck with defending this form of public housing in the face of mass dissidence within the working class itself, not so much with the principle of council housing as the tenants' lack of control over design and management. That contradiction has left the party divided within itself and divided from its own constituency – the working class. It is exemplified in the resistance of councillors to tenants' own mobilisation. 'Yes, we've got a terrible profile on repairs,' said a Coventry councillor, formerly of the Left but driven into the arms of her old protagonists on the right of the party by other Left councillors' support for tenants.

I've got this gut reaction. I represent areas with stinking housing estates. Those people are in a housing misery situation, and people will write papers and dossiers about it – but they won't get the repairs done. That offends me. I'm not denying people's right to do it, but politics is about power, and suppose the Social Democratic Party moved in and swept the board, what would we do then? I remember a tenants' association was set up and they demanded that we meet them. They'd brought a poor young woman with a baby in a pushchair and we traipsed all around, in and out of houses, it was bitterly cold, and at the end of the exercise I felt we could have saved a hell of a lot of time. If they'd come straight to me we could have quietly got it done. Why make such awful examples of those people? It was conflict's sake, what the tenants' association didn't want was a solution, it wanted a lovely, publicity-generating conflict. Stunts. When all they needed to do was lift up the phone and have a quiet word. The problem is when you talk about organising the tenants, who are you organising them *against*? We thought we were building a new Jerusalem, but these people seem hell bent on destroying Babylon.

Housing offers the greatest opportunity of all for local self-determination. Perhaps the crisis in public housing gives concrete evidence of something the Left longs for – the marriage of representative democracy through the institutions of the state with tenants and residents exercising direct democracy in defining and managing the community's homes. But if the Labour Party is to survive the consequences of its defence of bad housing, it is going to have to surrender the belief that it is the only voice of the people. Its future depends on a different kind of alliance with the class that created it who won't for much longer be reduced to the status of clients dependent on the whim of their political godfathers.

Mothers
on the Rock and Roll

... the working class think nothing of getting married on the dole. It annoys old ladies in Brighton, but it is proof of their essential good sense ... families are impoverished but the family system has not broken up.

George Orwell, *The Road to Wigan Pier*

Women are the poorest of all. Women are responsible for family finances but they have none of the power that goes with possession. Having it in their hands never made money their own. A flinch of recognition flits across women's eyes when it comes to men and money. Sexual inequality describes their experience of the political economy of the heterosexual family, it's an open secret. Yet while we readily blame employers for their extra exploitation of women as cheap labour, and the state for regulating women's economic dependence on men, we protect men from the shame of their participation in women's poverty by keeping the secret. Family budgets are seen to be a *private* settlement of accounts between men and women, men's unequal distribution of working-class incomes within their households is a right they fought for within the working-class movement and it is not yet susceptible to *public* political pressure within the movement. It's no good measuring poverty by averaging out the incomes of people living on state benefits, we also have to describe the differential between the sexes, enforced by the employers, and state and last but not least by men. Forty years ago a Sunderland shirt-maker married a shipyard pattern-maker. The shirt-maker gave up her job, and they both lived on the pattern-maker's relatively high pay.

I don't know how much he earns. It used to be murder talking about it. He gives me £54 a month and I have to pay all the bills out of that ... It used to bother me at first, it doesn't now. We've got a joint bank account, but I don't use it. He'd cut my fingers off if I used it.

Another elderly woman in Sheffield who occasionally spends her afternoons playing dominoes in a community centre, where we met, says she's never had her own money. Does she buy anything for herself? Once a year she gets her hair permed and once a year she buys face powder. What else? 'Curling pins and clothes now and again, not a lot though, I make do.' Apart from domino afternoons, she never sees friends, never goes out, never goes to meetings. 'I used to be active in the church but not now, there used to be hell on if I did things in the church. We never go out together. We get ice cream every Friday – that's my treat. He says I should be thankful,' she says, and all the players laugh. Then it's quiet again and one of them murmurs, 'Aye, that's how it is.'

An 85-year-old Wigan pensioner is now looked after by her daughter – the mother applied for a grant for the daughter, because she is immobilised by arthritis. It was turned down. She's never had a wage 'I never worked – he wouldn't let me, though I'd have like to.' The day we met her diet was soup at dinner time, pineapple and cottage cheese for tea with a packet of crisps and a cup of tea.

It's old ladies who show all the signs of a long life on subsistence, though they wouldn't necessarily see themselves as having been poor, because their husbands weren't necessarily poor. I spent a wonderful afternoon with some women pensioners in Barnsley. They wear macs in mid-winter: many never had winter coats. For them, getting a winter coat was a big thing, it was to many working-class women what getting a car is to many men. No winter boots – everything has to be all-purpose, for all seasons. One eats meat once a week, and only two ever ate fresh fruit. Their handbags are shopping bags, their holidays are day trips, and occasionally going to a son or daughter. Often they say, they had no friends until they become old women, widows. Widow's liberation. None had worked after they married, except 'little' jobs now and again. Some had never had a job because they'd looked after their mams and dads. Most never knew how much their husbands had earned. Although they're among the poorest people in the community, many feel better off than they've ever been – they've got money, time and friends *of their own* for the first time.

Today's generation of old women may be the last to live a lifetime of socially accepted wagelessness. Their daughters now in their sixties, fifties and forties, were the post-war generations of married women who found their way back into waged work, who disrupted the equation between the bread-winner and masculinity which has been inscribed in both the wage system and in the state's system of income support. And now the sense is spreading in the old industrial communities that wives with 'wee jobs' are becoming bread-winners. They may be the sole earners in households where men and teenage children are all unemployed. Although mass unemployment has hit women badly, not least those women with the 'wee jobs', the fact is that the pattern of unemployment is unevenly distributed. Sex segregation in the labour market puts men and women in different jobs, often in different workplaces, susceptible to different impact as the recession bites. The dramatic collapse of work in steel and cars and shipbuilding, for example, has largely affected men because these industries were large employers of mainly men.

But there is another factor. The massive increase of employment among married women in peacetime has changed the culture we all inhabit and the legal rights of women. Of course, that hasn't happened without resistance: married women's re-entry into the labour market was usually conditional – it was designed not to disturb women's primary responsibility for domestic work. So although women's relationship to wages and work changed, men's didn't. Not surprisingly, part-time women were usually left to management's mercies and when recession struck they were usually the first to go. But the fact remains, something is afoot in English society which has prevented the promotion of a back-to-the-kitchen-sink strategy to meet mass unemployment.

When documents from the Conservative Cabinet's Family Policy Group were leaked in 1983, they revealed that the then Employment Secretary Norman Tebbit believed women should abandon waged work and return to their homes. But that belief did not, and could not, find expression in the official policy of his party. While the Conservative Party claims to be the party of national consensus, the common sense party, it is both the architect of common sense values and the prisoner of them. No party would now dare go to the voters promising a prohibition on women's right to work and to a wage. So, times have changed.

But the phenomena of women breadwinners is in no way equivalent to the experience of the male breadwinners – the new breadwinners are poorer, the legacy of a wage system based on women's economic dependence. The failure to equalise men and women's earnings leaves households headed by women poorer than they would be if the breadwinner were a man. In Sheffield I met an assistant in a hospital clinic. She takes home £201 a month. She keeps her boyfriend, who has been unemployed for four years. A couple of times a month she has a drink with the women at work, which is the only time she goes out. She pays £12.50 a week for a one-room flat, so the couple are constantly in each other's company. 'He gets depressed and then he'd rather shout at me than talk to me.' She has no winter coat or boots and she eats meat once a week, 'and by the end of the month it'll be beans on toast or a can of soup between us. *The women here are paid pin-money, but we are breadwinners.*'

A Coventry school-dinner lady in her late fifties, like many women of her generation, carries with her part of their collective memory of poor old times. 'I've worked all my life, I've never not worked, even if it was housework, and I haven't a penny in the bank. I've worked all these years and I've got nothing. When I started this job in school dinners I earned £7 a week. Now I bring home £70. It's no different.' During the summer of 1982 she drew £400 holiday pay during a six-week school break. She put by the rent for the six weeks, and laid out everything for the bills – she usually pays £6 a week for gas, £6 electricity, £6 phone, £1 television, £2.68 news-papers, £2.80 milk, £2 club for her son's clothes, £25 to £30 for food, £2 fares and £2.75 for school dinners in term time. By the time she has budgeted for these basics she has £50 left for the six-week holiday. Her husband has been out of work for three years, but her life as the breadwinner was quite unlike his. She, and many of the women like her whom I met, still does all the housework, just like before, and on top of that has to manage the effect of her husband's traumatic discovery of something women have always known – what it feels like to be economically dependent. Another school-dinner lady in Wigan told me a typical tale:

We had a terrible time when my husband was made redundant five years ago. He was in a rotten mood for months. Even now, five years later, I've got to be ever so careful – because he feels it's my money we live on. The other day he was ratty and saying 'all I hear is you are the breadwinner and we've got to be careful, we can't have this or that because we can't afford it'. I saved up for us to have a holiday, I booked a caravan and paid the coach fares and then on the morning we were due to go he said, 'I'm not going without a penny in my pocket, I can't, I can't.' Up to the eleventh hour he wouldn't go.

Men's economic dependency seems to face many women with a contradiction over housework – they need the men to change, and yet they feel the need to protect men in crisis. Only rarely did they talk of their men willingly taking over the housework and servicing their breadwinner wives. A hospital cleaner in Barnsley works part-time because she's got two small children, taking home £26.50 for seventeen hours. Her husband is a steel erector on short-time: six weeks off and two weeks on. When he's off he qualifies for unemployment benefit, which makes their joint income £49 a week plus child benefit. Until the 1982 health service dispute, she'd never been involved in a trade union, nor had she ever gone to any meetings about anything. But during the dispute she became a shop steward.

He didn't support our strikes and we used to row about it, but not now. Because we could row for ever and a day, so we've decided not to. Anyway, he knows I'm not going to back down. And I like the job, the women are great and I believe in what we're fighting for. Now that he's on short time he's doing more round the house. I used to do it all, I had complete control of the house, now the situation has changed completely.

A cleaner in a Sheffield hospital has four teenage children, all unemployed and all living at home, and an unemployed husband. She takes home £38 for nearly thirty hours. She says:

My husband does a bit of housework. He didn't do it before and he doesn't like it, but he does a bit. I'm the breadwinner and it looks like it will stay that way. Mind you, it gets me down sometimes – I'm getting out to work every day and they're there sitting around.

Another hospital cleaner in Sunderland takes home £35 a week. Her husband is on short-time and two sons are unemployed.

Me being at work causes friction at home. I'll get back from work and one of our boys is just getting up, or another day they'll all be just sat there, and you'll find all the bread's gone. I've had to get a padlock to lock it away. If I buy three tins of beans I lock two away. The other boy will mash tea a dozen times a day – your house becomes a transport cafe.

There's another kind of breadwinner – women on their own with no regrets. A psychiatric nurse I talked to in Sheffield works twenty-eight hours and takes home £51 to keep herself and two children. Rent is £11.50 a week, rates £4.60, newspapers 75p, gas £8, milk £4, electricity £1, children's clothes club £5. That leaves £17 for food and the rest of life topped up by Family Income Supplement.

I put everything in piles. What's left goes on food – sometimes it's only £15. So the thing is, sometimes you just don't eat. I very rarely go out except to union branch meetings — they get me out and they cost nowt. Now I grow all my own vegetables – it's surprising what you can do. And I've enjoyed having the kids on my own. I've been going out with a bloke for about ten years, but I wouldn't marry him – I'd have to be in to make his tea! And I love working, it's like home from home. Next to my kids my work is the most important thing in my life.

No sooner had the women's liberation movement moved from the sixties to the seventies than it saw the economic conditions for its demands evaporate. By the eighties this produced a panic that the political conditions for feminism were disappearing, too. But they haven't. So much for the notion held among some people on the Left that politics is only an expression of economics. But although the impact of women's liberation remains resilient in the culture, a question remains: given the assumption that the road to liberation lay, among other things, in women's *economic* independence, what happens when employment ceases to be an alternative 'destiny'? The answer is a baby boom. Mothers who took time out from employment for motherhood in the seventies thinking they'd go back to work later, find there isn't work to go back to. Many of them are having more babies. And in the eighties, unemployed girls who've never experienced economic independence are doing the only thing they can – having babies, either getting married or not, but often staying with their mam and dad, and quite soon getting a council house. They never consider an abortion, often don't use contraception. They want children. Of course they do. There isn't anything else. Being a mother has a certain status after all, it makes you a grown-up person, something you can't feel, if, like a girl I met in Barnsley, you leave school, which you hated anyway, and did badly at, become unemployed, and there's no job except perhaps a

government scheme. She became a painter and decorator on
a government scheme for a year. She said she really liked it,
but wouldn't have carried on doing it. She didn't know why.
Now she's twenty, and has a five-month-old baby. Her friend
told me that this baby wants for nothing, it is the best
dressed baby in the neighbourhood. She lives with her mam
and dad, a cleaner and welder respectively, and does a bit of
housework, though her mam still does the cooking, and she
goes out once a week. Of course she doesn't appear in the
unemployment statistics because she doesn't register every
week. Already you can anticipate the grumblings of protest
against sex on the dole, taxpayers' money wasted on profligate and promiscuous girls weakened by the welfare state
and women's liberation. But if motherhood is for them some
sort of liberation, it isn't in the image of the 'liberated lady'
stereotype, Cosmo girl, sexy, single, childless and *employed*.
That stereotype speaks less for women's liberation than a
society which treats children as a disruptive influence, a
social nuisance. Women's liberation doesn't promote
emulation of men's separation from children but a challenge
to that peculiar public apartheid between men and children.
It is about motherhood and independence and it is about
having women and children *in* society, not exiled from it.

Motherhood *and* dependence was the knot women's liberation tried to untie, but the baby boom among many of the
young, unemployed mothers I met suggests that, rather than
these young women being in retreat, something more complex
and contradictory is abroad.

When they're still young, girls hang around bus stations,
leisure centres, bus shelters or each other's doorsteps. A gang
of girls I met in Coventry hanging around with some boys
who, like them, were unemployed, said that when they were
younger they did a bit of vandalising: 'When I got pissed I
smashed the windows of posh houses,' said one of them. Her
friend said, 'I don't do things without a reason, only when
I've got something against people, so we did things like
spraying walls, not bus seats, we didn't slash them because
people have to sit on them. But we smashed a bus shelter

once just for something to do.' A third friend said, 'One time I used to go around with a load of boys who wanted to break people's windows, so I just left.'

If they were working they'd be going to discos, but because they can't work they stay at home, and because they're girls they do the housework, though they feel they are doing somebody else's housework. 'I do all the housework and the cooking, my mam and dad both work,' said an unemployed teenager in Coventry. 'I don't like beefburgers and things, so now and again I do proper cooking, like stews and puddings – that's the only exciting thing I do. I go to the pub a bit, but I haven't got the money, or I see my boyfriend, or I keep my mam company.'

For most of them sex happens in the same places it always did. 'We do it in fields, or up alleys, or at parties – that's the best.' The girls said some of them were on the pill, others weren't because their mams and dads don't know and they daren't go to the family planning clinic. They have no place of their own – either because they can't afford the Ritzy redoubts of the youth culture, or because home is a place where you're in the way. The only place left is the streets, and street life either costs money, or is dangerous. Hard-line street life doesn't sit easily with the girls' culture, and for all their stylish revolt, in the end the only way to belong seems to be to be part of the community of women. Faced with the alternatives of the dole, or the angry aggravation of the streets, motherhood brings a sense of belonging. More important, it offers a transition from immaturity made permanent by poverty, to a state of maturity.

So, one of the first things you notice in Northern cities hit by unemployment is babies, lots of babies, with very young parents. Unemployed men in denims and trainers pushing buggies. The sight of teenage fathers is striking because it is in such stark contrast with the role of their own fathers, who weren't seen pushing prams when they were nineteen. You don't notice the young mothers so readily, because they're doing what they've always done. The real change is that many are doing it alone. Men come and go in their lives, but there is no necessary connection between motherhood and marriage. They are going it alone not only because they happened to 'get caught out', but because it is an alternative to aimless adolescence on the dole. 'I always wanted to have a child,' said a nineteen-year-old woman living on a Sunderland housing estate with her parents. Youth unemployment there has reached 50 per cent. 'Having a baby makes me feel a lot older and more mature. At first my mam and dad weren't pleased about me falling pregnant, and they used to go on about how was I going to manage. The bloke denied it was his, I felt awful, though there's plenty have kids on their own round here. In fact the majority fall pregnant and don't get married.' After leaving school at sixteen, she went on a government course, painting and decorating, but after it finished she was unemployed. 'I went to the careers office – nothing.' She then got a factory job, earning between £30 and £40, for four months. Did she consider an abortion? 'It just doesn't seem right.' And what about sex, does she like it? 'Well, it's not everything it's cracked up to be.' She does it 'now and again' and never masturbates. Now, everything she's got goes on the baby. That's out of an income of £25 social security and £5.25 child benefit.

Older mothers watch their daughters becoming mothers with a wry recognition. 'Oh, they love it when the kids are babies, dressing them up and looking after them, everybody loves babies, but it's different when they get older,' they say. One of the women on this Sunderland estate told me they all recognised the drive: 'It's part of becoming a member of the community instead of just a reckless teenager. You don't need to get a job, when you're a mam. When you're a mam somebody *needs* you.'

In many working-class communities, particularly in the Northeast, women were never offered much in the way of waged work anyway and the girls feel that their own mothers gave birth when they were teenagers, so what's the difference? The difference is that more and more are having their babies at home with their own mothers and not with their men. But some have them alone. A mother in her early twenties in Coventry, who has been unemployed for most of the time since leaving school, said:

I wanted to get pregnant because I couldn't cope living at home. I wanted something of my own. So it was a way of getting out and I knew that eventually the council would have to rehouse me. A lot of people think that round here, several of us did it in my street because we wanted to get away. My family weren't bad, we were just overcrowded. Five out of seven girls in my street got pregnant without being married. Two got married later. And we all got council flats nearby. Life's easier on my own, I was lucky to get away.

But it's a road riddled with paradoxes. They are lonely and they are poor. Though if you're young and poor the surest guarantee of a council house is parenthood, only because the housing cataclysm of the fifties and sixties produced cold, damp deserts that no one else wants to live on. The young mothers take up the local authorities' slack stock.

The place I got, I used to hate going to bed – it was so damp, I had to listen to it dripping off the curtains. I had to wring them out in the mornings. For five months I slept with the baby, it was so cold. And I couldn't let him outside because there was a river just by. So half the time I felt like killing him, and I got agrophobia, because I was so depressed. I couldn't face seeing people. I had to go upstairs to tell the woman above that I was using the bathroom, because if she walked about above, the plaster fell off. One day a big bit of plaster fell off and hit him on the head. And the plaster was falling off in our bedrooms.

A single mother I met in Sheffield has got housing, but in a Dickensian block of flats, on the fifth floor, with no lift, a damp kitchen, bathroom and hall where the wallpaper seems to stand up only out of inertia because it isn't sticking to the walls. There is no place for the child to play. 'One day a neighbour opposite came to tell me my little boy was hanging over the other side of the railings on our landing. So after that I would never let him out to play, but then a social worker came to complain that I was keeping him in and away from other children.'

How do those young dole-queue mothers manage? A single parent living with her parents gets supplementary benefit of £25 a week plus £5.25 child benefit. If she moves into a council home of her own, her rent is paid direct through the unified housing benefit. Her cash income remains the same, but she has to stock her new home on that and whatever grants she can secure from social security for domestic hardware. These are increasingly hard to get – a Coventry welfare rights centre had so many claimants complaining that they'd not received their statutory entitlement to maternity grants that the centre has printed a special complaints form.

Fuel is these young mothers' greatest problem: it takes a large chunk of their small income, and many mothers are also housed on estates with either excessive heating costs or minimal heating provisions, which forces them to use expensive alternatives. Many of the single mothers I met had accumulated massive fuel debts of £200 or £300, and had had spells without gas or electricity or both.

A young woman living in a semi-detached house on an unpopular Sheffield estate showed me a letter she'd just received from the electricity board: 'A board employee will ... call at your premises to cut off the electricity supply on 9/11/82. If the board fails to gain entry it will use the law to gain entry to your premises.' The bill was for £19.23. 'I know I'll be all right because there's a few steps to go before it gets to that,' she said, 'but some of the lasses wouldn't know that.'

These mothers may seek maturity through maternity, but that's not the same as domesticity – they aren't into being earth mothers, mega-chefs or craftswomen. The poor, however, are often blamed for their own poverty, accused of budgeting badly or living beyond their means. But good budgeting means having a budget in the first place, having a surplus beyond merest subsistence with which to plan, bulk buy, meet the emergencies which crop up constantly. The

speed at which things wear out and break down rises fast
when everything you own is cheap. There's an unseemly
haste among people who don't have to live on £25 a week to
suggest how they could do it better, manage on a minimum
and feed the 5,000. Facing people with the budgets of the
poor often prompts the response, 'why don't they make
soup?' or 'Fresh vegetables are cheaper than fish fingers.'
But are they? Compare a typical fast-food meal for four with
several suggestions offered by people who *wouldn't* resort to
fish fingers. (See price comparison on page 70).

In an era of fast food, subsistence incomes don't make for
a culinary culture. The mass production and marketing of
family food expresses the dissolution of domesticity *as a way
of life*. Beanz Meanz Heinz exemplifies this, it is represented
as children's food and it is the moment of consumption which
is celebrated, not the process of its production. It's functional
and cheap and takes the work out of mothers' work – the
opposite of the colour supplements' fascination with food and
its production and the backlash against junk food, which
present a chic counterculture of cooking not as *work* but as
leisure and pleasure. But for the poor, food is always functional: 'It just fills a hole doesn't it?' said one single mother,
'I can't stand watching television because it depresses me,
there's always food on.' It's never the endless toast and tea,
beans, bread and chips which are the staples of poor people's
diets. 'Toast, I look like a piece of toast.'

Then there's the notion that poverty is mitigated by 'doing
it yourself'. Of course it is. But this doesn't take into account
the capital equipment you need if you're to be self-sufficient.
Nineteen-year-old mothers don't have sewing machines,
mixers, liquidisers, mincers, drills, paint brushes, *The
Readers Digest Book of Home Decorating*. Often they don't
have even baking tins, or enough pans. And only *half* have
that most ubiquitous machine, the washing machine, according to a Child Poverty Group survey carried out with the
Family Services Unit in 1981. The cost of launderettes is
prohibitive on a subsistence income – so the washing gets
done in the sink. The single parent building a home on

ten economy fish fingers	45p
2 lb potatoes (for chips)	20p
white sliced loaf	30p
	95p

potato pot

2 lb potatoes	20p
large tin tomatoes	28p
½ lb cheese	50p
onion	5p
½ doz eggs	35p
greens	20p
	1.58p

macaroni cheese

macaroni	35p
6 oz cheese	30p
1 oz flour	2p
1 oz butter	8p
½ pt milk	11p
	86

shepherd's pie

1 lb mince	1.00
1 lb carrots	20
2 lb potatoes	20
tin tomatoes	19
onion	5
	1.64p

supplementary benefit doesn't have the tools acquired by workers who've been earning for twenty or forty years. So the new wave of mothers exemplify the separation between maternity and domesticity already entrenched in working-class culture since married women reentered the labour market after the Second World War. Theirs is a rebellious motherhood, it's not an uncritical retreat into traditional femininity. But as a resourceless rebellion it also produces isolation and dependency. If motherhood *includes* them in the community of women, poor parenthood also *excludes* them from the public culture of their own generation. 'I got fed up of seeing people I knew getting dressed up and going to pubs or discos, because I couldn't and I didn't know what the latest was – and round here that matters a lot,' said a nineteen-year-old Wigan woman with a child. When it is youth culture above all which makes the pace and claims to define what is public pleasure, young single mothers, like young married sisters, are excluded. Their lives are entirely private.

Exclusion extends from pleasure to work. If having babies is partly a response to unemployment, it also becomes one of the causes of continuing unemployment. Single parents off the dole queue have the same thwarted desire for waged work as their married sisters – a *Woman's Realm* survey in the seventies found that 70 per cent of mothers full time at home would like a job, but had none because of the lack of childcare facilities. In the eighties, the prime reason is that there are no jobs, and for the few available, single mothers aren't equal competitors in the jobs market. A Coventry woman I met who had her child when she was eighteen said she had been 'on the rock and roll' since she was sixteen.

I hated being on social security and I tried everywhere for a job. At the Job Centre they were a bit funny about me going on government schemes because I had the baby, but I did get on one eventually. My mam looked after the baby and I did a job on a scheme looking after old people. I got up at six, spent all day cleaning other people's houses, from 8.30 a.m. until 4.30, with half an hour for dinner, for

£25. I did that for a year until the scheme finished. At least it felt like it was my own money and I was working for it.

Lack of childcare facilities not only blocks a job, even if there were one, it prevents single parents doing anything else to prepare themselves for a changing job market. A twenty-one-year-old mother living alone with her child on a Sunderland estate became pregnant the first she 'had sexual intercourse'. Having passed seven CSE's at school, she said, 'I reckoned that if I had a future then computer studies was where it would be. So I went to night classes at the college to do O levels. But after my mam died I had nobody to look after the baby, so I couldn't go any more.'

Many of the old industrial communities have long been a desert for women's employment. After the Second World War some became the sites of new industries located there specifically to draw on work-hungry women, but that respite lasted only two or three decades. The clothing and electronics factories have closed down in the Northeast, and the shifts specially designed for mothers, the part-time and twilight, were the first to go. But even they were no use to the unmarried mothers without fathers to mind the babies. The remaining jobs, cleaning or semi-skilled work in small factories which are surviving the recession, pay pin-money wages that assume that someone else, a man, is the breadwinner. They're not viable for women who are their own breadwinners. In Sunderland a single parent in her late teens told me. 'I worked in a factory making bingo books. It was winter, I'd go in when it was pitch dark at 8 a.m. and come out again in the dark at 5.30 p.m., still in the dark. We had Friday afternoons off and for that job I got £16 a week.' It wasn't enough to pay the rent, never mind to live on. For women on supplementary benefit, the economic benefits of having a part-time job, all they can manage without full-time childcare, are somewhat illusory, because it is taken off their benefit. 'If I was full time, I'd be taking home £40 a week,' said a Sheffield hotel worker who is also a single parent. 'But I can only work nine hours, three nights a week, and I take home £10.20. That counts against my social security.'

What about the absent presence – men. The mothers' courage in going it alone doesn't seem to draw on any *new* feelings so much as old ones. And it's less an explicit critique of men than a consensus shared between women – they share it as much with their grandmothers as with women's libera-tion. Women have always felt both complaint and commit-ment about domestic life with men – the difference is that today they can do something about that contradiction. A seventy-two-year-old Barnsley woman married a miner when she was twenty-one; she describes the contradiction:

When we got married there were no wedding cakes, no wedding do's, you were just glad to get married, you thought you were going to be better off, but really you'd no idea. Such a pity. The furniture you got was just little bits and pieces you could get hold of, and you had to go into debt for it. The men worked, but they often drank away what they worked for. All they cared about was drink. They didn't care about the home. You just thought this was your life, you just put up with it. The majority were like that. The men worked hard and as you got on in life you just thought this was home, although you hadn't the luxuries. As long as you had your mam! We hadn't a lot of room for enjoyment. Television was a marvellous thing, it shows you a bit on life, you'd never know all these things otherwise. And nurseries, they're good, aren't they? I always had to have mine with me, you got no babysitters then, you'd got nowt. I dragged mine everywhere. The men were too busy working or having their enjoy-ment, or in bed – that's been life! It shouldn't be like that. They used to torture women in them days, you know. But now women can just leave. You couldn't leave them in those days because there was no social security. It was worse than if you'd been single – you'd no friends. Married women just stayed in their own house. And when the men were in the house they were in bed. When they were out, they were out for a drink.

I always knew how much he earned, because he used to give me his pay note and I'd to go down and collect it. You got your own wages out of that and he kept the rest. I'd have liked a job but you couldn't, because the men had to be looked after, you just had to be there. And anyway he wouldn't have stood for it – a woman running round and doing things on her own.

I never had anything to do with the Co-op Women's Guilds or the Labour Party. He makes me vote Labour. I'm not up in all that, I'm not in the higher class, I just vote because he wants me to. And I didn't go to the women's guilds because I didn't have the knowledge. But it's different now, women can leave and have different men.

A twenty-year-old Sunderland woman living in a council house on her own with two children, told me, 'My boyfriend kept giving me a hiding. I wasn't very happy about that so I finished with him. He'd just come in and say, "You fucking frigid cow," and all that. But that's a regular thing up here in the Northeast. Only about two of my mates *don't* get a hiding. But I wouldn't put up with it.' They know they don't have to endure it, and they know, too, that they don't have to get married. They may *want* men in their lives, but they know they don't necessarily *need* them. That makes the difference.

The men are trapped too, though. They're young and poor and the patriarchal culture they inherit and the conspicuous consumption of their contemporaries sanctions their irresponsibility. Nonetheless, when they're there, living in, the nice little brown envelope with the weekly giro cheque arrives in their name; and when they go the authorities depend on the dependents to pay off the debts. Of course, some young fathers are fascinated by their babies and enjoy cohabiting co-operatively, finding more meaning in being fathers than their own fathers did. Parenthood promises them the same as the women – a future.

What about sex? Has anything changed for the single mothers of the eighties? Ever since the Pill revolution of the sixties, it's been taken for granted that the only obstacle to women's enthusiasm for heterosexual sex – fear of pregnancy – has been removed. The Pill was to be for the sexual revolution what steam was to the industrial revolution. It seemed to be the perfect solution – contraception without constraining the fountain of male pleasure. But this conflates two issues – pleasure and pregnancy – when they are in fact separate. Sexology and psychology throughout the twentieth century has been preoccupied with heterosexuality's problem – women. Only women's liberation, coming out of the decade of the Pill, permissiveness and the sexual revolution, inverted the question – women's problem was heterosexuality.

The Pill was as much about men's sexual liberation as it ever was about women's, because it purged *their* fear of paternity. The Pill seemed to symbolise the free woman – sexy *and* single, and so it seemed to prefigure the women's liberation movement's quest for pleasure and independence. But sexy and single didn't mean equal, and it didn't mean independent. The assumption that once women had freedom from fear of pregnancy they'd like men and they'd like sex, just like that, meant neither sex nor men nor the economics of women's powerlessness had to change. The sexual revolution escalated the pressure and helped remove the prohibitions on sex, but changed neither the form nor the content. It took women's liberation to politicise women's discontent with sex and men, but how far has that reached the young mothers inside the traditional working-class communities of the industrial North?

'Sex? I just felt pressured, it was all the bloody time, "You can't love me if you won't do it, everybody is doing it."' 'I didn't enjoy it,' said a woman who became pregnant when she was sixteen. 'He kept telling me I couldn't get pregnant the first time, but I did.' 'We do it once or twice a week,' said a woman with two children whose boyfriend comes over to stay. Does she like it? 'Sometimes, it all depends on what's gone on during the day. I used to before – when there was nothing bothering me.' Did she get what she wanted? 'No, it's just something to do. It's just because you feel affection from someone else.' Did she masturbate? 'No.' Had she heard of the clitoris? 'No.' Had she heard of orgasms? 'No, only slang words.' A nineteen-year-old Coventry woman who disowned any interest in feminism or politics – 'I'm just a fun girl,' – said she could never remember anybody talking about 'the clitoris or orgasms'. Did sex always involve penetration? 'Mostly, but not always.' Did she ever experience the magic moment equivalent to his ejaculation? 'No.' Fantasies? 'No.' Masturbation? 'Never, not ever, never fancied it.'

Today the young mothers on supplementary benefit hang on to the hopes that sex will be pleasurable and cohabitation will be companionable, but they often aren't and they're resigned to disappointment. Men come and go in their lives. When a man lives in, a woman's independence – her own name on the weekly giro – is automatically surrendered. The men become the claimants and the women their dependants. They lose control over both the revenue and the expenditure, often with catastrophic results: rent not paid, fuel bills missed, arrears mounting. It is conventional wisdom among advice agencies, local authorities and fuel boards that it's the women who pick up the tab for men's mismanagement. I heard a housing association official who visited a northern Women's Aid refuge for battered women being asked if she could help a woman who'd just arrived, eight months' pregnant, with two black eyes, find a place on her own. She said, 'I've rehoused women on their own before. Away from the influence of the husbands they cope remarkably well.'

Who knows what will happen? Will unemployment hasten the domestication of men? People seem to assume that it will, but although women may expect it, there's nothing coming from the men's movement, the working men's clubs, the trade unions and the Labour Party to encourage that transition. Among the women themselves there's the feeling that you hope for the best and expect the worst, a deep pessimism that patriarchy rules and scarpers without paying the bills.

For feminists like me, who live through the political processes of women's liberation, which turns sex inside out and reforms relationships with men, even if it doesn't revolutionise them, talking to these young, single mothers proves that gains won in sexual relationships are not necessarily permanent or universal. It's an encounter with women on the edge of transition, discontented and yet disarmed. Sex hasn't changed, men haven't changed enough and mother-hood shrouded in poverty is what it always was – gains and losses.

For me, this seemed to be symbolised in the living room of a teenage parent living in one of Coventry's worst housing estates. It was a home, her own home, even though every-thing was scavenged second hand, except for some net curtains, a coffee table and a picture on the wall above the mantelpiece. It was the only decoration in the room, a picture that hangs over thousands of mantelpieces, bought in a chain store. There were no other pictures, no photographs of weddings, babies and holidays, no parade of faces across a china cabinet or TV, no chronicle of births, deaths and marriages, nothing to be nostalgic about. The painting showed a child's face with a teardrop falling like a pearl from its cheek, an ecstasy of agony, a secular martyr. The picture bore no relation to the blotchy, snotty, shouting face of angry childhood. It was utterly serene, with no sign of rebellion, no struggle. It wasn't a real child, it was a mature face with the wisdom of hindsight passively bearing the pain of the past. Meanwhile an ebullient three-year-old bounced over the peo-ple and the furniture, clamouring for conversation and met with exhausted expletives, 'Shut up ... get off ... don't ...' The same tug of war you see in any family when the beauti-ful love affair with a baby becomes a demanding relation-ship with a little person with an invincible will. What did that painting symbolise? It seemed to hold something that couldn't be articulated, like Christian icons of Christ's martyrdom, suffering, but sweetly. It seemed to filter pain that couldn't be felt. The women's liberation movement builds on those kind of feelings, the guilts and disappoint-ments of the most passionate relationships, and provides the process in which women can say the unsayable and put personal pain back into politics. That changes how women feel about themselves and generates a web of activities to pick up the pieces kept hidden when pain is kept private.

However, the dole-queue mothers aren't just victims,

suffering women. Nor are they the 'fallen women' of the past.
There is no shame in their situation and they are participating in the disintegration of the moral force of respectability
which would once have shamed them within their own class
and community. If respectability was undermined after the
Second World War by married women refusing dependence
and returning to waged work while also having children, it is
being undermined again by the new wave of dole-queue
mothers who find a measure of independence in motherhood.
Both disrupt the rules and regulations of respectability,
which was about nothing if it was not about controlling the
social status of women. These single parents care about being
mothers but they don't care so much about being married
and they care even less for being rendered dependent.
Unemployment steals from them the economic conditions
which supported the new wave of feminism in the sixties and
early seventies, but the welfare state, the provision of child
benefit, minimal as it is, and supplementary benefit, mean
they can survive in the absence of jobs and wages of their
own. At least they can get out when the going gets rough, as
their grandmothers couldn't. And at least having babies gives
the appearance of self-determination.

Nevertheless, their rebellion is paradoxical – it may mean
a baby and a home and an income, but it also means exile
from the culture of their own generation and the political
resources available to the employed, respectable working
class and its representatives. Single mothers are disrupting
the conservatism of Labourism, they confront the patriarchal
principles of women's dependence which is embedded in the
old labour movement's codes of behaviour, in housing policies
and in the distribution of incomes. But their dissidence is
cauterised by their isolation and poverty. Worse than that, in
practice if not intent, many local councils, including Labour
authorities, treat them as though they were rough and rootless
by banishing them to barren reservations. They seem to
regard them as patients or problems; the last thing they do is
help them *organise.* Labourism has failed to produce a
politics of private life which is not patriarchal; at best it

pities the dole-queue mothers, at worst it scorns them. The only politics which I saw representing them are those organised by tenants and feminists campaigning primarily around housing, health and children. So their revolt is fraught with contradictions – resilient and yet pessimistic, they have the stamina to survive and not enough to spare. What they need is not a man to take care of them, but a new kind of working-class politics that would take care of them and take care of the radicalism of their case.

A Safe Place

On the day when there was a full chamber pot under the breakfast table I decided to leave. The place was beginning to depress me. It was not only the dirt, the smells, and the vile food, but the feeling of stagnant, meaningless decay ... It struck me that this place must be fairly normal as lodging houses go, for on the whole the lodgers did not complain.

George Orwell, *The Road to Wigan Pier*

If a woman needs to go underground from the unsafety of her own home, she can find sanctuary in the network of 'safe houses' set up by the Women's Aid Federation. When I arrive outside the refuge where I am to stay for several weeks, it is a house with no name. You'd never know it was a refuge.

Inside, the first room you come to is the office, full of filing cabinets and waste-paper bins, in-and-out trays, directories and box files. But it isn't just the arbitrary assembly of objects and colours of alienated workplaces: there is a kettle and cups beside the directories, a mirror, photos, postcards, kids' paintings, a hairdryer and deodorant, a barbecue stand, a knitting machine, a cassette playing Randy Crawford and armchairs – the miscellany of bric-a-brac that says this office is lived in.

A woman with big beautiful hands who smokes too much writes down my name and what she needs to know and what I need to tell, and another worker goes through the same routine with a serene and rather silent woman in her early thirties, with three children and two plastic bags containing toys and toiletries – the mark of a mother on the run, all you can grab in a quick getaway.

Along the corridor from my room, which is spartan but clean, is a former railway clerk, who lives on £30 invalidity pension. She'd moved in two weeks earlier and always corrected the spelling of her name when it was written wrongly on the cleaning rotas. She took me up to see her room, which she had to herself until she was joined by another-middle aged woman without children. On her neat bed is a folded nightie, there's a threadbare rug on the lino beside the bed and a library book on the bedside table. Hanging on the door is a dressing gown and in the wardrobe a change of clothes given to her when she arrived in the refuge with only the clothes she stood up in and a shopping bag. Everything is scrounged and second-hand. 'Lovely isn't it?' she said.

Next to her is a twenty-one-year-old woman sharing her room with two little girls, two teddies and a wardrobe full of clothes acquired in the refuge. At the end of our corridor is the playroom where the children not yet in school spend their days with playworkers – unemployed women who'd been signing on the dole before getting these 'work experience scheme' jobs funded by the Manpower Services Commission.

For most of the mothers this is their first experience of childcare outside their own families. For all of them it means that the children have somebody's attention all day. The mothers can sit alone with their preoccupations, or share tea and sympathy and cigarettes with other women, or sort out social security, injunctions, divorces, custody struggles and hassles with housing officials for a new home.

Once a week we have a health visitor who checks to see if the women and their children are well. 'It's all confidential,' she says, 'you don't need to tell me anything if you don't want to and nobody else sees these records. I'm just here if you need me. If you need a doctor there's this group practice nearby, or that one. Do you need to see a doctor? Are you having treatment for anything?' One other afternoon a week

her desk is occupied by a quiet, middle-aged woman book-
keeper who does the accounts. She'd got the job after being
made redundant and signing on at the job centre. There are
nine workers altogether. Two administer the refuge, work
with the women and their children, order supplies, negotiate
with the local authority, housing agencies, lawyers and social
workers, plan the annual budget, apply for grants, raise
funds, scavenge for second-hand furniture and clothes,
bargain with local firms and charities for equipment. Most
importantly they provide a safe passage for women living
through the most traumatic encounter they are ever likely to
have with men, the law and the state.

For women whose kitchens have been their own, it seems
to come naturally enough to share the domestic space in the
refuge and at least here they have a room of their own –
possibly for the first time in their lives. I never saw anyone
make a cup of tea (nobody drinks coffee, it's too expensive)
or smoke a cigarette without offering the same to everyone
else. Meals are different, everybody cooks for themselves and
keeps their own cupboard with the universal staples –
potatoes, beans, bread, eggs, cornflakes, tea and sugar.
Mine's the same. We live on chips and beans on toast. When
one of the children asks his mam for some coffee she says,
'We can't afford coffee any more, son.' That's the thing I
miss most, a thick, black cup of freshly ground continental
roast, a kick in the head. But one day somebody buys a
salad! 'I can't face chips or beans or toast again. I spent 35p
today on a roll and a cream meringue.' There's a large sitting
room with worn sofas and chairs and ashtrays and a television high on the wall, it's always on with the sound turned
low. People sometimes look but rarely listen except when
'Coronation Street' is on. And on the mantelpiece there is a
book, Marilyn French's *The Women's Room* which somebody
is reading. The kitchen has two cookers, a big plastic dustbin,
two sets of tables and chairs and a tall fridge, which rarely
has anything other than milk in it. Behind the kitchen
there's a utility room with two industrial washing machines,
bulk cartons of soap powder and an industrial dryer. The

place has a minimum of things, nearly nothing new, but enough of what the 200 women and about 400 children, who pass through the refuge every year, might need. 'I used to think these places were terrible, before I came here, but it's marvellous,' says one of the mothers whose two boys regard the refuge as 'our new house'. They cling to her hands, legs, skirt constantly, except when the playworkers arrive. Then they dart off upstairs.

Something about the place is summed up in its smell – the secret life of a space. It challenges the myth that refuges might be safe but they're squalid. In any one week there could be a dozen or more children spilling their beans, wetting the beds, hoarding old crusts. Like any over-populated, under-capitalised place, it could stink of smoke and shit and sick and sleep. But it doesn't, it smells of work, the wiped-up smell of pine and lavender.

That evening, once the children have gone to bed (little ones at 7.30 p.m. and big ones at 9.30) we're all in the sitting room for the monthly meeting between the women, the workers and the management committee who operate as a support group. There are as many people as turn up at an average Sunderland boilermakers branch meeting. We learn that there's a forthcoming regional meeting of a group planning a pamphlet for Women's Aid. Who wants to go? One of the workers and one of the women, who's never attended meetings of any kind before living in the refuge, want to go. After the business we're still sitting around. The older woman looks tense and upset, and says she's missing her bingo, but daren't go to her old club 'because he might see me,' but if she doesn't go she'll miss the annual trip and, 'if I don't go on that I'll never get out.' She hasn't been outside the refuge properly for two weeks. 'Well, why not go to the local bingo round here,' somebody suggests. 'We can check what's on easy enough.' No, she wants to see her old friends. This was getting serious, the clatter of people talking all at once dies down until there's silence. 'Are you missing your friends?' somebody asks her. 'I'm missing everybody,' she says. Her head is in her hands, holding on hard to the tears.

She needs to be held, but that seems dangerous, everybody is hanging on to themselves. We're mesmerised. 'I bet the budgie's dead,' she says, 'he won't remember to feed him.' One of the workers touches her shoulder, it is only the slightest touch and only for a second. 'We'll go and see,' says the worker. 'And he hasn't asked about me,' says the woman, who still loves her husband and worries about whether he's eating and whether he's well. She cares for him, 'but he doesn't care.' How did she know? 'I phoned one of my neighbours to find out if she'd heard any noise from our flat. She said, "Why? is anything wrong?" I told her I wasn't there, I'd left, and I thought he'd smash things up and my china cabinet would be the first.'

By midnight an expedition to the bingo is planned, half a dozen from the refuge will go with her in the minibus, and a couple will go to the flat to rescue the precious possessions, the budgie and the china cabinet. When they get there the china cabinet is still in one piece but the budgie is dead.

This woman arrived at the refuge early one summer evening in 1982 after a row over the dinner.

The day I came here I'd gone down to Age Concern – I used to go there for meetings and bingo – and I told them I wasn't stopping because I'd no money. Anyway, one of them told me to stay and gave me a raffle ticket. And I won! It was groceries, peas, baked beans and things, so I went round to somebody's house and asked if she'd like to buy the Weetabix because I wanted the money for a pie. I bought a steak and kidney pie, heated it up with the peas and some potatoes and put a couple of spoonfuls of peas on my plate to kid him I'd had some. Of course, he played war that he'd got rubbish for his dinner, but he'd got everything I could give him. That's when he started. He threw a punch at my scar. [She'd had a breast removed some months earlier.] I swerved, went into the bedroom, found my shopping bag, packed my nightie and three library books my neighbour loaned me – I knew I'd have to give them back. I just went through and said, 'I'm going out for some cigarettes,' and went out, and I've never been back. I walked to the nearest telephone box and asked the operator if she could put me through to the refuge – I didn't have a single penny. The refuge just told me to stay put and they sent a car round for me.

A few of us sit around talking into the night, women's talk about operations and illnesses, birth, blood and death. The convention of body talk among women creates an impersonal intimacy, by means of our bodies we bare our souls. 'It's *my* body,' says the oldest when we're complaining about doctors never telling you what's happening. It takes us aback, perhaps because such a bold outburst connects her un-expectedly to women's liberation, and yet, of course, it affirms feminism's faith in women's wish to reclaim their bodies and in body talk as the great leveller. It is also shock-ing because it confronts us with *her* body, an old woman's body with cancer, only touched when it is being cut or hit.

The young woman who arrived today talks about falling ill while her baby was sick. 'My husband just crumbled when I felt it was me that needed to crumble and somebody to help me. I had to keep the house going and look after the kids. I was ill too but I couldn't consider my own feelings. I never really felt cared for, ever, not in the way of support.' Nobody takes care of mothers. She wept and we listened. 'Goodnight,' we said, and a houseful of women slept safely alone in their beds.

Within a day or so the newcomers have appointments fixed with social security to get some money and when it looks as if they're staying, negotiations begin with schools to admit their children. Meanwhile it's sunny and the climbing frame is hauled over to the paddling pool, newly built in the back garden, and the covers are lifted off the sandpit. The pool is filled with water and bubbles and the kids scoot down the slide attached to the climbing frame into the bubble bath and the arms of a playworker who picks up one of the children and kisses his little red bum. The mothers are sitting around on the grass while the playworkers look after the children. One mother of two small children arrives back later in the afternoon looking ashen. She's just picked up the children from a rendezvous with their father who had an afternoon's access, and he'd shouted at her and them in the street and threatened to take the children away. Plans are laid, a couple of the workers will take the children next time and pick them up and a lawyer is contacted to deal with the harassment. She sits down but doesn't join in the conversations, her face is distracted and her hands move constantly as though she's talking to herself. She always looks frightened. 'I was always that frightened,' she says, 'he screamed at me all the time and the kids. He didn't play with the kids, he used to hit them, he'd take it out on them more than me. He said I neglected things, it didn't matter what I did it was never good enough.' Before she married she'd lived alone in a bedsit and worked in a factory for ten years. After they married they got a council flat on the second floor overlooking a main road. 'So there was nowhere to let the kids out to play. It was terrible, I just sat in the house all day and when my husband wasn't working he'd just scream at me and the kids would be screaming and he'd be hitting them.' When he was on the dole they lived on £114 a fortnight. 'I never had any pocket money, he spent it all. I even got a job cleaning for £26 a fortnight and he spent that too, that used to make me feel dead small. Now I feel like a millionaire and I've got peace of mind.' The rows were always over money and housework: 'He'd just go berserk till two or three in the morning, bawling and shouting, and I'd just try to sit and hold his legs. One time the giro came and it was only £2, so when he went out to phone the social security I just shoved the baby in the pram and walked out to phone social services. They told me to go home and talk it over. When I was pregnant many a night I've run out and slept in passages till the morning. He wanted the place immaculate but he'd never tidy up, he just sat there in his chair from morning till night and got at me all the time about the housework. I had no friends, I felt as if I had nobody.'

One morning the lobby is loaded up with furniture being shunted into a spare room to be stored. It belongs to a woman in her mid-twenties. Seven or eight months pregnant with bruised arms and a purple bruise round her eyes. She believes she can't stay in the refuge because her husband knows where it is – they live nearby – and she can't stay with her relatives because he's threatened them, too. So the refuge arranges for her to visit the housing department, and later that day to meet a housing association official who will come to the refuge. In the afternoon she returns with another woman, who waits for her. The housing association official asks if she was a joint tenant of her council flat. 'Yes.' 'Well, we can't treat you as homeless because you are a joint tenant. We have policies which we have to stick to very rigidly.' 'But I can't stay here because he'll come round. And he's keeping the flat.' She points to the newcomer and explains, 'I met this woman at the council housing department and she said I could stay with her.' 'I can't offer you anything because you've got a tenancy. Have you got any arrears?' The woman explains that she probably still has, though she understood they were being paid off and the rent was paid direct through the DHSS. 'That would have to be sorted out before you could become a tenant of ours,' says the official. 'But my husband gets the giro. He's got the money,' says the woman. 'You've had that money equally, though,' says the official. 'We won't do anything until that's sorted out and if you give up your share of the joint tenancy.' 'But I can't contact him,' says the woman. 'The council will handle that,' explains one of the workers. 'But nobody knows where he is, what'll I do in the meantime?' 'Well, there's very little you can do. Do you want to live in this area?' asks the official. 'Yes.' 'Why, if he's so violent?' 'Why should I leave?' the woman replies, 'All my family live round here.' 'You're in a right state with yourself, aren't you?' declares the official.

The refuge worker suggests ringing up the council to check the arrears and clarify the next move. The council's housing officer says she's got to go back to her flat with an injunction, otherwise she's making herself intentionally homeless, and he says the arrears are £400. 'But £400, that's impossible, the DHSS has been paying it direct! What am I going to do?' 'Well,' says the official, 'nobody can help because of all the rules and regulations – we don't make them but we have to abide by them.'

She doesn't stay here, but the workers stay in overnight – they often work fifty, sixty, seventy hours a week – just in case her husband comes looking for her. The women are terrified, Carol biting her nails, Irene panicking about a ghost.

It seems surprising, but there isn't much talk in the refuge about marriage or men. There's also no pressure to come or go, no one scorns the woman who's left home five times and who still goes back, who loves her husband and wants to be wanted. Everybody knows why she does it. Equally, everybody knows why everybody stays, they've been through all the arguments a hundred times before and now they don't need to any more, now they know they're not to blame and their husbands aren't the homicidal maniacs some theorists would have them be.

Suddenly it all seems very ordinary, it's civil war on the home front about all the obvious things. 'The rows started because of money and him going out all the time,' said the woman who arrived in the refuge on the same day as me. 'If he wanted something in the house and I didn't have it he'd say, "What did you do with all the money?" He always made me feel I was doing something wrong. He'd go to football training, he was into physique, and he'd have a couple of pints after, and at first he went out Fridays and Sundays. He was typical of the men we knew.' She worked in a clothing factory before her pregnancy. He was a carpenter earning about £120 a week.

He gave me £50 for my wages. I didn't like that because it was less than half and all the bills came out of my wages – £13 rent, £100 electricity bills in the winter for the central heating, £5 gas and £7 a week for other bills. He'd give me money to buy clothes, but I had to keep asking for it. We had the same bills after he got made redundant. Some days after I'd been to the supermarket for the week's shopping I'd be smashed, there'd be nothing left. I always tried to buy some kind of meat, mainly for my husband, chops or rabbit, mince, a couple of chicken joints for a casserole. If I got him a chop

I'd have a sausage or an egg with the bairns. I ate the same as them. We'd have fresh vegetables about twice a week and fresh fruit not very often. I felt angry with him because there wasn't enough money to buy what he wanted. When he first got made redundant he got earnings-related dole, about £75. He had about £7 for himself, but I never had money of my own. He very rarely helped round the house, because he felt we had different jobs. I'd ask him to clean the bath when he got out or occasionally hoover, but he wouldn't so we rowed about that, especially after he got made redundant. I'd be working away while he was just sitting. He'd say, 'Leave it, it doesn't matter,' but if I'd left it the place would be a pigsty. I felt I'd tried everything, I'd tried to be a good wife, mother, mistress what else could I do?

She tried to work herself, and got a couple of nights barmaiding, but he didn't like that, and he didn't like one of the children going to nursery. 'He thought the kids should be at home with me.' And when he started going out all the time, she started going out occasionally,

I went out with the lasses, we were all married women, and I'd get a babysitter for £1. He never did. I got several black eyes during the rows and eventually I left – I left several times and always went back. I was just fed up with the whole situation. I'll work as soon as I can, I'd like to do something nice, but I expect it'll be barmaiding.

One of the youngest women in the refuge, twenty-one years old with two children, worked before she was a mother as a shop assistant:

I'd wanted to be a nurse or a policewoman, but I had to leave school right away and help support my family. We never fought when we were engaged, and I thought we'd just get married and have our own little home, I thought the bills would get paid and we'd be closer than we were before. He adored the baby and would help when she woke at night. He gave me £30 a week and I'd pay for the bills, £12 rent, £5.50 for two bags of coal and the rest went on food. He liked proper meals, he lived on liver or chops, his bait would come out of the family allowance and I'd not eat during the day, then eat the same as him at night.'

Like most of the other women in the refuge, she never went on holiday after she was married, never went to the pictures and rarely went out.

I went out half a dozen times in the three years we were married. He went out three or four nights a week at first and then every night. After a bit he got a job in a brick works and picked up £80 a week on day shift and £100 on night shift. My wages went up to £40. I asked him for more but he said that with the family allowance we had the same. I got offered a part-time job in a bakery at the weekends, and he said he'd look after the kids, but he never did, so I couldn't do it. After we had the second child we had the rows, he'd not let me go to her when she cried. He'd make me sleep with the kids, then he'd make me come back to bed with him, in and out all night.

She said he threw the baby around, tried to strangle them all and ripped up the furniture. Eventually a social worker told her she should leave. 'Mind you I wasn't pleased at all, because I wanted my own home. I knew *I* could stand it, but not the kids.'

The oldest woman in the refuge had worked as a railway clerk, in a sausage factory, a pop factory and in a factory making bingo boards until she stopped working a few years earlier and was put on invalidity benefit. Her husband is disabled too, and worked until a year or so earlier.

He got £3 pocket money when he was working, but when he finished and we were both on invalidity benefit, that was the worst part. Because he had too much time, he'd go to the club afternoon and night. He has to have his £5 on Friday, and he wouldn't take any less than £2 a session, we both smoke, so that would be a total of about £6 a day at least, and then I'd spend £1 on our tea alone. Often I could only afford a small steak and kidney pie and I'd give it to him, or a chop. I'd have potatoes and cabbage and gravy.

Out of their invalidity benefits, which came to £60, rent

took £10, coal £5.10, and he expected to spend £4 or £5 daily on drink and cigarettes – at least. That left £10, or less, per week for food.

He always liked to say what was going to be done, he was very domineering. I'd generally talk him round, but never answer back. He'd threaten that I'd not get any money the next week, but I always managed to. I got a social worker and she suggested I get a bus pass, so I could get to town. I tried six times but got turned down because I wasn't sixty. I couldn't afford to go anywhere, I can't walk far, so I had to buy stuff locally where it was dearer because the bus fare was 64p.

The last new clothes she had was when she married twenty years before.

Apart from that it was jumble sales or what I got given. Generally I'd buy him a second-hand suit and take it up. I used to have a sewing machine, but I had to sell it when we got into difficulty with an electric bill. The last time I saved any money was my redundancy pay, but that soon went. We never went to the pictures and I never had any pictures on the wall. For a treat for myself I'd occasionally buy a cream cake. The social worker said I should get out of the house, so I got enticed down to Age Concern and passed the afternoon there. We played bingo and had a cup of tea and a laugh.

The violence had begun about two years before:

He was always crafty, he'd hit me where it was covered, on the body and the legs, never on my face. One day I darted out of his way and he broke his hand on the settee. I rushed him to hospital and the doctor asked how it was done and I said he'd fallen over on the step. He hit me a lot, but I suffered it till I couldn't stand it any more. Everybody knew and said I should leave, but it's not so easy to leave your home and all the furniture I'd bought when I was on the railway. I think it wouldn't have been so bad if he hadn't swore at me so much, that was worse than hitting me.

She is a Christian woman and she whispers some of the

words he called her. As the weeks go by she begins to receive
visitors at the refuge and when she begins to feel the marriage is over, with the workers' help she starts negotiating with
the council and housing associations for a new flat, although
she also feels the refuge is home, a safe space that is becoming more and more difficult to leave. After several months
she moves into her flat. Within six months she has died of
cancer. The only mourners at her funeral are the women
from the refuge.

During my first few days in the refuge, I feel myself
descend into depression. The quest for social pain becomes a
preoccupation with my own pain – after all, feminists usually
start from their point of identification with other women, and
I have my own troubles too, like I'm also 'intentionally
homeless', a person who's got out in order to get up. So I'm
getting sadder and sadder among these women who are
getting stronger and stronger. Then there's a jolt – I'm not
the same as these women, I have no children, no dependants
and I have skills I can sell without impediment. Only women
who are not in the same circumstances as most women can
up and off for six months. I'm *able* to be in the refuge
because I choose to be – nothing is keeping me here. I have
the one thing most women don't have – freedom of movement.

Staying at the refuge becomes very comfortable, it's very
companionable and the women are very nice. There are
forms of care which are absent, certain kinds of intimacy,
and friendship, no touching, for instance, but it's compensated by other kinds of care which are possible and not
risky. Like tonight: Sylvia didn't come home and everybody
was worried about her. The only people here are women and
everybody feels safe and understood.

The refuge has been more revealing about people and
poverty than I'd expected, because what it's revealed is the
hard edge of the sex differential. The women who come to
refuges do so because marriage is unbearable *and* they have
no resources to give them anywhere else to run to. So the
question of economics is central too. Also, they are mainly

here because they have small children and no earnings of their own.

All the women in the refuge are poorer than men, all are allocated less money, distribution of resources, food, drink, clothing, money and time within their own families. They aren't just poor women, they are *battered*. In breaking away they aren't just leaving home, they are changing from the victims they once thought they were into survivors, transformed by their own flight into a little bit of freedom and safety among other women. Unlike the hostels for the homeless, places of last resort where inmates feel treated as if they have no rights, the refuge is a place of first resort, where women learn they have rights and how to exercise them. Feminism has generated this network of refuges. (If they'd existed in George Orwell's day, when they were needed at least as much as now, we'd have been spared all his sentimental fallacies about the perfect symmetry of family life.) But feminism never prescribes its own politics for the inhabitants. Firstly, because it goes against its grain: women always have to find their own way to where they're going. Secondly, it doesn't need to – the feminist consciousness which builds the refuges is only the commonsense of its clients. This gives the lie to the notion that women's liberation is only a middle-class indulgence – the refuges are a complex resource maintained by a poor movement for poor women. They are where sex and class meet – the women are there because domestic violence, like rape, is something men do to women, not because they're mad or homicidal maniacs, but as an expression of *ordinary* domestic conflict between unequals. The violence is only the exercise of an ultimate weapon available to men. And the women are poor because they are working-class and women. The refuge is more than that, though – it is a new kind of politics with the power to change lives. It isn't about only opposing, it isn't about passing resolutions, formulating programmes, making demands of something or someone else, or administering consensus. It does what is necessary *for itself*.

But the Women's Aid movement is more – it is a radical

intervention in the law and order debate, it goes beyond a puritanical protection of women which reproduces their vulnerability, and it transcends the limits of the Left-Right contest between police authoritarianism and police account-ability. It was no accident that when I was writing this, the Conservatives had just been returned to power in the 1983 election, and one of their first moves was to try to disguise popular discontent with the police by the restoration of the rope. For one awful month, it looked as though England was about to sink irretrievably into barbarism. But we were pulled back from the brink; the attempt failed.

However, it is worth reflecting on another dimension of the law and order forces. We may too readily have mocked the Tory ladies in their funny hats advocating primitive retribu-tion, for what the socialist movement has not registered is that these ladies articulate a collective fear which women share. Their catalogue of culprits – muggers, rapists, robbers, child molesters – are categories of men.* The Tory ladies add to these another – trade-union bully *boys*. What is absent, not surprisingly in the context of their rhetoric about the family, is that home is where many women endure violence against their person. The Tory concern is not with that kind of domestic warfare, but with war on the streets. Their response is authoritarian. The Left's response, quite correctly in some respects, is to counter the authoritarianism of the state with demands for public control of the strong arm of the state, a demand which has found force in the escalating evidence of state violence in Ireland and in England police abuse of the people in the name of protection of the people. However, the Left has ducked the problem of widespread fear of violence within the working class, arguing that violence is the result of deprivation – once the people are no longer deprived they'll no longer be depraved. The difficulty with this is that it is an appeal to the future, and it concedes the debate about the present to the Right. It took women's liberation to formulate

---

* I'm grateful to my friend Frankie Rickford for pointing this out to me.

a different kind of positive intervention, one that seeks to protect the casualties and raise consciousness about the causes of violence. It has thus politicised the problem of violence beyond the parameters set by the law and order debate. It does what the Tory ladies can't do, which is to name women's fear of men. It shows that domestic violence, sexual harassment, rape, incest and sexual assault are commonplace manifestations of a dynamic based on men's power and women's subordination. In setting up women's refuges and rape crisis centres it does not seek revenge, it seeks to take care of the survivors and to change the policies of state agencies.

In a different context, feminists have worked within trade unions to mobilise grievance procedures to protect women who complain of sexual harassment, either by their bosses or by fellow workers. In specifying what sexual harassment means – anything from pinups and sexist jokes to assault and rape at work – its policies against sexual harassment raise the consciousness of men. What is truly radical about this innovation is that it intervenes in the quality of life at work, the culture shared between men and women workers, *on the side of women.* By adopting policies against sexual harassment they are opposing hitherto-accepted codes of normal masculinity and their effects in exercising power and control over women. In other words, they take the side of women against forms of male power. In so doing, they enable women to organise against their own victimisation and create the conditions in which men themselves may take responsibility for the reform of masculinity. Feminism's concern with sexual politics extends into the whole range of representations of sexuality, masculinity and femininity, from advertising to pornography – it intervenes in the culture and in so doing seeks to change the ways in which men and women inhabit their masculinity and femininity.

Every day during my stay in the refuge the women would go out to see social security officials, the housing department, lawyers. Meanwhile I'd go round the town interviewing trade unionists, redundant workers, councillors, tenants and community associations: the *reform of men* was not yet part of their agenda. And yet in their own city, hundreds of women and children every year crawl out of the front line into this trench. If it were Northern Ireland we'd call it war.

Baths and Bosses: the Miners

The machines that keep us alive, and the machines that make the machines are all directly or indirectly dependent upon coal. In the metabolism of the Western world the coal-miner is ... a sort of grimy caryatid upon whose shoulders nearly everything that is *not* grimy is supported.

George Orwell, *The Road to Wigan Pier*

The socialist movement in Britain has been swept off its feet by the magic of masculinity, muscle and machinery. And in its star system, the accolades go to the miners – they've been through hell, fire, earth and water to become hardened into heroes. It is masculinity at its most macho that seems to fascinate men.

Miners are men's love object. They bring together all the necessary elements of romance. Life itself is endangered, their enemy is the elements, their tragedy derives from forces greater than they, forces of nature and vengeful acts of God. That makes them victim and hero at the same time, which makes them irresistible – they command both protection and admiration. They are represented as beautiful, statuesque, shaded men. The miner's body is loved in the literature of men, because of its work and because it works.

It is the nature of the work that produces a tendency among men to see it as essential and elemental, all those images of men down in the abdomen of the earth, raiding its womb for the fuel that makes the world go round. The intestinal metaphors foster the cult of this work as dark and dangerous, an exotic oppression, visceral and yet alienated. It constructs the worker, the miner, as earth-man and earth-man is true man. And it completes an equation between some idea of elemental work and essential masculinity. This romance is duly mirrored in working-class politics – miners are the Clark Gables, the Reds of class struggle.

The cult of masculinity in work and play and politics thrives only in exclusive freemasonries of men with their secret codes which render women immigrants in their own communities. There's nothing like secrets to thwart democracy. But the exclusion is all-important because women's presence would dissolve the symmetry between men's work and masculinity. So it is that the fetish of masculinity is fashioned in men-only milieus – we look to footballers, boxers, soldiers and miners to find our real men.

But back to the body. Men who write about miners lavish poetic pleasure on their bodies, they seek to *explain* miners in the language of their statuesque and satanic physique. 'It is only when you see miners down the mine and naked that you realise what splendid men they are. Most of them are small (big men are at a disadvantage in that job) but nearly all of them have the most noble bodies; wide shoulders tapering to slender supple waists, and small pronounced buttocks, with not an ounce of waste flesh anywhere,' says Orwell in *Wigan Pier*. It is a familiar fascination; D.H. Lawrence had it, and more recently Vic Allen in his history of the Left's rise in the National Union of Mineworkers, *The Militancy of the British Miners* (Moor Press, 1981) writes about his attachment to these men. They evoked for him images of hard, unrefined men, distinct and separate from other workers, hewing in the mysterious dungeons; they are dirty, strange and attractive because they are masculine and sensuous.

In Orwell's celebration of the glamour of miners, Orwell can't resist a ruling class analogy: they've got a 'figure fit for a guardsman,' he said. No doubt it was the finest accolade from an old Etonian, and no doubt it meant something *then* when miners were regarded as dark, ignoble savages both by the respectable Brighton ladies who are a typical target for

Orwell's abuse *and* among the respectable, washed working class. But looking back on his tribute to the miners, it is a *flawed* masterpiece. It isn't that his pleasure in masculinity is suspect so much as that all that sensuous attention tells us something else about the cult of masculinity among men. Clearly it involves a mass narcissism which is supported by the social structures within which they work and play. Men can see themselves as the ideal human type because they live in structures in which they are dominant. Women don't have that collective narcissism because they are a subordinate sex. But the form of that narcissism tells us more about men's love of men: it is masculinity *in general* that they love, and there is a contradictory corollary in the iconography of miners – it both suggests and suppresses sexuality. Orwell epitomises it, he eroticises his 'black and naked' and 'splendid' men, but his elegy is punctuated by a brisk and brutal denial of desire in what his biographer, Bernard Crick, calls his 'aggressive heterosexuality'. *The Road to Wigan Pier*'s wanton polemics against effete intellectuals and strident feminists are suffused by homophobia. Did he know how much he went on and on about 'Nancy poets' and namby pambies? Didn't any of his best friends tell him?

Orwell makes miners the core of his chronicle, they are the essential man and the essential worker, but the equation between work and masculinity depends on an exclusion – women. The suppression of sexuality which is material both to his affinity for and his analysis of coal mining is also a suppression of history. The equation is represented as natural, and that gives it the force of commonsense. It is typical of Orwell – recruiting the readers' commonsense to conquer history. Mining as men's work, as a natural and obvious essence of work, has a history, however. The archaelogy of mining reveals a historic struggle over the sex of miners. Just as men's muscularity was and is celebrated in the histories, so was another man fascinated by the muscularity of women who worked at the pitheads. A Victorian gentleman called A.J. Munby toured the Wigan coalfield talking to the pit brow 'lasses' who worked at the pit top sorting coal from

muck during an intense instance in the nineteenth-century
struggle to regulate the sex of waged workers and of men and
women. In Wigan the women wore trousers, they had the
strength of horses, and Munby loved that. But their very
strength, and their androgynous uniform, was invoked in the
campaign to abolish their right to the work, a campaign
which divided both male miners and coal owners during the
1890s. According to Angela John's history of the struggle, *By
The Sweat of Their Brow* (Croom Helm, 1980) opposition to
the women's work focused on control over their sexuality and
motherhood and on the employers' attitudes – some
supported the women because they were cheap labour. Some
feminists, too, supported the women's right to work. But the
men reacted to the women 'on the basis of sex solidarity
rather than seeing them as part of the working class'.
Although the colliery communities were never really associated with the cult of respectability, which was so important
in dividing the 'rough' from the 'respectable' working class in
Victorian England, nevertheless the pit brow women were
regarded as a moral threat. The purge failed in Wigan and
women were still working there and in a couple of other
regions until after nationalisation. Deputations of pit brow
lasses visited Parliament in the 1880s and in 1911 during
campaigns by the miners and some coal owners to exclude
them from the collieries. The women found support from
some local miners and coal owners as well as feminists. Many
pit brow lasses also did stints in Wigan mills, but they're
nostalgic for the hard, rough and often bitterly cold pit brow.
'The mills were hot and dusty, and we were used to the cold.
I know it sounds crackers but we preferred it,' said one of the
pit brow lasses who started working at the pit when she was
fourteen and finished when the women's work was abolished
after nationalisation. The women enjoyed their sense of
strength – some wielded seven-pound hammers – and independence. Nationalisation brought mechanisation of their
work which involved separating dirt – slate – from the coal
before sale. But the jobs in the new mechanised washeries
went not to the women they displaced but to men. Where

renewed attempts in Parliament to exclude the women in the early 1950s failed, the union succeeded. Feminism faded, women were domesticated and their right to work with coal was finally extinguished.

One of Wigan's local councillors, whose mother was active in the Labour Party women's section, remembers that she also worked on the pit top. 'She wanted to do it, she was one of the type who believed in doing it because she wanted to. She was a women's libber really, because she said they'd tried to stop the pit brow lasses, but it never came off.' So, the mines weren't always men's work. And the existence of such women is a memorial to a hidden history of intra-class conflict. These women weren't entirely defeated, and they weren't yet buried, their resistance could have been called to bear witness, but Orwell himself participated in the struggle for their exclusion by hiding their history. No doubt he could be forgiven for an inadvertent omission, but women more than most know that life, like history, is made up of inadvertencies.

In Orwell's time, Wigan was as much a cotton town as it was a coal town, and if his excavation of the elements of exploitation was to have been adequate, it could not have omitted the experience of women in the cotton industry. He ought to have known better, but he was blinded by his own sex-centredness. And given his own class position, as an emigré from the upper middle-class, a class serviced by the domestic labour of the working class, it is telling that he understands the contribution of coal to his class comfort, but doesn't discuss the contribution of that other 'service', domestic service. The census of 1931 which describes the distribution of workers at the beginning of Orwell's decade, recorded twice as many workers in domestic service as there were miners (about two million, compared with one million miners). And, as he warned us about the hewers of coal, we are as capable of forgetting that, as he did, 'as we forget the blood in our veins'. We would do well to transpose Orwell's transposition of Chesterton: the metabolism of the Western world is founded on the work of women more completely than we realise until we stop to think about it. Orwell doesn't understand half the world because he doesn't see it.

In the Bible of class solidarity, miners and men are the archetypes. Miners *par excellence*, depending which side you are on, are seen as the satyrs or the saviours of the working class, they are either the devils or the messiahs who will lead us out of the land of Canaan. Men have to beware of their fascination for these men whose solidarity in work and play is founded on the exclusion of women. Their solidarity was based on sex, their own sex, as much as it was ever based on class. Orwell broke with his class to express his solidarity with the miners in *The Road to Wigan Pier*, and he expressed his solidarity in terms of his own class position. 'In a way it is even humiliating to watch coal miners working. It raises in you a momentary doubt about your own status as an "intellectual", and a superior person generally.' Like Orwell, women's relationship to miners starts from the basis of exclusion and mystery, but women live with the drama and danger of the pits, they live their solidarity with the pitmen. Their story can't be written without the story of the men, but then neither could the story of the miners be truly told without including the women. The shroud thrown over the subordination of women in the mining communities has much to tell us about the myth of the 'archetypical proletarians'.

Let us look at their respective relationship to work and home. Orwell used the miners as the classic case of the working class; through them he revealed its suffering and its stamina. But the relationships within which women laboured in the coal communities would have told him even *more* about class struggle than did his breathtaking chronicle of labour down there in the dark. Or rather, the men and women's relationship to each other – unlike the work of hewing coal which is not *typical* of work in capitalist economies – that relationship, even in its extremities, was typical of something that shaped class struggle in Britain. It helps to explain the conservatism of our class struggle, and its failure to mature into socialist struggle.

The miners' historian, Robin Page Arnot, in his book *The Miners: Years of Struggle* (1950) briefly but pertinently shared feminism's concern with housework as labour that reproduces life and the capacity to labour. Unlike Orwell and his fetish, coal, he suggests that women's work was vital to life. 'Nearly every convenience which the nature of the miners' occupation demanded had to be furnished and maintained by the drudgery of the womenfolk.' That drudgery could have been transformed overnight by the provision of pithead baths for the men, and for their clothes, which were often so laden with dust that, as one old miner recalled, 'I used to bray my gear against the wall'. When the clothes were wet and were put to dry in front of the household's fire, they polluted the whole atmosphere with sulphurous fumes.

The history of miners' trade unionism throughout the twentieth century carried an oddly incidental commitment to transforming those conditions of women's work. The industry was unique in that the law prescribed for it health and recreational provisions, what we now call the social wage, for most of this century. All of human life was there, in the politics of coal, but half of human life had no voice and no vote. That meant that the unique opportunity to unite the whole community in demands of the coal-owners that would benefit the *whole* community were squandered. Arnot says it:

For the mining community as a whole there was one half unorganised, unsafeguarded, unrepresented in Parliament – the wives and mothers of working miners ... No government reports measured from year to year the changes in their conditions of life: nor do they figure in statistical columns beyond their place in the tables of births, deaths, and marriages. Their song, or their dirge, remained unsung, or at any rate unheard.

The story of the pithead baths bears him out. Under the 1911 Coal Mines Act, pithead baths had to be provided if two-thirds of the miners voted for them. Miners' leaders committed to the baths heeded the advice of a mining engineer at the Royal Commission which resulted in the 1911 act, whose advice was: if you win the women to the cause of pithead baths you will win the baths. After a tough debate within the Miners' Federation in 1911 – the miners were not united on the baths' efficacy – some of the miners' leaders collaborated with women activists in the labour movement and during the First World War brought out a pamphlet, published by the Women's Labour League, promoting pithead baths, including testimony from Robert Smillie and the well-known feminist Kathryn Bruce-Glazier. Above all, the cause was identified with the interests of women. Robert Smillie, who became the leader of the Miners' Federation, told the 1911 conference: 'I think it is a shame and a disgrace that the lives of our miners' wives, from four in the morning until 11 o'clock at night should be one long day of slavery.' He believed 'the dirt of the pit should be left at the pit'.

Successive commissions and reports amplified the case for provision of social services – especially baths and canteens – and recreational facilities, through a levy on coal, during the inter-war period. It culminated in the clean-up of the industry inaugurated by nationalisation after the Second World War. By then, though, many communities had their clubs and institutes, among the few places of pleasure on their barren landscape, or miners' 'casinos', as one aggrieved Durham clergyman called them. Only a third of collieries had pithead baths before nationalisation. The promise of the social wage, enshrined in the law, had given the miners remarkable room for political maneouvre to humanise their spartan communities. More important, it sanctioned struggle by *men* to mitigate the interminable labour of their *women*. But all the old miners I met, contemporaries of Orwell, remembered the arrival of the baths, thought they were wonderful, yet couldn't remember how they came or who fought for them.

Their construction became a treat for the whole community. 'It caused a little social outing in my family,' said a pitman's daughter who grew up in the South Yorkshire pit village where her father worked. 'It was in the mid-50s and I was about nine or ten years old. One Sunday my dad took us all up to see the new pit-head baths. We thought it was so smashing – it sticks in my mind because it was such a treat.' An old miner in Barnsley summed up the euphoria:

For all the pay rises in the world, the finest thing that ever came out of the pit was a bath. Nobody knows what a fella felt like then. I know what I felt like, I can't describe it. I felt like a fairy. The first time they went into the baths, you couldn't get them out. At first people kept their drawers on, then they'd lower them. And they started keeping their clothes at the pit. It was a godsend for the women.

Given the pleasure and benefit to both men and women, why was it never a primary campaigning focus? A much-respected retired Communist deputy in south Yorkshire summarised the pillars of working men's politics: 'Probably most were anti-boss though not necessarily anti-system.' Consequently, nationalisation expressed their political wish, but just as that didn't extend to an alternative philosophy at the economic or political level, neither did it extend to a radical philosophy of personal life. Men believed in mastery over women, keeping them in protective custody. 'We were never well off,' said a retired miner from the Durham coal-field, 'but I was always in employment and I wouldn't have liked my wife to work.' But wives did work, often longer hours than their menfolk. And so the explanation lies in the men's relation both to the culture of domesticity, power in the domestic sphere, and the sexual division of labour. 'Men worked very hard,' said the deputy, 'and there were no baths – it was accepted that women would do it all, they didn't think that the women were working all hours. I was unconsciously striving for something different; I got that from my mother who couldn't carry it forward for herself.' His first revolt against the culture of women's subordination was 'against my mother having to get up in the morning, like they all did, to cut the bread for the lads. I was only a lad. So she stopped. My dad, he thought she ought to do it, and he was amazed at me taking a stand.' Another retired miner in Sunderland, whose wife had never earned her own living and who never wanted her to, was similarly affronted by the extremities of the power relationship:

The men were domineering. I know it with my own missus. I remember talking about domination with people older than me, and I didn't think it was right. Some men thought more about their whippets or their pigeons – they thought nowt of slinging the wife out on the street. Men were brutal then. People used to say, if you didn't get your own way in your own house, where would you get it?

The miners' capricious commitment, or lack of it, to the baths and canteens – the communal demands – can be treated as a classic case of patriarchal priorities in class struggle. Their political passivity about these communal services can't be understood without taking into account the benefit of keeping it all in the family – for men it secured their surveillance over the time and labour of women. That was their stake and it detonated the kind of politics which are the stuff of socialism in our society. The patriarchal principle surrendered class solidarity to myopia and minimalism. The loyalty of the women of the mining communities to their menfolk is, of course, legend. It is invoked as an instance of those communities' internal solidarity. But that loyalty was mediated by a common critique of their own, shared in kitchens and over doorsteps, of the authoritarianism endured by the women. Yet the memoirs of these survivors, their dirge, is rarely inscribed in the chroniclers' sentimental journeys.

In the small coal communities, the pit was as often as not the sole source of wage-earning incomes. The women's exclusion from the pit separated them from a share in those incomes. The failure to socialise the work of washing and feeding confined women's labour for the miners, and indirectly for the coal owners too, to a private economy in which women were subject to vigorous authoritarianism and economic powerlessness. For all the discomfort of going home covered in evil-smelling dust, of whole living spaces colonised by the drill of the tin bath and the miner's ablutions, and the pollution produced by the suphurous rags, the miner had some advantages: the home revolved around *him* and his needs. His woman's labour was for him. It was a personal control over the labour and time of women. For the employers, that stake in personal power also provided, *at no cost*, the work that made miners' work possible.

After nationalisation in 1948, the pits were transformed by the universal provision of baths and canteens – social places to perform the private work of women. For many women in coal communities it provided the only wage labour available to them, and for the first time it provided wages for the work they'd always done. The pit canteen is the only women's workplace, for example, in a pit village of fewer than 100 households I visited. The miners' welfare club put on concerts – their only social entertainment – and provides space for a mothers' and toddlers' group where there is no nursery. A woman I talked to, a single parent, gets up at 4.30 a.m. every morning. By 5.15 she's in the canteen where she works until 7.15 when she clocks off to go home and get her children to school. She's back in the canteen from 9 a.m. until 3 p.m., when she goes home to the children and her working day starts its next shift. For that she takes home £55.60 a week. Another canteen worker in the same village told me she does a shift from 11 a.m. until 4 p.m., returns home to work for her family, then she's back at the pit from 7.30 p.m. until 10.45 p.m. The shifts vary to cover all the hours of the men's comings and goings. A woman who worked 9 a.m. to 5 p.m. said, 'My husband works the same hours. You live with them and you feed them here – a lot have their main meal here in the canteen. Otherwise I'd have to go home at 5.30 p.m. and I'd have to start all over again.'

I spent an afternoon in Sunderland with an old miner in his eighties, who wasn't a club man or active in the union, with this lovely voice, talking about first going down as a trapper – he sat all day when he was thirteen by the trap doors which the paddy wagons carrying coal had to pass through, all day in the pitch dark. He wasn't a political man, spent his leisure going out shooting rabbits for 'snap' (food), and it was obvious that his most intimate relationships were with his dogs and the land I'd forgotten – coal-mines are often almost 'rural'. He got married during the general strike. Like all old miners, he remembered the coming of the pit baths, they were the best thing that ever happened, he said. And nationalisation: that was great because it got rid of the old bosses. Again, such powerful memories among the very old of pre-war Britain, and their sense of very injured oppression. He hated the bosses – no wonder. Another old miner, a beautiful, gracious man with a graceful mind, but breathless with pneumoconiosis, showed me a list of disastrous explosions in the Yorkshire collieries in the thirties and early forties – there were major explosions nearly every year. Sometimes, he said, they worked with only two feet of air along the roadways, not enough to breathe.

Everything changes but nothing changes ... 'I work on the face now, and there are always dodgy situations when a lump of rock falls and just misses you. It doesn't frighten you so much as remind you where you are,' explained a young Barnsley miner. Miners today work with advanced coal-cutting machinery and hydraulic props, they're safer and they're better paid. But coal is coal. And getting to it can mean one man hauling himself through a two-foot tunnel for half an hour in six inches of water. Skill makes men dextrous, but that doesn't diminish the spectacle of a man leaping like a fox around corridors of coal too low to stand up, cramped with hydraulic props and coal-cutters. If it is like hell, it is sometimes a cosy sort of hell, snug with the smell of clay, but the work is treacherous, and the machinery has brought with it some new risks. But miners don't suffer alone. They have compensations few people have – the community itself, and its women at their service. Miners may strike in support of nurses, but that doesn't make them fighters for the equality of women or for women as women. I spent some time with another elderly miner in Sunderland. In one piquant moment, he was standing in the middle of the living room talking, while his wife scurried about making a bit of food. They're a very companionable couple, and enjoy spending time together, they go to political meetings, have the family round, work in their magnificent garden. Anyway, there he was, the subject of the company, everybody around his villages loves and respects him, and his wife also talked about how loved he was. There was no formal power play there, it was just that the very fabric of his psyche was about being central, the central person, the interesting person and everybody collaborated in that. His wife talked to him, about him, used his name, named him, registered him, but he never referred to her, never named her. He was lovely but watching him in that living room somehow said it all.

I met a very nice old man, an NUM moderate a couple of times. We talked about the general strike, family, marriage, work, the union, the Labour Party. He's lived life in a tiny community, a respected member of his class. I asked about his wife. He said she didn't do anything and wasn't very bright. I asked to meet her. She came into the working-men's club one lunchtime and got her bottle of stout. There she was, wearing a mac, a crimplene frock over her body which just seemed to hang like a cheese from her shoulders, a little woolly hat and NHS specs, and the inevitable shopping bag. 'Hello pet,' and we shake hands. I asked about her work before she married. She'd rarely been at school, went into domestic service, couldn't read, but can write her name, then got married. She's in her seventies now. No, she never had a paid job after that because he wouldn't like it. No, she hadn't any friends, because he wouldn't like it. No, she never was in the Co-op Women's Guilds, because he wouldn't like it. 'I just stopped at home.' She was wonderfully direct, straight-forward and honest. Nothing to hide. It was different now, she said, some women didn't get married, or had three or four men. What did she think of that? It was 'all right,' she said. Contraception? 'Oh God, we never had any of that, but some women used to soak their feet in mustard, or have operations.' I thought she was a lovely person. Her family were good, she said, 'never caused us any bother', and her husband was good, 'd'you know, he's never been to court in all his life.' He was very nice. She was very nice, too. He fought for things we'd disagree with, like wives staying at home. It

wasn't his fault, but that belief formed the backbone of much
of his politics, actually. She never had any politics because
she wasn't allowed to. It's the same with most of the old
ladies I talk to, and frankly it breaks your heart.

Still many miners don't welcome women in their political
midst. A woman in the Northeast involved in a campaign to
improve colliery houses arrived at a lodge meeting with
material on the houses for the members. 'They told me
"we've never let a woman on before and we're not going to
now" and they didn't.' Part of the culture of miners'
militancy draws on the religious motifs that moulded
working-class ideology – the more you suffer the more you
deserve. What used to be pie in the sky when you die has,
quite rightly, become pie now, please. But it is still pie for
Orwellian man, who suffers to save us all:

It is only because miners sweat their guts out that superior persons
can remain superior. You and I and the editor of the *Times Lit.
Supp.*, and the nancy poets and the Archbishop of Canterbury and
Comrade X, author of *Marxism for Infants* – all of us *really* owe the
comparative decency of our lives to poor drudges underground,
blackened to their eyes, with their throats full of coal dust, driving
their shovels forward with arms and belly muscles of steel.

It was the meeting of martyrdom and militancy that
brought their ascension to the top of the manual wages league
in the 1970s, and secured them their place as the romantic
heroes of the class war. But that same militant masculinity
has to be seen for the contradictory and often conservative
force that it is. Mining communities are committed communities, but they are not equal communities. With the
introduction of baths and canteens, there is now work for the
women that carries a wage with it. But no woman manual
workers in the industry yet earn as much as any of the men.
The lowest paid man working on the surface in 1982 earned
£94.10 minimum. The highest paid woman manual workers,
supervising a canteen with 11 or more staff under her, earned
a maximum of £88.68. Only when it was discovered that
some men, formerly working on the surface, were working in

canteens on the lowest male rate – higher than the female rate – did the union begin to campaign for equal pay for the women. But women's right to earn as much as men on the grounds of their economic equality with the men of their community had not prompted an earlier campaign. The very argument that had supported the miners' own rise in the wages league during the 1970s – that the work was difficult and dangerous – counted against an egalitarian measurement of women's skills. The image of the miners as gladiators for women during the Grunwick strike by Asian women in London in the late seventies and the hospital workers' strikes during the early eighties veiled their reservations about the rights of women in general, which have been entrenched in the culture of their community. The sexual apartheid has been reinforced in the assumptions about men's social rights and women's domesticity. Male activists are out every night unless they stay in for the wife's one night out. They may spend Saturday night together, and as often as not you see the men holding up the bar with their pints and the women sitting at the tables with their shorts. It is part of their folklore that the men go out to the pub or club at Sunday dinner time and there isn't a woman to be seen. They share that with thousands of working-men's clubs throughout the country. The men are drinking and the women are cooking their dinner.

A Sunderland miner described his week to me: 'I'm at the pit every weekday. I attend at least one meeting of an evening, the union and the Labour Party. Most nights I go to the miners' welfare or a pub, or a club. Most of the people I knock about with are in the union. The wife stops in, and one night a week she goes out with her women mates. That's fairly routine up here. For anybody in my circle that's fairly routine.' And a South Yorkshire miner said: 'My day starts at 5 or 6 a.m. Start work at 7.30. Then I'm home between 2.30 or 3 p.m. or if there is a meeting it is 4.30 p.m. I eat something, have a nap or watch telly for an hour, then I'm out. It's very rare that I stop in, so I see very little of the wife and kids.'

Shortly after the miners elected their new Left leadership
in 1982, the executive of the union launched a national tour
through the coalfields in support of their annual claim. Four
thousand miners packed Sheffield's city hall one night that
winter. It was an extraordinary moment in their history – a
united leadership led by the Left, returning to the coalfields
to campaign for their agreed claim. Out of that 4,000 I saw
maybe a dozen or so women. It wasn't a policy-making
meeting, there was no vote and no debate, so any women
could have gone. But the wives weren't there, though, of
course, they were implicated in the result of the ballot in the
claim, as they always have been. Robin Page Arnot was right,
the women were disenfranchised before nationalisation, and
they still are today.

The lads had turned out to hear their lads. For Yorkshire-
men the meeting was like the town turning out to greet the
local boy who scored in the Cup Final. This was 'our Arthur'
at his first big political contest on home ground since his
election to presidency of the union. It was an exemplary
Scargill performance in the long and honourable tradition of
working-class orators who combine politics with pleasure –
hard facts, immaculate timing and lots of jokes at the
expense of the class enemy. There were more standing
ovations than I've ever heard. A Yorkshire miner said retro-
spectively that he'd wanted Scargill's successor in Yorkshire,
Jack Taylor, to match Scargill. 'I were thinking when Jack
got up, "make us get to our feet." That were one of the best
nights in my life, the charge we gave Arthur he gave it
straight back to us.' What had excited him was the message
– 'it's us against them. That gave me a charge that we could
take back to our members. It were enough for me to take
back to our branch and say "it's us against them".' I got a
real feeling of class anger and class loyalty, of belonging to a
class, even. Quite something to witness, and often not part
of feminists' vocabulary. It was an amazing meeting, very
much a men's meeting. The Scottish miners' leader, Mick
McGahey, granite-faced and gravel-voiced, brought them to
their feet when he concluded: 'This is a united executive.

We'll halt the retreat and start the fightback in the Labour Movement.' The roadshow now belongs to the mythology of the miners, the leadership had made the effort, they'd gone on the road, and they'd been rewarded by a clutch of standing ovations. What really moved the men was the ignition of the class war, the excitement of climbing out of the trenches for the long march against the class enemy. Both the Right and the Left share the same awe at the thought of the miners on the move – they bring down governments, they are the labour movement's prizefighters, our local heroes.

But the miners' roadshow didn't work. The attempt to bolster the pay claim with the fear of closures failed. Having hauled themselves to the top of the manual workers' pay league, the reduction of miners' political offensive to an economic demand foundered on the success of economism during the 1972 and 1974 pay offensives. Having secured miners' place at the top of the manual wages league, there was nowhere for that economism to go. The conviction that what moves men is money became a commandment among the Left of the labour movement during the unprecedented waves of industrial militancy in the 1960s and 1970s. And even though it was obvious to many before the 1982 ballot that the miners were not ready to go over the barricades for a pay rise, the Left leadership couldn't think its way out of its own economism.

On the way home from the Sheffield spectacular, I talked to a veteran Communist miner, thrilled at the thought of 'the movement' when it's moving. I enjoyed his excitement with politics. Class lives. But he corrected me when I mused on the potency of class hatred and class anger in the Sheffield meeting. 'No lass, you're wrong, it wasn't class hatred, it was class love.' He was right; certainly there wasn't what goes with class hatred, class envy. And it was lovely to hear a middle-aged man talk about love as instrumental in men's politics. But he was also wrong. It was a love of miners.

I went home to the woman I'm staying with, a single parent with three children aged between two and nine years. She doesn't get a newspaper and had to ask the social

security for new shoes for the two children at school where
their last pair of trainers got holes. Today she was up at the
crack of dawn, 4.30, to make breakfast for her man friend.
He'd come round the night before after playing pool, and
they'd stayed up late, so today she is shattered. I arrived
home at about tea-time, we talked a bit, the children were
charging around until about 7 p.m., when they had their
baths, and by 9 p.m. they were in bed. By then I was in front
of the television with tea and biscuits watching the news.
That felt quite odd. I've noticed how rarely women watch
the news. There were two major reports on the news, one
showing mass rallies in Spain on the eve of the elections
there, hundreds of thousands of ordinary people crammed
into sports stadia to hear their party leaders, and the other
on the miners' ballot, with interviews among the miners who
travelled in busloads from coalfields in Derbyshire and
Lancashire for the Sheffield rally, interviews with Michael
McGahey on the road about the vilification of Scargill, and
the sight of Scargill himself appealing to the miners to vote
for their union and against the National Coal Board. The
miners' ballot counted as a matter of national public concern,
a mini-general election. But unlike the Spanish rallies, there
were almost no women at Sheffield. The woman I'm staying
with comes from a mining family, and as I was watching the
news I heard the ironing board creaking in the kitchen. She
was still working, doing the ironing at ten o'clock at night.
She missed the news. It had nothing to do with her anyway.
The following day brought the news of the miners' ballot –
despite everything I've said, the news was terrible. There was
no comfort in that result, a vote against industrial action,
even though it confirmed the suspicion that gone are the old
ways of fighting the class war that we've all been raised on
and still have the power to excite me. Because they did try.
I'm very glad to have been at that rally in Sheffield, because
it was a historic moment. But it's reminded me of one of my
father's books about the First World War, in which the author
writes about the demise of a certain kind of army and a
certain kind of warfare: cavalries organised in elegant

A retired miner and his wife. Miners have a special place in
the cult of the working class, they're the archetypical
proletarians. But who is the proletarian here? Marx's
companion Frederick Engels said that within the working
class men were the bourgeoisie and women the proletariat.
And miners' historian Page Arnot said that the voice of
women in the coal communities was a dirge, disenfranchised.

Maggie Murray – Format

Le Corbusier called homes 'machines for living in.' Only the working class live in these machines. They're commodities for the public's private life. The property-owning democracy doesn't extend this far, no 'For Sale' signs up here.

Raissa Page – Format

Nobody asked to live here, they've never secured any popular mandate, we didn't vote for them. We see the symbol of mass modernism we love to hate. But what don't we see? Damp, crumbling concrete, cold walls, exorbitant heating bills, a place to play, pleasure, the builders' profit.

Unemployed youth on a Right to Work March, Trafalgar Square, 1981. Maybe we have forgotten how the street presence of the poor has always evoked fear and loathing. Here are the new folk devils in the iconography of unemployment – big bad boys who conquer the streets.

Wigan 1938, photographed by Bert Hardy for *Picture Post*.
It's now part of the iconography of unemployment in the
Thirties. Why? He is hurt and humiliated, isolated and inert.
His pathos incites our pity. This still street life constructs our
collective memory of defeat and despair. Yet it is opposed by
another image of the Thirties, the Hunger Marches, when the
poor took to the streets together.

HARD TIMES, SOFT LOOKS.

The gentle lines of this hand-made Donegal tweed echo the romantic look of the Thirties. The suit £225, calf shoes £45, cashmere scarf £26, linen collarless shirt £37, pure wool tweed cap £28.

Gloria Chalmers

Fashion advertisement 1983.

'Who controls the past controls the future'
George Orwell, *1984*.

Just as photography fashions history, so history makes fashion.

Which is fact, which is fantasy?

Gloria Chalmers

'Futurist Night' at The Pier Club, Wigan, 1983

'In a decade of unparallelled depression, the consumption of all cheap luxuries has increased. You may have three halfpence in your pocket and not a prospect in the world and only the corner of a leaky bedroom to go home to; but in your new clothes you can stand on the street corner, indulging in a private daydream of yourself as Clark Gable or Greta Garbo, which compensates you for a great deal.'

George Orwell, *The Road to Wigan Pier.*

Queuing for 50 jobs in a Sheffield diner, 1983. Fifteen hundred applied.

Shipyard workers in Sunderland.

formation for the war of movement. The thrill of the rallies before the miners' ballot was that they evoked echoes of that kind of military manoeuvre, disciplined, exotic troops, mobilised in precise, obedient formation, like ballroom dancing. The rhetoric of the rallies had a kind of doom about them. The very optimism of the possibility that the miners might be on the move against the government carried with it a premonition of pessimism, that the miners would save the working class when it could not save itself. But meanwhile, the hospital workers had been dug in for another kind of long war which can't be won the miners' way. Round about the time of the miners' ballot, hospital workers were holding meetings in South Yorkshire hospitals where only months earlier they had voted for all-out strike action. Now they were holding awkward, sometimes acrimonious meetings, badly managed and very sad, because they knew it was all over bar the shouting. None of us expected the hospital workers to save us from Thatcher, and yet they tried harder than most. The odds stacked against them show that industrial action today needs a leap of the political intellect. It needs more than will, it needs the imagination to find a way. The miners offered to support the hospital workers. Did they also wonder if they had anything to learn from them?

A young lodge leader in Barnsley took a party of us down his colliery. We were all women, including the daughter of a miner, who had been married to a miner and whose son was now a miner. Her home overlooks the pithead and the haunting winding gear of a colliery where an explosion once killed over thirty miners. We also included some women workers from the canteen and a cousin of one of the miners. As we swept down to the seam in the old iron lift we all grabbed each other's hands in simultaneous panic. After we came up out of the dank womb of the pit, we went for a drink in the welfare club. Apart from the barmaid, we were the only women there, and the two youngest women in our group had a long discussion: one defended the secret solidarity of the men, the other said, 'it's no place for a woman, I couldn't stand it.' She's working as a secretary in a solicitor's office now.

Work

This business of petty inconvenience and indignity, of being kept waiting about, of having to do everything at people's convenience, is inherent in working-class life. A thousand influences constantly press a working man down into a *passive* role. He does not act, he is acted upon.

George Orwell, *The Road to Wigan Pier*

George Orwell based his journey on the simple task of discovering the essence of working-class work and monitoring the degenerate landscape of mass housing. It was a straightforward if shocking portrait then. Today the terrain is a quagmire. There is no archetypical proletarian, no homogenous working class, no symbolic essence of labour revealing the condition of the class, no essential culture expressing its interests and ambitions. On my journey it quickly became clear that there are many stories to tell and no generalisation will serve. How can we compare the story of a secretary with a steelworker? How does a cleaner compare with a capstain setter? Does a car worker *feel* the same as a hospital worker? And do the politics produced in their work speak with the authentic voice of all those experiences – does the current *form* of class struggle express what people feel about their work? It is also clear that there are bitter conflicts of interest within workplace politics and among workers. Would a printer say he should always earn more than a secretary but doesn't begrudge comparison with a miner? Would a miner say he should always earn more than a secretary because

he's a man and skilled and he suffers, but not necessarily
more than a printer because he too is a man and skilled, even
though the printer may share the same skills as the secretary? In the end, miners and printers tend to believe that you
get what you bargain for, and that whatever that is, it should
be more than the secretary – it may not be much to do with
skill but it has everything to do with sex. Most men grieve for
the loss of their skills, but don't notice the de-skilling of
women in their own communities through marriage to
themselves and then motherhood. When a secretary, lathe
operator or cook turns to part-time cleaning in the prime of
her life, isn't that as tragic as an engineer reduced to lavatory
cleaning in his mid-forties?

These questions modified the temptation I felt during my
journey to do as Orwell did – to seek out the typical worker.
Would it be a car worker? A typist? A man or a woman? But
I got nowhere with this – there is no essential worker, no
archetype. Nor is there a politics which expresses such a
mythic essence. Both Right and Left have compounded
Orwell's error in settling for the present commandos, the
shop stewards' movement in the shipyards and the car
factories, as second only to the miners in the hierarchy of
honours. Many men on the Left have criticised this kind of
primitivism, and the critique is even more important for
women whose experience and collective self have rarely been
represented in these symbolic male traditions.

So my aim was not to produce an alternative sociological
survey of the working class, but as a jobbing journalist, to
listen to both sexes with all their different skills, to report
what they say for themselves, and to bring to bear on this the
questions that people are asking about the state of the
working class.

Let's start with the modern paradigm of the working class
– car workers. You rarely meet car workers who like their
work. They don't like the way they work or what they make
or who they work for. Alongside their alienation there
flourishes an anti-work culture that produces a kind of
political pessimism. It is difficult to fight *for* something you

believe in when you work in an industrial environment which only produces alienation. Fighting the bosses may produce the first condition of class consciousness – solidarity. But when the bosses are among the biggest in the world, it may stay stuck in alienated aggravation ceaselessly renewed in a relationship of retribution. Throughout the postwar years the employers have sought to discipline their allegedly recidivist workers – through constant and coercive surveillance, through campaigns to lengthen the working day by abolishing tea breaks and washing times, through all the wars of attrition over small changes in time and place fought by workers to let them stop, rest, sit together, talk and become human again.

When modern assembly lines were introduced in the first decades of the century in the United States by Henry Ford and General Motors, they were enforced by hired hands to police the industrial population. It caused a kind of moral panic – national enquiries were inaugurated by politicians to investigate the degradation and de-skilling of workers. But in Britain during the postwar period, the sense of assembly-line work as inhuman has been veiled. It has been mitigated by car workers' own organisation and then mocked by the trivialisation of their resistance, and their reputation as the millionaires of the labour movement. The effect has been to represent them as undeserving of even the most basic rights. Now they're not even allowed to wash off the factory's filth in the factory's time.

During the post war boom years their world of work was a secret shared by the car workers alone, it was not yet the subject of sympathetic study by the media or scholars. I remember as a child hearing about the legendary struggles over tea breaks, which were announced on the television news as just the silliest thing, the workers being bloody-minded again! The car workers were represented as inhuman, isolated and unreasonable. They weren't nice. In fact, tea breaks and washing-up time were among the most important struggles those men waged over the quality of life at work. They challenged the idea that, once through the gate, your time is only the company's time, they tried to hold on to their time when it was being held to ransom, and to their right to time off while on the job. A Coventry car worker told me those struggles were among the most memorable in his life.

They made us give up tea breaks by introducing vending machines. We said we're not going to give up the tea break. So we got an agreement that we could have as many tea breaks as we wanted, but we had to take them on the bench. The hooter stopped going, but in the end everybody would have their twenty-minute tea break anyway. It didn't make any difference. The thing was, we were on piecework, if you had 200 items of production to do, you made sure that by hook or by crook you did them, and you'd work faster so that you could keep some stored by, so you could take a break. The foremen knew that we did, so the management didn't get away with it.

Breaks were important in mitigating the worst conditions. 'As a steward my objective was to win maximum breaks,' said a shop steward in a paint spray shop.

I won twenty minutes every hour, and for the sprayers half an hour every hour. This was done by achieving a proper labour loading, which had to be fought for very hard indeed. Management would be looking for eight men to do a job, and I'd be looking for ten men. We had a whole load of compensations like that.

Several stewards I met recalled that the companies tried to trade off their 'sacred breaks' against the forty-hour week. But breaks were sacred because the work was a clamour of concentrated, brain-bending production. Twenty minutes off the bench or the track meant so much more than they seemed. It was time off the job and away from the job, and while the car companies seemed to be shortening the working week, they lengthened them by banning the breaks.

Stories of sabotage are legion in the car industry, where the regime of discipline and punishment generates a permanent state of siege. 'Can you imagine what it feels like to walk into work everyday and to be *blamed* for everything?' said a Halewood worker. A bad day, and every day is a bad day, just becomes a worse day by the look on the foreman's face. And the regime has toughened up since the seventies when many car factories, multiplied the lowest levels of management to watch the workers. 'Under the old piecework system you'd have one foreman looking after 100 workers. After they introduced measured day work in the seventies you had one foreman for twenty-five workers in our place,' said a setter in a Coventry car factory. 'It's just not economically viable to have a load of foremen jumping on you all the time.'

A redundant paint spray shop steward reflected,

I never had any comfort in the place. I never enjoyed it at all. The place needed massive investment for a start, the stewards were on about it all the time. We demanded that the plant be demolished and a new plant built, but it never was. The effect was that the place was very dirty, so we have a rate of 70 per cent rejects because the dirt mucked up the surfaces. Mind you, that meant there was plenty of overtime to redo stuff. But I said, 'Look lads, this can't last,' and it didn't. It closed.

The environment is degenerate, the authoritarianism absolute, and assembly track work annihilating. An assembly line fitter in Coventry said:

You're expected to produce any figure thrown at you. The track was such repetition and you were doing your best but it was never good enough. Often problems blamed on you had nothing to do with you, like shortages of supplies – that was their bad management. The job just got on top of you, it was like a permanent depression. You just sold your body to the highest bidder. By the time you were thirty-five you were too old to work on the track.

The intensity of supervision produces the atmosphere of a police state. 'There was a lot of resentment,' said a track man. 'All the pressure was on to work harder and harder, you are treated like a piece of muck, you're expected to change gear just like that. Mind you, the money I was on was damned good, make no mistake.' Miners, they often feel they've inherited their work: 'You were just born to it'. You never hear a factory worker say that. A fitter in a Newcastle engineering works told me about his first day in the fifties in what seemed like hell:

I'd never seen anything like it, it was a gigantic multi-assembly shop about a quarter of a mile long. The bit we worked in as apprentices we called cells, it was actually like a caged-in fence. It was a terrible experience, the smell, the danger, the hustle and bustle of factory life. Safety wasn't like it is now and a lot of people took short cuts with the machines because they were on piece rates, so they were under pressure. We had to wear cumbersome, hot overalls and there was always the smell of oil on them that stayed with you, because you had to travel home on the bus wearing them. There was no such thing as overall schemes in those days. I took my bait in a tin and ate it on the bench.

The industrial landscape is characterised by clearly visible generations. Most recent of all is factory chic, those elegant monuments to modernism you see in the new towns, or, most spectacularly, along the banks of the Tyne where Vickers built their new factory with government grants. They're usually corrugated sheds in modest shades, with exits and entrances in geranium red or primary yellow. Before them were the postwar industrial estates, with their pink or red brick nursery units. And then before them there were the Dickensian barns, antique premises for antique processes over which the workers had no control – all their legendary inventiveness went into keeping the bits together and making them work. A fitter I met in the Midlands served his time on 'machines made of reconditioned scrap – they used to give me electric shocks.'

The *places* of work are as much an index of workers' powerlessness as their lack of control over the product. Here is the tale of a south Yorkshire steelworker.

Ours was an old plant, but we did a modern process. It just wasn't planned correctly. You'd have to cart stuff a quarter of a mile for one bit of the process, then another quarter of a mile for the next. The amount of handling of stuff around the place was tremendous. The same castings might be lying around for a month before they got out of the door. They had the room, they could have had a continuous process, but they didn't. All the time I kept telling them the stuff should go straight through. We used to bring it up at shop stewards' meetings, but the management didn't have to take any notice. Another thing was, under the Health and Safety Act they were supposed to discuss with us any new machinery – I suppose they did. When it suited them.

We used to throw castings into steel skips – they could have been rubber. It was like a big bell ringing out. The wind hammers could have had mufflers on them. Steel to steel – it makes a noise. You could wear ear muffs if you wanted, but that was yet more protective clothing – you'd be on your knees if you wore everything. There was a mask, a visor for eye protection. If it was hot outside it was even hotter inside and if it was cold outside it was even colder inside. We had a glass roof so the sun would hit you, it was chronic, and in the summer we had to take salt tablets. I used to go home peppered with little burns around my shirt neck. Not that it was really bad, it was just annoying. I worked in a big shop, twenty-five of us, you'd get castings from the foundry and you'd have to get rid of the muck and what we called fash around the mould and prepare it for welding and get it ready for machining. It was the only job I had for a long time, so it grew on you. Though I didn't like the noise and muck – it was below the legal limit, but you'd got wind hammers and grinders and welding tackle all over the place. You could get temporary blindness. If you were near a person you could talk, not otherwise. Well, I wouldn't say talk, you learned to lip read. There was a very high percentage of deafness. Some of them, if you went up behind them, they couldn't hear you. In my shop alone, out of twenty-five men, eight put in for compensation for deafness.

In some of the large workplaces, trade union organisation means workers can at least put their point, even if no one takes any notice. But thousands of workers particularly women, are stuck in small enterprises like this one in Sunderland, described to me by a teenager who worked there during the seventies.

We had no breaks at all. You'd eat as you worked, we were making saucepan handles and putting out 5,000 of them a day. It killed you.

There were no cleaners in there, we had to clean it ourselves, and if you didn't keep up with the work you were sacked. Actually, you were threatened with the sack all the time. They liked young people because the wages were low, it was slave labour. I took home £30 for a full week. And as soon as you mentioned the union you were sacked. That factory wants reporting. I'd come home with little lumps of the factory, it was so filthy, as soon as I got home I'd have to have a bath.

Amidst all this drudgery, what about the people who like work? People like working hard when the energy they put in feels productive, and they are able to enjoy their own culture. 'When I first started work,' said a former electrical engineer in Sunderland, 'I went straight into an accounts office. I decided I wasn't very happy there, so then I went to a hairdresser's as a receptionist. Then I heard a factory was opening so I thought I'd have a shot at that.' At first she found it a traumatic change, but when the firm introduced new machines and trained women in new, sophisticated skills things changed.

I thought it was marvellous. I must be honest, the money was fantastic. But basically I like it because I was good at it. And the other thing was, we had a good social life there. I'd a lot of friends, we'd a good life with the girls, trips, nights out. Everybody worked there such a long time, you knew people well – I saw some girls' children work there. It was a family place really. And I enjoyed working with women. We were members of the union, but I wasn't very active. I didn't go to branch meetings in the evenings because I didn't have the time, but I always went to meetings at work. I was a bit of a militant. A lot of people were scared of the boss, but the bosses never bothered me.

Another engineer who worked in the same factory for over twenty years smiled as she said,

I was *very* skilled. Oh yes, I loved the work, year in year out. The atmosphere was great. I've worked in shops and never got the same feeling. People would moan, but in the factory you told each other plainly what you felt. Factory work was looked down on as a lower level, my older relations called the girls the dollies going to work, and thought of us as a lower class of person. I didn't. But I went to work to make money, you are all there only for one thing – money. My friends always included women from the factory, and my friends were always women. I was always interested in the union, it had been very strong in our factory and in my family. But we were so good, you see, we were classed as the elite.

Among many skilled workers there is real pleasure in the skill of manufacturing things and in their skill being valued. there is also pleasure in workmates. Yet there is usually a feeling of powerlessness to influence the work process, and this seals the experience of alienation. With the expansion of the caring industries, the almost universal experience of alienation is eroded because, however menial the work, there is often a commitment to the job of caring for people. A geriatric hospital I visited in South Yorkshire exemplifies the rise of men and women, underpaid and overworked, who believe in what they are doing. One average ward had between thirty and forty residential patients. Officially it should have four qualified staff plus students. During the week I visited it, there were only three qualified staff on Sunday, two on Monday – one qualified nurse and one student; on Tuesday there were three students and one qualified nurse; on Wednesday, two nurses and four students – 'a good day'.

In fact, the wards were being run by students who had been warned that once they'd finished their training at the hospital there was no guarantee of a job there. I heard of other hospitals where married women students were told they needn't bother applying for jobs when their training was complete. At this South Yorkshire hospital the next year's intake were likely to be told that they should feel free to apply, but not only would there be no guarantee of a job, there would definitely be no job. Geriatric and long-stay patients in mental hospitals are probably the lowest priority in the distribution of National Health Service resources, unlikely candidates for privatisation. But it has among the highest levels of commitment in an already committed workforce, not only among nursing staff, but auxiliaries and orderlies too. That is not to say that they don't feel exploited – a take-home pay of £211 a month for a twenty-one-year-old student can't be anything but exploitation. But 'It's just great work, it's lovely, I just enjoy it. There's nothing lovely about it really, I just like it,' said a young nurse who works in the ward of long-stay middle-aged and elderly women.

The work itself involves a combination of administration, care and some basic therapy. 'We encourage them to do as much for themselves as possible, like get out of bed, which some of them will not do, get washed and get dressed – things to do with personal hygiene. We try to give them an interest in seeing to their own personal needs.' All this comes into 'care plans' designed for each patient. 'A broken arm is a broken arm, but a broken mind ...' says the nurse. Just as she talks about her care philosophy, a women walks across the ward in her tights and a pink frock, no shoes and no teeth. (All the women have their own sets of teeth but rarely put them in.) The tights are ruffled at the toes, like a pixie. 'Hello, Doris darling,' says the nurse, she was pleased because the woman had actually got up and dressed. 'Cigarette?' demands Doris, so the nurse gives her one of her own which Doris smokes for a while and then drops on the floor. 'She always does that, so you have to keep an eye on where they fall, otherwise we'd be up in flames.' Then a gimlet-eyed woman emerged from the corridor clutching a felt penguin. Within a quarter of an hour she is greeted joyfully by three members of the staff who give her a kiss. 'I love you, Dot,' says one of them. Another takes her by the hand to a desk with some paper for her to write or draw. The dark eyes watch the ward and without warning there is a wave of words, no sentences or phrases, just a quick, random babble. The nurses talk to her and she sits either mute, staring at them, or throws out an incomprehensible lexicon. At least it's a conversation. Somebody starts singing, and sometimes there's dancing, too.

The women are around fifty or older and many have been

there since their youth and they'll be there for the rest of their lives, being taken care of by people who are not paid to like them, but who do like them. A widow went to work there as a domestic several years ago:

I've always worked, but I'd been made redundant then I went barmaiding and then I came here. And I've always been in the union since I came. I like the job and if I'm honest that's because it's friendly, even though I have to do jobs I don't like doing, like cleaning toilets. The nice thing is being with each other. You see life in all its forms here, whereas in a factory it would just be the same routine day in and day out. Here, if you want to do cartwheels in the corridor nobody would take any notice – it's the happiest place I've ever worked. Although people outside think they wouldn't fancy it, I never mind coming to work. It's like a village here.'

Another cleaner said: 'We've all got problems. I've got an old lady here who always asks for a cloth, because she's been used to housework all her life. Just like us. This is their home now and we take on the family responsibilities. What's beautiful about this place is that people are treated properly.' Staff feel trusted with the job, they're not under constant supervision – 'We're committed to this place. These people are part of your family.' Some of the staff take patients out for the day and one, a shop steward, said, 'I always take two of them home for Christmas dinner.'

Health workers in the least prestigious jobs and the least prestigious sectors of health care do work unseen by the majority of people, even those who have been in hospital themselves. The passion of their work remains hidden from most of us and they, like any other workers, have their own anger about pay, conditions, staffing and the quality of their service, but they have no political language to express their commitment. Their discontent is discharged through the struggle over wages – though industrial action by health service workers in the late seventies and early eighties focused on money, it was fuelled by their feelings about the people they work with and for.

The wages struggle is the only form most workers have

available to them, but it is no vocabulary for their feelings. There are hardly the words to express their sense of loss of something they never have – power. I feel I need to learn more about the actual workings of the rank-and-file movement, and what they now feel about that deep conviction widely held on the Left that wages militancy expresses the highest form of contemporary class consciousness. Everybody I talk to loves to reminisce about the golden days of 'In Place of Strife' – the movement's greatest hour was fighting against an attack on the movement. People don't seem to have the same nostalgia about the wages offensives and they're wondering now what the hell they've been fighting for all those years, and did it *change* anything?

But trade unionism, even though it may only translate their discontents and ambitions into negotiations over the price of their time and skill, nevertheless stands fast as the only instrument of collective intervention in working life. A Coventry car worker who took early retirement at the end of the seventies reckons that

It was when I got interested in the union, that's when my life took off. It changed my life, it became my life. What excited me? Well, it was the thought of the workers taking part in their lives, workers having a say, the idea that you'd got the right to argue with the gaffer. I felt the blokes weren't going to go back to the old days before the war, they were going to have their say.

But having that say came hard, and it was a conversation capital desperately didn't want to have. An engineer in Newcastle remembers being vaguely aware of the union as an apprentice, but its right to represent its members always carried the threat of reprisals.

Apart from going to shop stewards with complaints I didn't realise that the union was there for other things. The only thing I remember the union doing for us apprentices was that the shop steward got us off components, stamping them with a number. We felt we were learning nothing and we said we wanted to learn. Suddenly the chargehand threw some plans at me and said, 'You want to be fitters, do you, well here, do this,' and you can imagine, we couldn't do it. So we had to ask the chargehand how to do it and, very begrudging, he showed us. That was the last job we got and because we were victimised so much we didn't dare raise it again. It sticks in my mind, that – the shop steward did something for us but it worked against us. In those days the foreman could still sack you, and the shop steward's job must have been very hard because of the powers that be. And blokes would tend not to use the shop stewards because they could easily get victimised.

Throughout the last fifteen years, the state has been obsessed with restricting the power of the new invincibles, trade unionists, who are accused of holding the country to ransom. To some extent the campaign has worked. More workers were trade unionists in the seventies than ever before, (though the numbers have dropped with unemployment): yet they are represented as unpopular now as never before. But none of the workers I talked to ever experienced the things for which they are feared or attacked or admired – real and constructive control over the work they do and how they do it.

Workplace Politics

... the English working class do not show much capacity for leadership but they have a wonderful talent for organisation. The whole trade union movement testifies to this ... no genuine working man grasps the deeper implications of socialism. ... His vision of the socialist future is a vision of present society with the worst abuses left out, and with interest centring round the same things as present – family life, the pub, football, and local politics.

George Orwell, *The Road to Wigan Pier*

Could the conservatism of the 'genuine working man' have anything to do with the fact that he's a man, I wonder? I think Orwell is right, but why does he assume that working *men* are the working *class*? What makes men think they are the radical sex? We know something about what men want, or think they want because they have a men's movement – they run every trade union and political party in the name of the working class. Their history, however, is as much about their rights as men as it is about their rights as workers; they exist in symbiosis. We are yet to conceive a labour movement in the image of women in which class struggle is shaped in a symbiotic relationship to women's interests *as women*. The contradictions are manifest in the different meanings of money, time and power.

The redundant convener of an electrical engineering factory in Sunderland, once a jewel in the crown of her union, because she was a woman, believes that women's priorities are no different from men's: 'It's money,' she said. So she fought for her part-timers' money. Women would usually disappear from the place once they married or had children, only to reappear a few years later on the twilight shift, working from 6 p.m. to 10 p.m. for twenty hours a week. They were paid below the hourly rate – which is usual for part-timers, their punishment, presumably, for being mothers – and had no employment protection.

Management wanted to get them doing the work at home, because the factory was overcrowded. They said they'd take the jigs and materials to their homes and bring them back. We told them they weren't on, because we'd have no idea how many hours those poor women would be working, they'd have no protection against the acids used in the process, no facilities and it would just be cheap labour. These were very experienced women we were talking about, it was just that they were twilight. So we asked the management to ask the women what hours *they* wanted to work and to give them a contract. So the women got various shifts, whatever suited them, but we insisted on the contract. If we'd not put the pressure on we'd have had the lasses working all hours, and we insisted that they got the same rate as the rest of us.

These words lead us into the minefield that makes the breach between men and women: their workplace priorities. These diverge along the curves of their life cycles and their work elsewhere -- in the case of women, at home and with children. But it isn't even that simple. Women trade unionists feel that it is they and they alone who put women's concerns on the agenda, so much so that concern with part-timers is usually a reliable index of commitment to women. Many trade unionists feel that part-timers are not cost-effective as trade unionists and share the age-old view that part-time isn't proper work and doesn't qualify for proper protection, a view which is also inscribed in employment legislation. It is summed up in the reports of the National Board for Prices and Incomes, which investigated low pay during the late sixties and seventies. Many of its subjects were poor, part-time women. Their low pay was ratified by the board, as often as not, on the grounds that because they were part-time they were dependent on another wage, not their own, to sustain themselves. But part-timers *are* bread-winners, either jointly or on their own account. When free collective bargaining was restored in the late seventies, it was to restore differentials (a euphemism for inequality). White, skilled, full-time craftsmen had had enough of equalities. The *collective* bit of bargaining hardly extended to parity for part-timers. Many of the workers in Lord Cooper's industry are part-time shop workers. The conflict of interest between part-timers and full-time workers is also manifest in the trade-union policies which support their sackings as the first round of redundancies.

Conflict of interest also arises over men and women's pay. Women and men who support equal pay have had to move against one of the canons of British trade unionism since the nineteenth century – the belief that men are the bread-winners and that their pay should get preferential treatment. A skilled woman electrical engineer in Sunderland recalls that, until the late sixties, all the workers in her department making telephone equipment were women. After the Equal Pay Act was introduced men came in.

I didn't like that. They got more basic pay and more bonus – can you imagine! We were very skilled, and if you were a bit militant it would really get your back up. It drove us wild, because we produced more and got less. We talked about it from the beginning in our union, but the other unions weren't interested, of course. We were in one union, but they were in two others. We couldn't get it changed. The men loved it, getting more!

A convener in a Sheffield engineering factory said, 'There are always differences over money.' The majority of his members are women on the production line, with only a minority of male members – skilled maintenance men and male labourers.

The skilled men always wanted the biggest increases. The women were against it. The women's argument was that we all have to shop in the same places and it costs us all the same to live. It's been a sore point with me, but there you go, that's how skilled men are, well that's how men are. Over the years the women got a better deal. Even though the skilled men wanted more, they were in a minority. Our district secretary, George Caborn, used to say, 'Keep the women happy. Do your best for the majority.' I resented it, too, because the rates of the skilled men went below the district level. The women would say, 'Yes we understand, but ...' However, times like these prove how women are discriminated against, because the firm would rather keep the men. In my case, because the majority are women we've got to keep the women's support.

He explained the company's 1982 pay award: $8\frac{1}{2}$ per cent across the board. A vote on an original offer of 8 per cent had been rejected by 80 per cent of the members in a secret ballot. So the company came back with an extra rise for the skilled men – nothing for the mass of women workers. That was rejected too, in a secret ballot, not surprisingly. So the union asked for extra to be extended not to the majority but to the male labourers. Again, not surprisingly, the majority rejected the award. 'Our problem was to get them to accept. This was also embarrassing for the management because they like secret ballots.' Asked what he thought about the women and their priorities, he said: 'I don't think I've ever thought about it. No I've never been particularly impressed by their priorities.'

What do these tales of trade union life tell us? They show the parts the Equal Pay Act couldn't reach: the resistance of men to the Act, both employers and workers, and the exclusion of many categories of women from its terms of reference. In retrospect, however, the Equal Pay Act changed more than perhaps we thought it would. Squeezed between the flamboyance of the sixties and the pessimism of the eighties, the seventies – the decade of equal pay – risk being consigned to a past which seems no longer palpable. In the seventies women's economic interests were put on the political agenda as never before, consummating decades of frustrated effort by women trade unionists and their supporters. No one expected much to come from the Equal Pay Act, and analysis of its impact shows that women had formidable forces ranged against them. It was a limp law backed by bad faith. Employers, industrial tribunals and, not least, some male trade unionists mobilised behind their corporate fortifications to minimise the impact of a minimalist law. Some trade union leaders in the sixties still believed that equal pay should be achieved through free collective bargaining – it was part of a common enough view that industrial relations should be free from state interference. Yet collective bargaining had not only failed to budget the sex differential, it was implicated in bargaining *for* it.

What makes us think the trade union movement is any different from anything else? It's only another place where men and women live out their conflict of interest. It's only another site of struggle in which women have often been defeated by what feminist labour historian Barbara Taylor calls men's 'sexual Toryism'. This is borne out in the experiences of the women of Sunderland and Sheffield quoted earlier. There are of course, examples of solidarity between men and women, and women have found solidarity with each other. But solidarity between workplaces is memorable because it is exceptional. The intervention of the industrial mobilisation generated around it during the seventies disrupted those habits of lifetimes. Certainly the implementation of the law depended on collective bargaining, but the experience in general and our particular examples also show that collective bargaining was itself implicated in the industrial inequality between the sexes.

That timid law soon became a tired law and its exhaustion in the last years of the decade produced contradictory results – it prompted many protagonists within the trade union movement to probe deeper into the structure of inequality and come up with demands to meet it head on, fuelled with the energy and experience of struggles in the seventies; it also exhumed a pessimism, briefly buried during the era of equal pay, that the return to collective bargaining, freed from the constraints of the Labour government's social contract, would lead to a resumption of normal life and restore the sex differential. That fear was vindicated: the gap between men and women's earnings began to grow, and women were chagrined by the response to the recession and the retreat from egalitarianism in English politics at the end of the decade. It was expressed not only in the rise of the radical Right and Thatcherism, but in the failure of egalitarian nerve within elements of the trade union movement itself. The restoration of free collective bargaining rehabilitated differentials in the minds of some trade union leaders. Equality was still a sometime thing in workplace politics. Redistribution between men and women seemed to depend on an economic boom. Faced with the real test – recession – a 'smash and grab' strategy of every man for himself moved into the political vacuum.

These kind of observations usually provoke pious protest from some trade unionists, whose defence of free collective bargaining confuses the principle of trade union autonomy with the practice of collective bargaining. Those on the Left who are guilty of this conflation between form and content depend for their defence on the suppression of conflicts of interest within the working class and fail to take responsibility for formulating a democratic and egalitarian offensive on incomes. This problem becomes more acute as the lessons of the seventies are learned and as we assimilate the changing profile of the working class itself – women now constitute 40 per cent of the waged workforce, ghettoised in sex-segregated jobs and rates of remuneration. Women workers are poorer than men, and they therefore have the greatest investment in a spirit of egalitarianism which still seeks legitimacy in a labour movement stripped of hegemony in these poor old times. They have powerful allies among those prominent members of the trade union movement not only on the Left who still adhere to a quest which gained ground in the sixties and seventies to modernise bargaining practices and priorities. Writing about the need to find forms of bargaining 'that eliminate as far as possible the sex bias', David Basnett, leader of the massive General Municipal

Boilermakers and Allied Trades Union, and hardly a Leftie, argues that, for example, semiskilled and skilled clerical workers should be compared with equivalent levels of skill in predominantly male areas. 'A shorthand typist should not be compared with anything less than a skilled manual craftsman', a view that thousands of men would find anathema but that would be music to the ears of thousands of women.*

Basnett and other men and women like him across the boundaries of Right and Left within the trade union movement are not confronting residual attitudes so much as dedicated recidivists who fear reform because generations of patriarchal pay bargaining have protected their relative privilege. It is they who promote divisive inequality in the name of unity and it is they who give the trade union movement a bad name. It is among the women workers I met that the reformers find their natural allies.

Men's and women's priorities diverge not only in the politics of pay but in the economy of time. For women, time is precious in particular ways. First, time away from waged work is rarely free time, it's always another kind of working time – home work. Secondly, women see time as a gain that can't be eroded. 'Our women go for time, shorter working time and time off, because that's something the bosses can't take away from you,' says a woman shop steward in a Wigan factory. 'Money is important, but tax or inflation take it away as soon as you've got it.' Male trade unionists have been very slow to see time off as a positive benefit. They have tended to treat women's premium on time as a lack of commitment to waged work, and their own campaigns for a shorter week has often only been translated into more overtime. Though shorter working time is now increasingly part of men's agenda, this is often as an alternative to redundancy. In the past, 'the lads always wanted to work more time,' said an engineering union negotiator in Sunder-

* *The Future of Collective Bargaining*, David Basnett, Fabian Tract 481, May 1982

land. 'They wouldn't have gone on strike for longer holidays
or better conditions. They'd only strike for more money.
whenever there was any attempt to reduce what they earned
they'd strike at the drop of a hat. It's mostly women who
want more time off, because they've got homes to look after
as well as work.' And a former convener in a Newcastle
engineering factory recalls bitterly:

All my life I was faced with a situation where if we were working
overtime I had a happy factory. If there was no overtime for a few
weeks it was amazing how many problems would come up. People
looked towards overtime because it meant less time at home.
They'd work every night and every weekend, I'm not kidding. We
had people who would rather not take holidays, they'd rather work,
or they would complain viciously to the shop stewards if there was a
bank holiday and they'd have to stop work for the weekend. People
didn't want more leisure – some wanted the opposite. Most working
lads have the attitude that while there's money they'll grab it. The
ordinary bloke is slaved to death. The employers would never
negotiate over time anyway because they said their fellow employers
wouldn't. Employers like to play each other off. Ninety-five per
cent of working men would put money before holidays. Lads were
going in to work seven days a week when some were being made
redundant.

Only once have I heard a male trade unionist fight for
shorter time or flexible time on the grounds not only that
women preferred it, but also that men should take more
responsibility for domestic labour. And he'd been talking to
feminists.

I heard that some office staff were interested in joining the union,
but there seemed to be a problem so I went to see them. One of the
women, a Tory actually, said paying dues wasn't the problem, so I
tried exploring other ideas. Like women versus men. They said the
men never told them anything about meetings, or what was happening. So I talked about flexible hours, and this woman's face lit
up. Great! she said. I said it would be good for the men, too, to think

about their hours, because it was always an excuse for them not doing anything at home. They like that.

It is men's dependence on women's domestic work and their passivity as parents that enables them to put a premium on working most of their time and playing the rest of it. And it is those same conditions that make possible the doubletime worked by most trade union activists. The life of the labour movement lives off women's unpaid domestic labour. 'Knowledge of kids is very limited among working-class men,' said a father of five, a redundant shop steward in Coventry. 'Certainly myself I was very engaged in outside politics. This is a vital thing because it is a great problem with the working class. The man invariably comes home exhausted, rests for an hour, you eat a meal and bloat out like a boa constrictor eating a pig, and if a man feels like a pint or two that's the night gone.' A dedicated organiser in the Midlands describes his life:

Politics first, family second. We had two kids. I had a good job, a good salary, that solved the problem as far as I was concerned. She might not have me but she could have anything else. My life was circumscribed by the union and politics, five nights a week and every weekend. I worked very hard. So my socialism was front door socialism – it began when I shut the front door and it ended when I came home. I didn't drink, though a lot of people in my job do, but I smoked a lot. I never read a novel for years. I was a person who lived for action. Give me pressure and I respond beautifully. I loved addressing meetings and being the centre of attention. I was committed bordering on nobility. I'd come home and say I'd had a terrible day. The wife would say, 'Well, it's not been too great here.' And I'd say, what are you talking about, I've been dealing with thousands, you've been dealing with two. I was always prepared to stand firm and I was always in trouble with the hierarchy. I gave my all to disputes. But when it was over I'd be down, I'd retreat home and of course there I had my emotional sponge.

Most of the men I met are not as self-aware or reflective.

They wouldn't admit to having an emotional sponge, she wouldn't have a name, not even her own name. She would be *the wife*. I never met any woman who said *the husband*, though they'd refer to 'him' as *him* or *your father*, but at least that meant he was specified as a person in a relationship.

Women workers often complain that something many men call harmless fun or flattering flirtation prescribes a relationship which the women regard as a presumptuous intrusion. A typist in her forties in a Wigan factory summed up the complaint in her account of a meeting addressed by a man. 'I asked a question. "If you give me your name and telephone number …" he says and giggles. The swine. I was livid.' Men tend to think of women in relation to themselves; they don't see the otherness of women as having anything to offer, save to service themselves; or they tend not to see women's difference save to do it down. They don't see themselves as a problem and they don't even see themselves doing it, which means they often don't see very much at all. The result is that many women see trade unionism much like any other institution, like the Boys Brigade, unless the unions *do* something to show they're different. This women is not alone in her feeling that getting into the union is like qualifying for the masonic lodge. Most of the women in her electrical engineering factory in the Midlands are part-timers and most of the men full-timers:

I asked the men when they had the branch meetings and they said, 'Why do you want to know?' They had them in another town nearby. Well, how could I go? I didn't have a car and I had kids, I went to work on a bike – they never did. They were in the union because it gave them some personal power. So the women regarded them in the same way they regarded the male supervisors. The reps were often the most rightwing and racialist people, though they might sound socialist in their class attitude against the boss.

Men like this think the union is primarily for them, not the women. This is reinforced by the pressure of workplace politics which brings maximum competitiveness to the fore.

And the time trade unionism takes often excludes women representatives who have to bargain for time with their own men at home. As a result, women's demands simply die or are filtered, with some honourable exceptions, through eyes that cannot see women's lives or women's militancy. One union official I spoke to in Sheffield feels that his work as an organiser legitimates aggression.

I was very aggressive, I was the most aggressive person I knew. So the job I was in was beautiful for letting all that out. I felt I could say anything I wanted. The trade union world is macho and brazen and it is all about wearing your credentials on your sleeve. You rise to it, you try to outdo in smartness or militancy the speaker before you. But how do you change it? I don't know. I've talked to other officials about it and we've been wondering whether leadership is the thing – I'll say it's got to be the workers who decide things. It's got to be, because the other way doesn't work. But because morale is so low now, it's very dangerous, because one of the things people look to you for is some confidence. Stewards come to me and say, 'What are we going to do?' I'd like to be able to say I don't know, let's talk about it. But the bricks of trade unionism don't allow room for reflection. There's no sense in which you can just sit around and talk.

A male convener at a factory in Sheffield took me round to meet some women machinists. 'I don't know what you'll make of them,' he said. 'They're a great lot of women, they're class conscious all right, they're militant, but I don't know what it is, you'll have to find out for yourself. I just don't understand it. They're not political, maybe that's what it is.' These women, a minority in the workforce, had still not secured a regrading claim they'd struck for ten years earlier. Whenever the stewards collected the priorities put forward by each shop for the annual claim, the women put a shorter working week at the top of their agenda – then money. The men always put money before time. The company had refused point blank to negotiate reduced working time, flexible time, compassionate leave or any other kind of time off. It was always the first item to fall off the agenda. So the women never got what they wanted. Not least because their demands were always processed by representatives who didn't share them. The effect has been to create a chasm, a crisis of representation between men and women in workplace politics.

Most women feel that the men who represent women just don't see that gulf as a problem. The women are simply *blamed* for the *effects* of a conflict of interest, they shrug their shoulders and shut up. The men never think they're the *cause*.

An experienced shop steward among clerical workers in a big Coventry car factory told me she used to trawl her members for ideas:

I once went round all the girls in my place to see if they felt the union was looking after their problems, and one said, 'You've got to be one of the lads,' so I said I don't want to be one of the lads, I'm a woman trade unionist. One of the best compliments you could be paid by men is that you are one of the lads. So it wasn't surprising that if you mentioned nurseries on the shop stewards' committee it just died.

Her husband was an active trade unionist in another factory and an active Labour Party member. He protested at this. It wouldn't happen, he said, and anyway there were enough nurseries.

Her: Tell me a time when I could have said I want our kids in a nursery and there'd be a place.

Him: The Labour Party has always supported nurseries.

Her: But there were never enough places.

Him: There was a need for women workers so they provided nurseries.

Her: But they didn't. Our own daughter couldn't get her kids into a nursery, so what are you talking about?

Him: All right, I concede.

We talked about the differences between men and women and their workplace *politics*.

Her: During pay restraint, our clerical people went for holidays, because that is something they can't take away from you. It meant people were thinking about something else other than work and money. But basically the shop stewards' movement is about wages. I rang every lady rep. I knew and said, if we ask the company to bring in the cervical smear facility from the council, would you want it? They all said yes, great! The company said they wouldn't because we would have to provide clerical support. I said, don't worry, we'll do it. There was a real interest. I even went as far as chatting to the women about getting a nursery at the factory and they were really interested. But the male reps wouldn't entertain it. 'You can't do that, the company can't afford it,' they said. I said the women were paying £15 a week on child minders anyway. But there was such resistance from the men, they said the women should stay at home. There's resistance to those things, but it's not from the women members.

Him: I'm trying to think of the kind of political things we did in our factory – we raised things about civil liberties and Northern Ireland, the Liaison Committee for the Defence of Trade Unions, Vietnam.

Her: On the shop stewards' committee, yes, but not among the members.

Given the acute sex segregation that divides the workforce, most men and women never do the same jobs in the same places. Most men who organise workers only come into contact with other men. 'I just never meet any women trade unionists,' said a Sunderland boilermaker. And a Newcastle engineering convener – 'We never had any women in the works, so I never had the problem of worrying about women's rights.' Many men spend all their time at work with other men, they go to union branches full of men, to trades councils with the same men, and to the club or pub with men. The lives of women never impinge on their world view. They never have to think about how they treat women, or about their own unconscious resistance to women who raid their territory. When the women's sense of exclusion produces a reaction a patriarchal piety is rolled out to condemn them.

'You wouldn't believe the chauvinism among some men,' said a Coventry convener. 'I remember during one strike, some of the wives organised a protest picket. You should have heard some of the chauvinism from some of them – they were saying "Get back to the washing machine ..." "Now if that was my wife!" Terrible.'

The Wear runs though the middle of Sunderland. Riding over the bridge late at night is better than crossing the Thames on a moonlit night. The banks are deep and on either side there are crane yards and ship yards with monumental, modern sheds and great hulks in the river being built, in repose. It's a working landscape and a worked landscape, and work is inextricable from home; the presence of work is everywhere, and yet the shipyard workers and the home-workers live in different worlds. I met some boilermakers and shipwrights in a working-men's club, where they spend every weekend. They've got 500 members in their union branch; fifteen turn up for meetings. The union structure hasn't changed to meet the changes in shop floor organisation, much to their chagrin. Every one of the men in the club I talk to justifies the ban on women for the committee. We talk about anything and everything, from the shipyards to what they talk about in their working men's clubs, how they spend their spare time, what they want the union to be about, how impossible it seems to be to mobilise any town-wide initiative on jobs, or on the NHS dispute. They're asked about women and children. One says he was very involved with his son when he was little – 'we used to go for walks'. Their wives don't come to the club. 'Mine doesn't drink ... mine likes to stay at home.' They talked as if women were marginal to their lives. I became aware of my own invisibility in relation to the men. It's strange, trying to create the right kind of co-operation and tone that enables them to speak their minds, yet aware that they are not consulting my opinions or feelings in any way, and I'm not consulting them either. In this line of work, you are in control, you are responsible for the con-versation, even though you are not its subject. It's about them, after all, not you. During this journey I spend all my days talking to people about themselves, each conversation influenced by the last. And when I'm not doing that, I'm setting up contacts through other contacts. That's only one kind of loneliness though, and you have little devices to deal with it, mooching around, taking a ride between one appointment at midday and another at teatime, or buying a bun or a peach, a comfort-treat. Talking with people, it's rarely a dialogue, it's an arranged monologue. Rarely do the men ever *ask me* anything, like 'who are you?' 'why are you doing this?' 'what are you getting at?' I'm struck by their lack of curiosity. It's only been women who've asked, 'What's this for anyway?' who put this book into their story, into our exchange. Perhaps it's people's deference to some idea of an expert, perhaps the appearance of assurance forbids people's questions. All that makes the companionship of my hosts all the more important, to go home at night and muse over the day's experiences and make sense of them with them, makes the journey more than a job.

I'm reminded that during the journey only rarely did I ever experience anything overtly sexist. No doubt that's partly because as a journalist, I'm in 'control' of the conversations. But a redundant steelworker I met in South Yorkshire disclosed something more oblique but systematically sexist. He'd come from Ireland and he'd worked for thirty-two years in a steelworks before being made redundant and he now works in a welfare advice centre. He wore a tie, a neat jacket and pressed trousers and he talked with the elegant vernacular of an Irish gentleman, he was a lovely man. He talked about his confusion at the beginning of his stint in the advice centre, because he not only had to learn the labyrinthine lore of the welfare system, he had to learn how to cope with the 'liberated women' among his colleagues, who wouldn't be called 'girls'. It totally bewildered him, he said, but eventually he grasped their point of view. 'I'd always worked with men,' he said, 'and I'd always had authority and commanded respect.' Suddenly he'd had to learn to work with women who knew more than he did and to whom his authority meant very little. It had been shattering.

Steelworkers just weren't used to women, he said, and consequently 'they're very conservative.' I never heard any of the women I met saying that because they don't work with men they don't know anything about them. Women know about co-operation with men, they do it all the time, not least at home. But if men's experience of women is only at home, they say women are beyond their ken; they don't listen.

A married couple in Sheffield, both middle-aged, active Communists and trade unionists, talk about her work as a school dinners supervisor.

Wife: With the recession, the quality of meals has gone down. When I started nearly twenty years ago – it was the only job I could get that fitted with the kids – we had two crates of milk to cook with. Now it's all powdered. No fresh milk at all. We used to have roast beef and lamb. Now it's all dehydrated beef and mutton and we have to supplement it with soya. We do one meal a day for free meals kids, a load of rolls, with egg and cress, for example, sausage rolls, beans, chips. In the old days we had to give them a nourishing meal. Now a kid might have sponge and chips and sausage rolls – look at the starch they're eating. It changed because the numbers were so low, it was to attract the customer. Tuck shops were open in dinnertime so the kids buy sweets. That raises money for the school to buy things that the authority should be buying. An icecream van drives *into* the school grounds – we've been fighting that and we've asked the authority to ban them. Anyway I've asked them to ban the tuck shop, too. I've brought the quality of school meals up in the branch – but he's a bad union secretary and he doesn't follow things up. I've brought up the question of South African goods, and the authority has agreed not to take them, but they still appear on our lists of purchases even though they're banned. The branch secretary is really on the management's side. I'll tell him things like this, or I'll complain about our hours being cut – these days they don't just make you redundant they cut your hours – and he'll say, 'I spoke to such and such,' and he sits and has coffee with them. Or he'll say, 'I've got to be a bit careful ...'

Husband: Now that's a bit unfair, he's got a hell of a job. A lot of the women, like it or not, don't have to work, and a lot of the cooks don't win the kids' support, and that's due to their indifference to the work. You can't go too hard on some of these people.

His wife lets him say all this then she reminds him that the secretary was a rightwinger, his predecessor was a leftwinger, energetic and a good listener. 'He'd come over and he'd work for the women, something this bloke would never do.' 'That's rather sweeping,' replies her husband. What he couldn't see and she couldn't say was that school dinner staff have been among the few workers in England to fight redundancy and to fight for improvements in their product for the consumer. And what he couldn't see and she couldn't say was that he was defending a lazy rightwinger against her women *because he was a man.*

Too often men's self-centredness makes them see women only in relation to themselves, subordinate satellites in their orbit. Talking with men and women together brings it out into the open. The men talk about themselves – naturally they've spent their lives *doing* things serviced by women whose own participation in life is constrained by men's dependency. The women talk about themselves and the men too – they refer to them, mention their names, accord them recognition, give them cues, give them respect, honour their past, bring them into conversations, in short, include them in. The men I met would usually hear out their wives, but rarely say their names, draw them in or give them an equality of presence, usually they'd wait for them to stop. Many men side with other men, even their political opponents, even men they've never met, to maintain sex solidarity.

Much debate within trade unions today is about the modernisation of both national and rank-and-file organisation to make it match the formidable resources of employers in motor manufacture, engineering, electronics, and the state, who are among the biggest employers of labour in England. Against their might, the shop stewards' movement appears like a mighty mouse, starved of resources, and a most important weapon of class war – information. The consolidation of shop stewards' combines is a vital means of

sharing resources, it generates an important politics of parity
between plants and can be an irreducible resource for the
basic strength most workers possess – solidarity. But the
fight for combines, which expanded during the postwar
period, has met with the enraged hostility not only of the
employers, but also of trade union bureacuracies which have
found it hard to countenance any trespass across the
boundaries of inter-union power and procedure. But it wasn't
only the forces without which undermined the growth of rank
and file solidarity, it was prejudice within. The Right and
Left, myself included before talking to scores of shop
stewards during this journey, have their own myths about
trade unions, but what unites them is that they give to the
rank and file an infinity of power, a profusion of militants.
They confuse the rhetoric of class war with its reality, and
most important of all, they think the rank and file naturally
believes in unity and equality. The rank and file may be the
major resource the working class has got, but that doesn't
make it magic.

The combines' most distinct feature, like most trade union
leaderships, is that they are peopled largely by men. That
didn't happen naturally. Since the war, when thousands of
women were drawn into engineering in particular, much
manufacturing industry has been reduced to one sex. Many
car workers, for example, can remember women in the
factories after the war until the industry was hit by sporadic
redundancies in the fifties. Redundancies were endemic,
then as now, and when production picked up it wasn't the
women who were taken back. One carworker remembers a
factory he worked in where they laid off three-quarters of the
labour force. 'The union won an agreement that when work
resumed those workers would be the first to be taken on. But
they wouldn't take everybody back, so they only took the
men. We should have said those women were in the union
too, and should be started back, but we didn't. I never looked
at the issue of women until this last year or so. I just never
thought about it.' To many other men it comes as a surprise
that there were ever women in their factories. In some, of

course, the women were allowed to be there. Others just vaguely recall that they were there once, but they vaguely disappeared. This absence of women from work reflects and reinforces antipathy to women working. A redundant assembly line worker in Coventry said that when he began work over twenty-five years ago, he believed 'that our role as men was to be the breadwinner. We all did, it was our duty to provide a home. I didn't want my wife to work, yes, definitely a man should earn enough to keep his wife at home.' If you work on the assumption that most women work for wages most of their lives, and bear in mind the statistic that women make up 40 per cent of wage labour force, it comes as something of a surprise to discover how many men don't take that for granted. They don't like it and they don't believe in it. Many have adjusted to it, but they organise their politics as if it hadn't happened.

Men's belief in their role as breadwinners has subordin- ated all other dimensions of their workplace politics to the politics of pay – their own pay. They have stopped planning strategies concerned with *ownership* of the means of produc- tion, a pessimism which was reinforced by the fate of the nationalised industries, and – with memorable exceptions – they have stopped imagining their own *control* over work, its pace and its produce. That is not to say they don't care about these things – much of workers' continuing class conscious- ness comes directly from their discontent about the conditions in which they make things, what they make, and the experi- ence of being mismanaged and misrepresented. But they rarely have an operational vocabulary or procedure through which to express their ambitions. Workers who believe in their work, like hospital workers who talk about their feelings in the last chapter, likewise rarely have any arsenal with which to fight for and improve the work itself. For the language of struggle has been translated into sabotage, shadow-boxing the boss, compensation for hardship endured, or wrangling over the price of their time. All this puts a premium on pay.

The struggle over pay escalated in the seventies when many manufacturing employers launched an offensive against the most effective gladiators in the wages stakes – the shop stewards' movement. It was believed by both employers and workers that the piece-rate system of payment gave the stewards their strength in day-to-day attrition. After years of resistance, the employers managed in many factories to establish a measured day work system whereby people are not paid by individual piecework results but according to a measured rate of work to be done over a period of time for an agreed rate. This aimed to stabilise employment, production and wages and, therefore, eliminate the endless war over the price and pace of work and, therefore, wages.

'I thought it would, too,' said a Communist convener in a Coventry car factory who was made redundant at the end of the seventies:

But it didn't because the workers found ways round it. If they couldn't earn more by working harder, then they could by reducing the measure of their output. They would do less. Productivity did go down. So shop stewards moved into other things, like safety. Before, the workers would have thanked you for that. People found all sorts of ways of beating the system, but it wasn't an advance for the working class in any way. It could have been but it wasn't. It was negative.

The car workers became the pay pacesetters. A union official in Coventry remembered that during the boom times 'production managers would say, "Settle, for Christ's sake!"' which gave the impression that the Coventry shop stewards were fantastic trade unionists. But even when the industry was beginning to decline, the impending doom was veiled,

because the stewards were fantastically good at screwing money and of course there was everything that went with that. The image I had was that everybody wanted a wife, two kids and a holiday in Spain, a mortgage and if possible two cars. It wasn't really like that, of course. But there was very little plant bargaining on anything other than pay. There were very few written agreements when I started in the sixties. The operation of custom and practice meant that workers had a measure of control, but that was when times were good. Pay figured prominently because the employers had a softer line on it, because they were making money.

Another Coventry convener believed that this was the source of some of the Left's infatuation with the shop stewards' movement.

This is where the Left outside the factories made a big mistake. They saw the great power of the shop stewards' movement. But it was always based on economism, it was all about pay. When a lot of us turned to political struggle they assumed we could bring the lads out on political issues, and some of us were fêted and flattered and invited to conferences. And of course that boosted your ego. But our problem was that our movement was based on what you could get for the lads, and the lads wanted cash in their pockets. And it was based on the boom mentality – get what you can.

The lions of the labour movement are 'the lads', and while their tactics may have been masterminded by the sea-green incorruptibles, the Communists and socialists who have spent their working lives servicing them, the motives of the movement have remained entrenched in the conservative common sense of the common man earning his breadwinner's corn.

Any programme for defence of the movement and the ground won during the good times would have depended on a rare degree of foresight. That foresight has tended to be passed on by the workers' informal bush telegraph. At least, trade unions have tiny research departments servicing hundreds of thousands of members. Match that against the computerised corporate planning of companies whose operations span the world. The growth of the multinationals has not been matched by a commensurate restructuring of the trade unions or the parameters of bargaining. Transplant combine committees remain a rarity, and although the development of shop stewards' combines in some industries have shown positive and relatively creative results for their members, there is a daunting individualism deep in the commonsense of trade unionism which opposes one of the movement's commandments – unity is strength. It is summed up in the attitude of a convener in a well-organised Sunderland engineering factory. 'No, I'm against combine committees, really because, let's put it this way, if you ask for a 10 per cent pay rise for your own 1,000 members you're more likely to get it than if you put in for 10 per cent for 10,000 people throughout the company, aren't you? So we go it alone.'

In practice, the idea of unity as strength sits beside an equivalent commitment to the principle that disunity is strength. That ought not to be surprising, but no doubt many people would regard it a sin to say such a thing. It's not surprising because the shape of British trade unionism is defined by its history in sex and craft chauvinism. People can believe contradictory things simultaneously. Many trade union officials don't like combine committees because they don't like rank and file upstarts poaching on their position, they don't like being deprived of their eyeball-to-eyeball contact with the bosses – one of the pleasures of working men's politics. And many rank and file representatives indicated that they fight shy of making contact with their counterparts in other companies. Too much of their history is enshrined in the competitive spirit.

Workers have an endless catalogue of grievances against each other which express deep divisions in the movement which, everyone knows, *need* to be overcome. But knowing it and doing something about it isn't the same thing. Staff and the shop floor have both crossed each other's picket lines, it is to be expected – the supervisors and foremen have been the shop floor's direct enemies – but they are also trade unionists. Sometimes not even mass sackings have helped them through their history of hatred, well grounded in a collective memory of mutual treachery and in real conflicts of short-term interest, which shroud their long-term unity of interest.

The growth of shop stewards' committees has rarely succeeded in overcoming these historic conflicts of interest –

between different categories of employees, staff versus manual workers, craft against semi- and unskilled workers, men against women, white against Black. Male and female rank and file activists from a car factory in Coventry discuss it in a pub one night:

Her: You didn't feel happy about sitting down with the other unions, did you, you were only forced into it.

Him: There was a fear about sitting down with foremen and staff because we didn't want to be associated with them.

Her: When we were fighting redundancies we should have sat down as a plant, but we didn't. There's that myth that if you get involved with the works, if you were staff, then you'd got to be militant, and the shop floor think the staff will sneak to the company.

Him: But they always do.

Her: So do the bloody shop floor. The shop stewards' movement has been a great strength but it has also been divisive, and it was plant based so it had difficulty moving outside the plant.

Him: The movement was based on what you could get for the lads.

Her: If you still had the piecework system's strength it wouldn't do you any good.

Him: I'm still convinced we'd be raising rates.

Her: When we moved over to measured day work – we all fought it, but we are nearly all on it – the pay negotiations became annual. But the strength didn't get displaced on to other issues.

Him: The lads aren't conscious enough.

These workers' accounts described both the weight of employers' power, despite the unprecedented size of the trade union movement today, and the political myopia of trade unionism. The latter has been the subject of long debates among people who study the labour movement, historians, sociologists and participants whose quest is to uncover the cause of economism as the movement's Achilles' heel. But it is clear that economism has a dimension rarely discussed among these scholars – it is a function of the political priority of a trade union movement based on men's self-interest as breadwinners, on a distribution of earnings within the working class based on the divisive legacy of differentials, and on individual families' self-sufficiency supposedly achieved through men's wage as the family wage. Women's economic equality is squeezed in the vice of employers' strategies, on the one hand, and men's view of the role of women, on the other. You don't have to fight for nurseries or an adequate child benefit if you believe that men's wages should support women at home with their children. The expansion of trade union parameters beyond the individual wage is unthinkable in a structure of bargaining based on the idea of the breadwinner. If the shop stewards' movement has become a paradigm of working-class militancy, it is also a paradigm of patriarchal economism. Fraternity conquers liberty and equality.

Redundancy:
How It Happens

It is only when you lodge in streets where nobody has a job, where getting a job seems about as probable as owning an aeroplane and much less probable than winning fifty pounds in the Football Pool, that you begin to grasp the changes that are being worked in our civilisation.

George Orwell, *The Road to Wigan Pier*

Why has the attack on the right to work been met with such a failure of resistance? Why have so many workers taken the money and run? And why have there been so few successful counterattacks by trade unions? You could say, and plenty of people on the Left do, that the Redundancy Payments Act is the cause of it all. It's a glib explanation which carries a kind of whine, 'the workers have betrayed us ...' Workers talking about their own redundancies show that something more complex has been going on. The most spectacular evacuation from work has taken place in the car industry, one of the fortresses of the modern shop stewards' movement, and car workers make clear how a hatred of work scatters the will to resist. I met a paint-sprayer made redundant from his Coventry car factory in the late seventies. He described how hatred of their work has fuelled the mass flight from work: 'People say now they wish they had a job, but in their heart of hearts they don't want that sort of flippin' job. In my case I accepted redundancy because I was sick of it. Even if we didn't have redundancy payments, we

still wouldn't have an effective movement.' Attempts to
preempt the closure of his factory fell on deaf ears.

You could see there was a great strength in the workers, but
management had a long-term strategy to scrap the place. I saw
signs of closure years before, but nobody took any notice, so we
never formed a strategy. There was a lot of opposition to action.
They just wanted to buy a little place or pay off their debts. So they
wanted to wait till it closed and collect a packet.

Though 1,800 people were involved in the redundancies it
was spread over time and even if there had been resistance, a
rugged strategy of attrition by management saw them off.

We went in dribs and drabs. We sat around for six weeks, it got so
damned cold in there I'd have been prepared to go in and do
anything. People sat around playing cards, walked around, did
anything. There were other sections who were underemployed.
Management were just mucking about. The thing was, they weren't
prepared to make full compulsory redundancies, but they created a
situation in which they forced you to take redundancy. No,
redundancy agreements don't really solve anything, because when it
comes to the crunch, unless there's a stand-up fight, there's no
chance.

Voluntary redundancies issued in yearly bouts avoid
confrontation but still shave the workforce down to a shadow.
In one of the few Coventry motor manufacture plants to have
survived, the first round of voluntary redundancies was
bought by offering massive payoffs. The shop steward said:

There'd never been terms like it.There was a terrible atmosphere,
people jockeying for positions. A lot wanted to go who couldn't.
When redundancies were announced people just rushed to put their
names down. The second time round they got so many surplus
volunteers, but the terms were reduced. The third time, people only
got the state minimum.

One of the stewards I spoke to who took early retirement
from this firm went because he couldn't stand the demoral-
isation any longer. Despite strong organisation

when the stewards said we wanted to join the 'Right to Work' march the young chaps were saying they didn't want to because they had jobs. They'd have a collection and chuck a quid in, but they didn't want to strike and lose a day's pay. And the unions are only interested in protecting their funds, they'll say don't fight, lads, because they're trying to protect their funds. I'd had ambitions to be a steward till I was sixty-five, but I took early retirement because I was knackered.

The workers who talked about their work in the car industry said they hated it, and that was why they hadn't the will to fight – they would have had to believe in their work to muster the emotional energy to take on some of the biggest employers in Britain. Many of the older men knew that going early at fifty-five or sixty would put a few years on their life, while staying under the pressure of the clock, dirty work and management's dirty tricks would have killed them, literally. Their former strength had depended on buoyant economy: 'We were successful during the boom years because the company could buy us off – that made people think we were strong,' said a car factory convener. But the beginning of the end came in the mid-seventies when Chrysler in Coventry planned to shed a third of its 25,000-strong workforce. 'If we lost that one, which we did, then a lot of us thought we'd lose the lot, which we did.'

Redundancies purged the motor industry of some of the most formidable rank and file leaders in the country. 'Even in the late seventies we could call meetings of 300 or 400 conveners in Coventry alone,' said one. 'Now we can't get a meeting of twenty. In my plant I had nearly 150 shop stewards at the end of the seventies, now I've got 50.' The total workforce in his firm declined from 32,000 to 7,000 in the space of a few years. For nine months everybody was on one day's work a week. 'You can't get a meeting together when nobody is at work, and you can't get industrial action when it means people losing the one day's pay they've got.' The official of one of the industry's small craft unions said:

I'll go into factories and I'll say in passing, 'I see your convener's gone.' It's the active people who go. We find that shop stewards are the first on the redundancy lists. They take all the pressure and there's not been any way to resist that. I don't decry them for taking redundancy, because they're under pressure from both the management and the members. Stewards have had enough. I can't tell you the number we've lost, they think, 'The quicker I get out the better.' And in the context of short-time I've heard conveners and stewards saying they're taking home £60 when they could get more on supplementary benefit. Meetings get smaller and smaller and I'm at a loss what we can do about it.

Once-busy union offices find themselves with little or nothing to do but administer redundancies. Phones that never stopped ringing sit silent, secretaries who became as expert as organisers, servicing members from their desks while officials were out 'in the field', read novels waiting for someone to call. In the mid-seventies, after the end of the wages offensives of the sixties and early seventies, other bargaining issues rose to prominence – health and safety, industrial democracy, pensions, workers' education, shorter working time. It was an exciting time for organisers and their staffs. In-trays were full and out-trays even fuller. Now all that has stopped. Trade union offices and city resource centres – viewed with so much suspicion by trade union bureaucracies when they first burgeoned – get panic calls from workers. 'We've been given ninety days' notice of closure, what can we do?' By this time it's probably too late, the orders have shrivelled, the books have been cooked and the workforce is terrified. The only path open to them is to take over, but they're not used to that.

The official structures of the labour movement, based as they are on representation of workers *in* work, don't seem to know what to do when they're out of work. Throughout the country, there are only a few branches for the unemployed, organised and serviced by the union structure. Some unions still keep former employees on their books as part of their historic role in acting as an agency for employment. But even some of these abandoned the practice when unemployment hit the 2 million mark. Former activists find themselves with no role – no one to represent but themselves. 'I'm an experienced secretary and I've been a shop representative for years, but the union never contacted me when I'd been made redundant to say there were useful things I could do for the movement,' complained a woman who represented clerical workers in a Coventry car plant.

Toward the end of the seventies there was a widespread fear among women active in the trade union and feminist movement that women would be the first to go. And indeed part-timers and twilight workers, usually women, are the casualties of management and union policies which don't actually say women should go first, but have the same effect by putting the part-timers and twilight shifts off first. And though many organisers working primarily with women, share the widely held commitment to work-sharing as an alternative to redundancies, they also fear that women are particularly at risk when work-sharing is actually just wage-sharing. 'Job-sharing often enhances the view held by most of my male colleagues that women only work for pin money anyway,' said a clerical staffs' representative in an electrical engineering factory employing a majority of women. 'It's very difficult to get a few hundred men together and get them to agree to fight against women being given half a job, because that's what they think the women should have anyway. The women are expected to do the wage-sharing and then go home and do all the housework.'

The expansion of services and public sector work and the introduction of new manufacturing industries after the Second World War brought thousands of women into industry in the industrial conurbations where the workforce was once primarily male. Many of their jobs, particularly in manufacturing, have disappeared. Nevertheless, many women are now breadwinners in these communities, either because they bring up children alone or because their men's industries have been decimated. In the Midlands, where the motor industry is a men's ghetto, thousands of jobs have disappeared, but many still have wives and mothers who are cleaners, canteen workers, clerical staff and public sector manual workers. Among these women workers, and those in manufacturing enterprises employing mostly women, union representatives have noticed a growth in militancy. 'We had a meeting of our white collar staff, about 60 per cent men and 40 per cent women,' said a shop steward in an electrical engineering works threatened with massive but unspecified redundancies through new technology.

The vote went against taking industrial action. Partly it was because the skilled men on the staff side still think they're indispensable, they think the company can't do without them, while the women have grabbed the chance to be retrained. They know what's coming, you see. It was the men who voted against industrial action, and I reckon 90 per cent of the women voted for it. But they were in a minority, so they were outvoted.

It's not that the men are stupid, or that all women are voting for militant action. Rather that many women *appreciate* the change in their economic circumstances and don't want to lose it, while, many men are having to change the beliefs of a lifetime. Being a skilled man in the working class promised the same kind of economic security that the Treasury or the armed forces meant to the 'upper' classes. While women have been used to moving in and out of the workforce, men were encouraged to seek stability above all. Being a draughtsman was an ace job among boys I grew up with. Now those boys are watching computer-aided design reduce their numbers from maybe 200 men in a big factory to twenty or twelve.

The government's war against the public sector and its propaganda for the privatisation of cleaning services, in particular, has scored a direct hit against women workers, though not without a fight. Although government departments have been obliged to be 'helpful' to unions representing cleaners by offering private contractors' costings for their scrutiny, the Department of the Environment has in some areas simply refused to show these. A civil service cleaners' union official in the Northeast who doggedly services women in government departments which have provided many jobs for women where there had traditionally been few, complained that the DoE would only say that private contractors were 40 per cent cheaper than directly employed labour. That left the union unable to compare conditions and pay. 'They say we are more expensive,' said the official, 'but our costings include superannuation and National Insurance Stamps. That's very important because at least it gives our women a pension.' So the effects of privatisation are not only redundancy, but a casualisation of the industry that deprives the women of employment and pension rights. It involves a double impoverishment: lower hours and wages now, and an end to deferred earnings on retirement.

School dinner ladies have been among the most forceful in fighting back against local authorities arbitrarily cutting their hours or abolishing holiday pay. They were compelled to concede to modifications on these lines. If they refused, they were deemed to have abrogated their contracts and sacked themselves. In 1983 some Kent school dinner ladies took the council to court and won.

In what's left of the private manufacturing sector profitable companies have used the recession and the political retreat of the labour movement to rationalise the labour process, a fertile ground for redundancies. A Sheffield tool-making factory employing a majority of women as semi-skilled production workers, and men as skilled machine setters and maintenance engineers, had its workforce pared down from 1,400 to 700 within three years. 'We know people aren't going to fight. The management is in a strong position to prolong the fight and they don't care what it costs,' said a shop steward.

We used to have part-timers and twilight, but they went first, they just discontinued the shifts that were working under sixteen hours, and anyway it's union policy to get rid of part-timers first. Then there's job-splitting – the company gets a £750 premium for administering job-splitting. The company will do that to save the women going on the dole, they'll split their jobs. Our union district committee frowns on it, but our members prefer it, and I'm for anything that saves jobs. The union says don't negotiate redundancies, but you do. You end up conceding really unreasonable things when you negotiate flexibility. It might not seem unreasonable to get a woman doing two jobs, she'll get more money, but we lose a lot of control through losing demarcation – the employers are really getting through demarcation barriers now. And they are creeping in with new technology in stores and computer-controlled machinery on the shop floor – we've lost women that way. The company says it is the recession that's caused our redundancies. But we're knocking out the same amount as we were with less than half the women. They've bought a £5 million computer to control the stores, that will lose more jobs. We're supposed to be consulted, but that means they *tell* me. And if you start raising arguments they say you can't be Luddites.

The culture women workers inhabit today is radically different from that of the 1930s – even if the men haven't changed, the women have. No trade union leader these days would be heard saying women should pack in work for the good of their fellow men. And although the documents leaked from Margaret Thatcher's Family Policy Group in 1983 revealed Employment Secretary Norman Tebbit saying that women should return to the kitchen sink, the Tories, too, have not come out with outright opposition to women's employment as such. Men may mutter and they may push through misogynist redundancy policies, but at least today they'll be opposed. One clerical workers' shop steward in a truck company described a typical brush with old chauvinism: 'During our first round of redundancies, we had to lose about fifty jobs. One bloke on the shop stewards' committee moved that it should be the married women. So I jumped on him and the suggestion died.' Her husband interjected with some residual reservations, 'But you do feel guilty when both of us are working.' She replied, 'I never did.'

By stealth or shock workers are informed in the most peremptory manner that things are going to change and there's nothing they can do about it. Where workers concede piecemeal changes, they find new machines taking over jobs they were not earmarked to destroy. Employers are wrong to call resistance Luddism. It isn't the *machines* the workers are frightened of, so much as lack of control over their deployment. 'This time, there's going to be a bigger change for us than the industrial revolution,' said a machine-tool engineer I spoke to in Sheffield.

We've got a couple of computerised and numerical-controlled lathes, we've got machines that can be set up in the office to operate the machine. I was amazed when our firm suggested having one for certain specific jobs. We've got some clapped-out old machinery and the firm suggested looking at new stuff. So I went with the foreman to look at one. Now I've been in engineering all my life, but I couldn't believe it. This machine's cutting speeds were far in excess of anything we could do. It was beautiful to watch it work. It was doing things that are impossible for us to do by hand. And it was doing it like shelling peas. It took a year to install it and get over teething problems, now it's doing *our* work, which we hadn't been consulted about.

Workers watch the coming of the new age with mixed feelings. There is fear of losing the one thing they've got to sell, their skill. Yet they are mesmerised by the new machines, because it is they above all who *know* about machines. They watch 'Tomorrow's World' with wisdom and part of them loves the elegant purr of the industrial renaissance. But all they see is an epitaph to their own thwarted inventiveness.

Even if there's a will there has to be a way, and redundancy reminds us of something so easily forgotten – the unequal power of employers and employees. The media's ritual announcements of closures and sackings, on the one hand, and of shop stewards' declarations of determination to fight, on the other, don't disclose how much workers have to fight *against* and how little they have to fight *with*. The following accounts tell us more than facts and figures ever could about the odds stacked against workers.

A private steelworks in Sheffield watched its workforce
decline from 18,000 in the early seventies to 3,500 a decade
later; in the city as a whole the number of steelworkers
slumped by 20,000 in four years. The management of the
works gave the workers regular 'state-of-the-nation' reports
on orders, but at the end of 1981 the workers discovered
through newspaper reports that secret talks were being held
on a merger with the public sector. On their own calculation
2,000 jobs would go, 'we approached the management,' said
the works convener, 'and we got a categorical denial'. A close
relationship was established with the city council, which
supported a city-wide campaign to save steel jobs. And from
that date the convener began meticulously to collect cuttings
from the newspapers and stick them in scrapbooks. A year
later 'we were still like a terrier at a rag doll – they've always
denied it.' Eighteen months after the first clue, they got their
second clue, when the company had its auditors in. Not an
unusual event, 'but what was unusual was the BSC [British
Steel Corporation] auditors and ours were in hourly contact.'
In the summer of 1982 the unions got the management to a
meeting: 'We'd had denials up to then, but this time we got a
significant change – *no comment.*' By September, the merger
was agreed – 'And still they weren't telling us anything.' On
20 September the stewards received a letter announcing the
formation of the new company, Sheffield Forgemasters, and
at the same time management issued a press release. 'It said,
"The workers have been informed" – cheeky bastards, they'd
told us half an hour before.' The following day, hundreds of
redundancies were threatened. A month later the company
decided to close one of the old melting shops. The workers
went on strike, and the company responded to their campaign, supported by the local authority, by saying that if they
did not return 'this would be the end of Sheffield as the city
of steel', and that they were 'not facing up to any responsibility'. By the end of the year they were negotiating redundancies.

The workforce in a Coventry machine-tool factory heard
the first whisper of doom not from their own management

but from the wages clerk. Their convener, a semiskilled
engineer, described how it happened:

It was Thursday morning, and it's pay day and everybody is
excited. The wages girl came to me at dinner time: they'd come in,
the bosses, looked at the money and sent her out. She came out and
told us, 'There's something going on – they've just rung for six
taxis.' I thought, bloody hell! Half an hour later there was a tap on
my shoulder. 'In my office – now,' said the boss. I said 'What for?'
but they wouldn't tell me on the shop floor. In his office he said,
'Get all your members to switch off their machines and get them
into the fitting bay, I've got something to tell them.' So he came out.
'I've got a statement to make and it's not very nice. We've just had
a word with the bank, they've pulled the plug. You've got an hour's
notice to get out.' It took him about thirty seconds. He said, 'Don't
worry about the money, the government will pay.'

This convener was only in his mid-thirties and he'd been
there for twenty years. Some people had been there forty
years.

Even if you were expecting it you wouldn't know what to do. I
wanted to stop work – we'd nothing to lose anyway. I tried to keep
them all in till we'd had a word with the union at least. So I went to
see our union official – he said, 'It seems all right to me.' That was
all. Everybody was running about all over the place to get their stuff
out, all they wanted was out. I said OK, but let's have a meeting
outside. I got the staff representative and said we'll have a meeting
together – we'd never done anything together before. We still hated
each other, the staff side and the shop floor. I wanted to occupy.
But we agreed to meet the following morning. I contacted the
pension company and got an assurance that the company had been
paying in our contributions, and that they'd come and explain our
entitlements. Two years later we're still waiting to find out what our
entitlements are. Then I went to see our union divisional organiser.
He said he'd get in touch with the banks to check out the management's story. He's paid £13,000 a year to know everything, but he
hadn't a clue.

The workers watched the company go through the factory

like a dose of salts, stripping it of machinery, the stores, every nut and bolt and all the shelves.

When I saw them doing that I said, 'What are you doing?' They told me, 'We've sold the company.' They'd sold the blinking company! The blokes were already in shock that first afternoon, and they were in even more bloody shock when they saw this happening. There were no negotiations because they were emptying the factory as soon as possible. The members clicked – it wasn't the bank that had pulled the plug, it was the company. The union confirmed that. We learned later that the newest machinery had been moved to another plant. So we went to one of the creditors' meetings because we were creditors – that shocked the life out of them! And we told them what crooks we thought they were. We got on a committee of inspection, and we managed to oppose the company getting one of their people on. Being close to the office workers was very helpful, because they were able to tell us everything that had been bought and sold – we wouldn't have been able to record all the sales, etc., and anyway they're better educated than we are, and we're not in that kind of environment. It was several months before we started getting any redundancy payments. I used to call meetings once a week because people were so worried – but then the cost factor came in. People had to travel from other towns to get to the meetings, and they couldn't afford it, so we started to lose people. If we'd occupied we'd have made a better job of the place than the management, people had been there a long time, and we *knew* about the machines. With the staff and works together we'd have made a good job of it. Our basic product was making lights in the car and electrical industry. But we had never been able to have any influence on the product at all – we were told that wasn't our job.

This convener campaigned for two years after the closure to sort out redundancy money and various moneys owed, and liaise with the liquidators, including attending meetings of creditors in London. Finally an industrial tribunal awarded them thirty days' pay as compensation – but that was recouped by the DHSS who counted it against their interim social security payments.

It cost me a load of money in travelling costs to get that. That was the heartbreaking thing for some of my members. They were so happy and buoyed up when we won at the tribunal, and they thought they got something and then found it was nothing. Some were badly in debt by then. Our redundancy money amounted to the equivalent of thirteen weeks' pay. I got £1,324.96 – not much for eighteen years of your life, eh! I thought they were crooks at first. They're not – they just don't care.

A Sunderland crane-building works, part of a group of heavy engineering factories, well organised and relatively stable: 'It's a family firm, fathers and sons, the fathers keep the sons in line, it's been company policy,' said one of the conveners. Over recent years the management has forced union concessions over craft demarcations and in the week I went there the unions had just been told that one of the group's factories had to go. Management called in the two most senior representatives late one Friday afternoon and invited them to withdraw their current pay claim, which in any case was only for a cost of living increase. So the good news was a pay cut. The bad news was that one of the four plants in the company would have to close, it wasn't decided which. It depended on what assurances they got from these leaders. 'We felt terrible, because we were losing a factory. It wasn't nice. We felt that if we'd not given the right answer it could have been us. They wanted an answer that day, that hour, that half hour' – a full commitment that the shop stewards wouldn't rock the industrial relations boat. Already the workers had watched a dramatic drop in orders and the company's share value and had headed off redundancies by insisting on short-time. 'We'd lost many weeks' work but we'd hung on to our people,' said one of the conveners. There was no combine committee, and consequently no strategic planning between the four plants in the event of a crisis. On that Friday afternoon the two men not only had no time to consult their other plants, they had no opportunity to consult their own members before surrendering the desired assurances. But even then, they didn't contact the other factories.

Why not? 'Because it would have been embarrassing. We know we'll get their work. So you see why we wouldn't want to contact them.' They waited day after day for the first week, half expecting a phone call from the other factories. But the call didn't come. 'If it had been us I'd have had our gates closed and let nothing out. We've got to look after this area, it means security for our people. I've got a lot of sympathy for the other people, but if anybody's got to go, it's not going to be me.'

Most workers who fight and lose can at least remember a festive insurgency denied them in the boom years of abiding by proper procedures. In Newcastle, the Vickers factory stands as an elegant monument to modernisation, but for a few thousand workers who live within a mile of it, it is also a monument to a Jacobin offensive by the employers. The workers wanted the new factory, but they also wanted jobs there. Instead, their nineteenth-century shed was razed to the ground and their jobs went with it. They were given a formal ninety days' notice. Their convener, who had represented them for years, said, 'My mind was on telling the lads – go back, shut everything off, play cards, read the paper, please yourself, stop work going out. We'll have a sit-in. A strike would have been useless, losing money for nowt. I wanted a massive campaign.' They contacted all the other Vickers factories in the country; for once in their history they had reason and need for unity. Briefly it looked as if they'd got it: a huge march was organised, MPs were lobbied, collections were raised. But the 1979 general election intervened, and suddenly their support evaporated, it was all out knocking up the voters. The convener called a meeting of a half a dozen senior stewards. It was all a secret – they would lock the gates the following Monday morning. 'Nobody squealed, we put stewards on each gate, and when everybody was in we called a meeting. The vote was unanimous. Management turned up later and couldn't get in. They were furious.' The occupation consummated years of patient drill. It failed, but only because officials, frightened of fighting, instructed the stewards to put to the members not a plan of war, but a package of redundancies. 'It left us with no weapons to fight with.'

Workers at Plessey's electrical engineering company making telephone equipment in Sunderland heard that their plant was to close from the local television news. Their convener went into work the following morning amidst tears and shock. 'We had whole families working there,' she said. After sorting out voluntary redundancies, a core of the workers, a vociferous minority, decided to put up a fight. Nevertheless, it was difficult for some women, however militant, to take part. One woman, a committed union member, said, 'I wouldn't take part in it, though I'd always been a bit of a militant. Why stay away from home and sleep in? Lots did and they did a marvellous job! Apart from which, my husband – no way would he have allowed me to sleep on the site.'

We decided at 4.30 p.m. to occupy and within a short time everything was in there, it was amazing. We had air beds, a cooker, one woman even brought in her portable television. We enjoyed it, but it was damned hard work. We had to climb over the railings because security wouldn't let us in. Your poor ribs got so bruised. We were on the sit-in for days, but weren't getting anywhere. So we decided to pinch the chairs, so the workers couldn't work. But we overlooked something – they got the chairs from the canteen. All the workers were coming towards us, we thought they were coming to bash us up, but they just walked past and next thing they were walking back, each carrying a chair. A few days later some of the craftsmen unscrewed some of the equipment and put it all in a box. Some workers booed us because we were holding up the redundancies, and personnel couldn't work.

When the occupation ended they negotiated payment for putting the chairs back. 'And at least we improved the redundancy payments, so it was worth it.'

These accounts show that when they're employing labour, employers have more or less to reckon with workers' own organisation, but the absolute power of ownership is never more apparent than when they're discarding labour. They also show just how difficult it is for workers to unite with other workers in the same company. While the history of combination is long in England, the history of combines is short. For much of its history, the shop stewards' movement has been confined to domestic negotiations over pennies and pounds, on the one hand, and devolving the rights of representation to the workplace and breaking through the boundaries of political and craft demarcations which divide unions, on the other. So they have been trying to modernise the trade union movement, but often they've been starved of research and resources, other than those they rustled up for themselves. And although their efforts have necessarily been local, they have been often isolated from the community outside the workplace. Meanwhile their opponents have been crossing continents.

Redundancy:
How It Feels

... so long as a man is married unemployment makes comparatively little alteration in his way of life. The man is idle from morning to night but the woman is busy as ever. Yet so far as my experience goes the women do not protest. I believe that they, as well as the men, feel that a man would lose his manhood if, merely because he was out of work, he developed into a 'Mary Ann'.

George Orwell, *The Road to Wigan Pier*

Say the word redundant and what sort of person comes to mind? It evokes in my mind a shipwright, a toolmaker, a foundryman, the men who make the things that make Britain great. To put them out of work is to do violence to their class, because their history is often written as if it were the history of their class. As Britain sinks into the low-wage, de-industrialised pit of Europe we are forced to wonder, is this it? What is going to happen to them? Will they ever work again?

Men's unemployment transforms the social landscape. The first thing you see in Sunderland, Coventry or Rotherham is shopping precincts packed with women *and* men. In the middle of a weekday afternoon, men are sitting around on public benches once occupied only by pensioners and mothers, you see denimed youths of nineteen or twenty pushing buggies, queues of men cashing giros in the same numbers as women cashing child benefit and old people collecting their pensions.

It is the same thing on any housing estate at mid-morning.
You see the redundant man because you don't expect to see
a man at all. He's the shadow in the front window reading
the *Daily Mirror* from cover to cover when he should be at
work. It is as if he is stranded in a place where he's an
immigrant and doesn't speak the language – at home.
Millions of men have fought for their right not to be there.
They've spent most of their time not there, at work or out to
play with other men. For them, home isn't where the heart is,
it's where the wife is. Sometimes it seems the oddest thing
that they ever eat and sleep in the same place together at all.
It isn't a man's natural habitat. It may be his castle, but that
doesn't mean he finds it a 'good and comely' place. When
men go out to play it isn't in each other's houses but, so to
speak, in public houses, where until recently they managed
to keep women out. Northern working-class men still proudly
make women's inclusion in their clubs conditional, the
condition being that the women don't play them at their own
games. Pubs and clubs have formal relationships, they're not
the raucous, raw and needy clatter of home, they're institutions in which everything has its time and place.

Men's redundancy is seen as a special tragedy. What a
terrible thing to happen to a *man*! Because, of course, work is
one of the places in which men are made, it sorts the boys
into men. Cut them off from work and there's a collective
panic that they'll be no different from women; they'll be
beached, cut off from the sphere that sustains their difference, their culture, their skills and their organisation.
Redundancy propels them out of the supposedly public and
into the private, it starves them of the company of other
men, mates, men whom they love. Perhaps because we
always knew that men worked for money it never seemed
necessary to ask the question – why do men go out to work?
When men become redundant they then know, if they didn't
before, that they work for the money *and* the company. Just
like women.

Likewise it seems necessary to seek a sister stereotype to
match men's experience of redundancy, the women whose

skill and social strength is thrown on the same scrapheap.
But that quest falters on some false assumptions – we don't
see men and women's feelings about work as being the same,
nor do we expect their experience of redundancy to be the
same. For a start, society has not caught up with changes in
the facts of life. Skilled secretaries are not regarded as
national assets equivalent to toolmakers or technicians. What
is still not seen is women's skills, but what is seen is their sex.
The same applies to their struggles, headlined quaintly as
'petticoat protests' while men's politics are never differen-
tiated by references to images of their underwear. Nowadays,
most women go out to work for wages most of their adult
lives. The idea that women don't go out to work for money
derives from the idea that they shouldn't work, or that they
are dependent on another breadwinner and that they have
ulterior motives – to supplement the household income so
that they can line their homes with consumer goods. The fact
is that women's wages are invested in the capital equipment,
the hoovers and washing machines, which are the tools of
their second job – housework. Women go out to work for the
money *and* the company.

Work and wages provide men with more, however – the
means to participate in the public society of men. It is not
that redundancy is worse for men than for women just
because they are men or because their work matters more to
them. But there is still a difference, and it explains much of
what makes redundancy a crisis for men. It rests on their
relationship to the home, because it is unemployment that
puts men firmly in their homes, full-time, for the first time in
their lives.

Most women know what that feels like. Most women, like
men, become parents, but only mothers find themselves in
solitary confinement, deserted during the day by men and
unsupported by social childcare unless with other women
they make alternative arrangements. Their discontent with
the loneliness and relative poverty of economic dependence
of motherhood is common currency in the culture of women,
but it is an experience from which men have protected them-

selves. Men's organisations, trade unions and working men's clubs have supported a sexual division of labour that makes men strangers in their own homes. Why it matters so much now is that the recession pushes men into a poor and private world. And if you're unemployed you just watch yourself getting poorer and becoming more private. They used to describe people laid off or unemployed as 'idle'. It is symbolised in the imagery of the thirties, bowed men, hanging around street corners. Their passivity has become the motif of unemployment. 'Two thousand idle at Vauxhall,' they'd say on the television news. But the school dinner lady is never idle. For her the difference between being 'employed' and 'unemployed' is a wage. Our feelings about her redundancy are mitigated by the knowledge that she has at the least to look after herself, which isn't necessarily the case for married men.

Many of the 'working wives' I met with redundant husbands protect them in their crisis by still doing all the domestic work. Home and work are both workplaces for her, the question is only which pays her? That word 'idle' speaks volumes. It equates the man to the machine. When it is idle so is he. Like the word 'hands' used to describe workers, 'idle' is part of employers' vocabulary that reduces people to their work. But there is more to it than that. It equates a man to his work because it is possible to imagine that the only work he does is waged. Domestic idleness that was once his right then becomes a man's crisis when he's unemployed. It is a cruel come uppance.

Here is the story of a man I met in his early sixties; he was made redundant from a Coventry car factory about five years earlier. His wife is a part-time worker:

I don't do anything. I used to potter about in the garden, but that goes in winter. I'm not the kind who does housework. Most of us decorated the house first. Before he's unemployed the working-class man's home life happened at the weekend, or part of it. The average working-class man had little or no time to notice his children growing up. Working-class children are hardly noticed by their fathers. So this unemployment might give younger fathers a chance to understand what the hell is going on with the family. There was a period after I was redundant when gardening kept me occupied. But the whole day wasn't planned. Before, you came home, got washed, went to the club for a pint. But with no money, there is no purpose in time. There's no commitment to fill in an hour in any particular way. Time, it's aimless. Your social life is completely disrupted. The games you used to play like domino's when I was a club man, they're completely gone because you can't afford it. Your social life is the first thing that goes because you can't afford it. I used to go down the club in the evening when I had a certain amount of money through redundancy pay, which was used to supplement the dole. We used to get together two or three evenings a week, it was a little ritual. Because you're not tied to the nine-to-five movement afternoons have no meaning to you, or evenings.

After a year the dole ran out then I had a year of no money at all, because my wife was working. That was totally unfair for my wife. I wasn't regarded as an individual by society, I was just an appendage, which was sickening. If I wanted to go anywhere I had to scrounge from the wife. It was sickening. The wife was the main one I had to depend on, which was disgraceful. Of course, it makes you narky. I've met some of the lads in the town, and there were one or two cases where the lads were hopping mad -- one of them solved the problem by agreeing to part so he was able to claim for himself. The bloke wasn't prepared to be dependent on his wife, even though he might be quite fond of her, in order to qualify for a few bob. It cost the state much more because housing had to be found for him, as well as an income.

A former fitter in a Coventry machine tool works, a twenty-two-year-old father of two children describes a day in his life: 'I get up about dinner time and just literally hang about. Then I watch telly. I get absolutely and totally absorbed in "Emmerdale Farm". I don't just sit there blank.' Does he fulfill the conventional wisdom that it's all different among younger men, that they're more domesticated?

No, I never do any shopping, or housework, or washing, or cleaning. The wife does it all. We eat meat once a week at mam and dad's.

My main meal is beans and a beefburger, or a fry-up. I go for a pint
when the giro comes, and on Fridays I play in a darts match, and
every two or three months we both go out. We live in a flat and
there's no garden, so we always get on each other's nerves. I get
depressed and just sit and sulk, it's never physical but we shout a
lot. The two kids are small so they get on my nerves. I just generally
have the feeling that I'm about to blow my brains out, thinking is
this it? The only thing that used to make me feel better was the giro
– but that's over. Now there's no respite.

A few years ago a machine tool engineer in a Coventry
factory bought a new house as near to the country as he
could afford, with a large back garden. Before he was made
redundant he was on short-time for over a year, as the
machine-tool industry lurched towards collapse. His wife and
two sons worked in the same factory. The two boys lost their
jobs in the spring, his wife in the autumn, he himself in the
winter.

People who don't work in industry don't understand what it's like.
Every time redundancies were declared in our firm's other plant, we
all should've gone out to fight for them. But they cared as much
about us as we did about them, which is nowt. My youngest boy has
left school and he's on the dole. My wife didn't pay full stamps so
she got no dole. Initially we went to a lot of meetings when a lot of
companies were going down the nick, but we felt quite safe, we were
the best in the world. But they didn't improve the place, there was
no investment, and the only growth seemed to be in the size of the
management. I was there sixteen years.

We didn't go on holiday every year, haven't got a hi-fi, and we
rented a video, but that's going back for lack of funds. I very rarely
drink, and we never had a penny – everything was bought on HP,
and we always owed money. So we used the redundancy money to
complete the repayments, because they only let you keep £2,000. If
I get a job it will be less than before, and I couldn't have afforded
this mortgage if the wife hadn't been working. I won't be able to get
a smaller house because I won't be able to get a mortgage. It's Catch
22. I had to exhaust the redundancy money before going on the
dole, and now when I've finished paying the mortgage and the rates

we finish up with £40 a week for three of us. Our last gas bill was £140, that's £10 a week. That leaves us with £30 for everything else. The money's run out and we've missed two months on the mortgage. I've worked hard, I paid in to the sick pay fund but I've never had a day off and I've never claimed anything in thirty years, so why should I have to give everything up?

What do I eat? Eggs, chips and beans and meat only on Sundays. I never go out, never see any friends, only ever see a convener from another plant who sometimes calls me up. Sometimes I think my brain is dying. I get depressed – sometimes I shout and bawl. I'm not going mental, but I feel I might like to damage somebody. I can't watch Thatcher on TV. I listen to 'Question Time' on radio, and she talks different you know. The way she talks to her peers is very matter of fact. But on TV when she talks to us, it's like thirty words a minute slower, she treats us like morons. When she's on I turn the bastard off. No, I don't go to meetings now. I've been in the engineering union for thirty years, since I was sixteen, and now I don't even go to my branch. The reason: two words – Terry Duffy. I may not be articulate, but he's disgraceful, he's let my class of people down.

What do I do with my time? Well, there's the garden, but I'm not a gardener, I'm not going to garden for victory yet. I do nothing. I've got the tools you'd need for anything, but I never touch them. It's very difficult to get motivated, I've got a lot to do, like redoing the kitchen, but I can't. We're both avid readers, sometimes I'm awake reading till 2.30 a.m. I used to buy books now I'm in the library. I'm just reading Wilson's memoirs.

A constant rattling noise came from the upstairs. 'Don't worry, it's only the wife's knitting machine. She knits for people.' As we talked, a three-year-old boy toddled in and out: 'Grandad, grandad ...' 'Just a minute darling while I talk to this lady ...' 'Grandad ...' 'OK, let's find a biscuit ...' 'Grandad ...' 'Tell you what, why don't you play with some water! What about filling up the sink and you can stand on a chair, darling, and we'll take your teeshirt off so you can get wet ...'

I see him every day, he keeps me sane. It's like a drug, I think I'm not going to go for him today because I've got things to do, but I usually do. I really love him, I worry about him if he's got a cold. He phones me up, you know. Anyway. Now, I do the cooking. When I left work for some reason I wanted to bake, so I asked her and she taught me to make pastry, and I make a couple of apple pies every week. Your life is a load of crap. What bothers me most is that surely to christ they're not going to keep me on the dole all my life.

He was a big man with big hands. After a while his grandson decided he'd had enough of the water, and they both returned to the sitting room with a big towel. The grandfather wrapped it round the little body and patted his back and chest dry and then gently lifted up the boy's elbows and dried his armpits, in a gesture of the most knowing intimacy, while the big hand held the little back, which seemed no wider than the span of his fingers. As he dried the boy we talked about Margaret Thatcher. Suddenly, his hand clenched into a fist, like a bomb. 'Thatcher, I *detest* that woman.'

Coventry's motor manufacture and machine tool industry collapsed in the late seventies and early eighties, producing unemployment among one in five of the workforce. On whole housing estates half the population are on the dole, permanently hibernating at home while children go to school. A fitter made redundant from the track in a car factory spends most of his days pottering about. His trousers, suspended from braces over a nylon teeshirt, swirled round his hips and legs – only when he turned round did you notice that he'd got darts stitched up the back by the waist. His feet seemed very big – a pair of shoes a size too large, passed on by a friend. By his kitchen door was a car battery, a toolbox lay open across a worktop by the draining board, together with a disabled television and somebody's discarded radio. There wasn't a dirty cup or a draining dish to be seen. He lived alone in a council maisonette with an exquisite garden, and he'd learned since his divorce to look after himself. He had an orange three-piece, a 'contemporary' carpet, a postwar utility table covered with a cloth which covered an antique television sitting on the floor, a formica coffee table and a large free-standing television, presumably for watching. He had worked for over thirty years in car factories as a skilled engineer and took redundancy in 1980 when he was in his late forties.

I took voluntary redundancy because I was cheesed off. Track work annihilates you. It's a permanent depression. It's still with me now, after all that time. You sell your body to the highest bidder, you're expected to grow up, get married, keep a wife, have kids and work. But at thirty-five you're too old to work on the track. I'd have done anything involved in building axles, but you were expected to produce any figure they threw at you. Two or three years before I went there was no work at all, so they had everybody in there painting everything – everything! Tools, cupboards. I'd grown up thinking I should be the breadwinner with the means I'd got available, but the means got meaner and meaner. People thought it was a boom town, but you needed two wages. A man should be able to earn enough to keep his wife at home. Although with the redundancies I wouldn't have supported the women being made to go first. One of the most deplorable things I ever saw in the fifties was a woman with three kids to support being made redundant.

Another reason I took voluntary redundancy was seeing people with mortgages of over £230 a month -- they couldn't manage that without a permanent full-time job, so I decided I'd rather see myself go. What do I do with my time? Decorating, gardening, a bit of drinking, fix things, and I like to find a bit of immoral crumpet. There's nothing nicer than a good dirty woman. We'd all say if you had a woman you'd be all right. You need to be able to touch people – not having that is like taking a person's legs away. I'm a randy git, I like all I can get. They're selling everything with sex. You open page three and I think to myself why doesn't one like that come through my door?

If you are alone like me then a twenty-four-hour day feels like an eighty-four-hour day. You've been on that jig all those years, you end up moulded to it. Mind you, I never think about that job now, because it was unimportant. It's like we are housewives without any kids.

I have no breakfast, and I eat when I feel like it because I don't live by the clock or calendar. I have one meal a day although I can't really afford it. I can't pay the TV licence, and every time I shop it's a toss up over things like washing powder or toothpaste. I bought a second-hand overcoat -- before being on the dole I wouldn't have entertained the idea of second-hand clothes.

The other day this man had a visit from the DHSS to check that he wasn't working. He's now qualified for a supplementary benefit book, instead of receiving regular giros through the post: 'I call it my ration book.' As a skilled man he is under special scrutiny by DHSS snoopers, whose targets are skilled manual workers able to earn a bit doing odd jobs, and single mothers. This man occasionally commits 'fraud'. 'If I earn a couple of quid fixing something, I'll buy a big sack of potatoes for £1.50 and sell half of it.'

On my way to an interwar housing estate in Coventry I was looking round a street corner wondering which way to go. Two painters standing outside a private prewar semi nearby shouted, 'Where do you want, love?' I told them. 'Ooh, you don't want to go down there, watch it, it's rough.' What is this, Harlem? Down there was a thirties council estate, the type which when I was a kid always seemed more respectable than ours, probably because the tenants were older, and there weren't so many kids making the place untidy. These streets had seen several generations of households with children. They had back and front gardens with roses, cornflowers, grass, ailing armchairs, retired twintubs, redundant pokers, recycled motorcycles and a miscellany of potential spare parts.

When I reached the house I was making for, a big man with a Zapata moustache opened the door. He was wearing neat jeans and a Wrangler shirt. It was a small house with an old but not threadbare brown square carpet, with lino round the edge of the room, a utility three-piece suite and a formica wall unit holding a hi-fi, letters and a bottle of whisky. 'I won that in a raffle, I can't afford things like that now,' he said. On a chair was a pile of jeans and shorts, freshly washed in the sink and dried. He was in his mid-thirties and lived in the same house as he'd grown up in with his parents, both now dead. He'd been made redundant two years earlier from a Coventry engineering factory where he'd started work twenty years before, when he was fifteen. He was a semi-skilled machinist and like many workers suddenly made redundant his first year of unemployment was governed by the habits of a lifetime.

I used to get up at 6 a.m., like I was going to work. I thought I'd get a job in a couple of weeks, but now it's a couple of years. That's frightening, my confidence is going. When people ask me how long I've been out of work, I think, shall I lie? When you're unemployed, you feel like you've committed a crime somewhere, but nobody tells you what you've done. The first thing that happened to me was that I realised I'd become almost illiterate after years working in a factory. I fall asleep a lot, it happens if you've got nothing to do. I have some toast for breakfast then I go out and get a paper and have a read of that until about 10.30. One bloke round here, the only place he goes out to is to sign on at the dole. Sometimes I think I'll go barmy. Of course you get depressed, you convince yourself it's you. Sometimes I feel really ashamed, especially with things like Christmas. This will be the first time I've ever not given my sisters something for Christmas.

I used to eat steak and things, and a chop, tomato and bread and butter. Dead easy. Now it's bread and butter. First I went down to bacon sandwiches, now it's just sandwiches. One of my sisters will come and drop in a jar of coffee or a tin of salmon. Sundays I go alternately to one of my sisters, who give me a meal. I eat a lot of bread, so I've put on a stone, usually I have a bit of cooked ham or spam. I don't make meals very often. I used to have eggs on toast or a luxury meal was beans on toast. And I have a few pints a week. I've bought no new clothes since I was made redundant. My sister buys me jeans for Christmas. I used to go to a folk club, but I can't afford that now, and I used to go trout fishing, but a day's fishing would cost about £5 or £8, and if we had a boat it would be another £5. Then we'd go for a drink, so even if I scraped the money together to do it, I'd have to sit outside while the rest were in the pub. If I haven't any meetings to go to I might go for a walk or just sit or play a record – I listen to folk and blues. I go to a lot of meetings. After I was made redundant a Labour Party councillor came round and we were talking about the estate, it's falling down. He said come to a meeting and tell us about it, anyway he came back – the first guy who'd ever knocked on the door about politics and come back. That convinced me, so I joined the Labour Party. I walk everywhere, it's a bit embarrassing when you're a trade unionist. I walk to three or four meetings a week – at the union branch none of us is employed. Half the union's district committee is unemployed now, too. Usually I don't stay on after union meetings for a drink because I can't afford it, but I try to after the Labour Party meetings because it's usually most interesting then.

Sometimes I feel depression coming on. Things get to you, like programmes on television about people dying because of asbestos, or unemployed people killing themselves. If you're a bit socially aware it gets to you and you can't do anything about it. You're a waste of time as a human being. There's nothing to do except go to meetings, but you feel the fight going out of you. Somebody did something rotten to me – I went to join the library and when I was asked for identification I produced my dole card. They said they couldn't accept that, so I had to go back with a gas bill. You end up telling lies. If people suggest going somewhere I say, 'No, I can't come because I've got to go to my sister's.' And really all I do is sit in the pissing house. Before, I'd say I've got no money, and I wasn't ashamed of it. Now it's becoming natural to me to lie.

Since being made redundant he's got active in the local Labour Party, because somebody visited his house canvassing, they had an argument and the bloke came back to see him next day. He does it because it is something to do. At least since he's unemployed, he gets letters, which he never did before. Regular little brown envelopes from the DHSS. The thing that affected me perhaps most, apart from the fact that he was such a nice person, was that there was clearly a point in his account of his feelings about it all beyond which one couldn't go, it would have been too dangerous for him. But, more than that, he was exactly the same age as me.

Actually, one month older. That made it worse.

Most unemployed teenagers correspond very little to the image of redundant workers because they've never had jobs save for brief interludes on youth opportunities or work experience schemes. Their 'idleness' is compounded by uselessness. They are nuisances in their own homes, littering the place with their pals, nuisances on the streets where they gather as the day wears on and the rest of the family comes home from school or work. I met a group of unemployed teenagers in Coventry, who spend much of their time sprawled around their parents' homes, or wandering the streets. Several had been on Youth Opportunities Programme schemes, some loved the opportunity to work, others regarded it as a waste of time. 'I went on a catering course, but they didn't teach us to cook,' said one of the boys. 'It was all about washing towels and table cloths. I told the supervisor that we weren't getting enough to do so she said do anything you like. So I didn't do anything.'

Some of the girls had learned to type at school, but none of them had managed to find work through the agencies. They get up round about mid-day, then visit each other, and later in the day start wandering around the streets, sometimes vandalising bus shelters or shops, or stealing from off-licences. 'Round here we're called "the toolmakers", we're blamed for everything. The sixth-formers, they're snobs. Kids from round here never stay on at school. You just thieve because you can't afford anything, or you smash things up because you've got to make your protest.' Most of the boys were skinheads who grow their hair periodically to apply for jobs. 'It's great, short hair, because you don't want to be known as a snob. Snobs, every one of us hates them, they treat us like nothing, they think they're better than us. Paki snobs are the worst.' There was some disagreement over this, particularly from the girls. 'But they work harder than us,' the girls said.

When Norman Tebbit said to the unemployed, 'On your bike', everybody knew he was a fool. Only a fool would go round the country looking for work, because there isn't any.

No doubt a number do, but I came across very few. In Rotherham I met a group of young Asians. Some of them are desperate for work because their families rely on them. One Asian teenager's father had returned to his homeland suffering from TB. He had to fight with the DHSS to restore his mother's social security, which had been cut off on the grounds that her husband should maintain her.

I'd get up and go round factories in Rotherham or I'd travel to Sheffield, though most of them won't let you through the gate. Then I'd come home and eat something, pick up a paper and if I saw anything I'd write off for it. Out of half a dozen letters a week I'd be lucky to get two replies. Once I applied for a driver's job and I got a letter back saying they'd had 150 applicants. But you can only do so much of that. I went regularly to the job centre in town then gradually I came to an understanding of the situation I was in, because a lot of people were redundant. At first I'd got to thinking it was because of my colour.

In South Yorkshire I also meet three young people who seemed to be Tebbit's dream children, intrepid itinerants who'd roamed the country looking for work, from the West Country to the Northeast and now Yorkshire. They turned up one day at a local unemployed centre where they didn't know anyone and, after putting up at a hostel for the homeless, spent their day in the centre. Late in the afternoon there is a pool competition. It is quite a ceremony, with a referee and supporters from the centre and the rival club. The two boys are absorbed in the crowd; their companion, a girl, sits on a chair and looks on with an air of polite blankness. It is October, thank god it isn't too cold yet. The girl is very pale, with cracks around the side of her lips. A little cream would sort it, but she probably hasn't the money. She has sunken brown eyes, an extinct perm, a cardigan, tee-shirt, red trousers with a gold thread in them and little red ballet-type pumps. Nineteen years old, left school at sixteen. Her passivity was formidable, but we talked a bit. I ask if she'd talk about her unemployment. She'd been made redundant, not once but twice. The first time, she says, she'd got a day's notice. The second, a week's. She'd worked in both firms for under two years so she hadn't qualified for redundancy money. Then she'd moved out of her mother's house to live with her boyfriend, a redundant roofer who claimed for both of them – £82.20 a fortnight. Rent was £40 a fortnight, summer fuel £8. That left £16 a week for both of them to live on.

The landlord pressured them out of the flat and they'd met some people in a pub. 'They told us there was jobs going in Durham, so we went there. We asked people when we arrived but they said there's no jobs going here. We didn't have anywhere to stay, but we met some people in a pub and they let us stay with them for a few days.' When they arrived in Sheffield they settled in another hostel.

We stayed in a night shelter for the homeless. We had to sleep separately. It was all right but you had to be out at nine in the morning until eight at night. It cost £2.30 a night for a bed and a meal, usually beans on toast or egg on toast or tomato on toast. Then we moved on. We're in another hostel, but it's rubbish, it costs £1.60 a night and you get a bed and food – soup and beans on toast. We always go to the job centres in these places, but there's nothing.

Nowadays, the unemployed stay at home. These three, on the move all the time, spend the infinity of time before settling in for the night at their hostels, hanging around strange city centres with no place to go because most places cost money. It brings to mind the imagery of the thirties, the apparently passive poverty of people hanging around street corners. If this young woman was standing on a street corner like that all day she'd be cautioned for loitering or suspected of soliciting. She possesses two cardigans, a pair of jeans and the trousers she's got on, four tee-shirts, one pair of shoes – the little red shoes – soap, and that's it. During her account of her travels she never said a word about how it felt. Did she ever get depressed, I asked, like the proverbial television interviewer? Silence. 'Does it ever get you down?' I repeated.

'I suppose it does,' she said. 'Have we finished, can I go now?'

I wanted to ask her more, but she didn't want to talk very much about the detail, which didn't seem very important to her. And yet detail in these things is everything. More, the detail is the bearer of your real feelings about it all, and yet your real feelings can't be disclosed. Why should she disclose her real feelings to me, after all? I've got a notebook, and a pen, and more than one pair of shoes, and I'm not revealing *my* feelings. So why should she? She's an itinerant person, of a type that I suspect is quite unusual now, traipsing from city to city looking for work. That's a hard life, and there's winter coming on and she's not got a winter coat, a pair of socks or winter shoes. So what could she feel? Usually, people do tell me some of what they're feeling. But I was struck by this woman, by her pale, blank, numbedness. That kind of itinerancy isn't hard only in terms of the hardware that makes up life, but you're thrust on your emotional resources all the time, you have to negotiate places and people several times a day who are complete strangers. What does *that* feel like? And who's got the right to ask her? A few days later she and her companions were arrested for stealing a chequebook.

For women, particularly mothers, employment usually means over-employment – doing two jobs, one at work, one at home. Unemployment means that they've got less to do and less money to do it with, but it is still within the continuum of women's experience. Because, of course, women *know* both worlds of workplace and home, and being in either doesn't disturb their femininity. Unemployment as a day-to-day routine is like being 'just a housewife'. At the same time, they are not easily sent into domestic exile, rather the opposite – the few outbreaks of organised resistance to closures and redundancies have often included women, and some of the most spectacular resistance, like Plesseys in Sunderland, Lee Jeans in Scotland and school dinners has been led by women. However, women do seem to be more serene survivors than men.

A Coventry car worker tells her tale: after working for twenty-five years as the sole breadwinner bringing up her children, she was made redundant from her job trimming car seat covers in 1980.

We liked the work well enough, though it was an awful fumey sort of place, it was a good crowd of people who made a good little life for themselves in the factory. I worked shifts because I didn't really mind and I needed the money – on my last job I took home £65 a week. My first job was in an electrical engineering factory but because I was always trying to better my wages I ended up in a car factory which paid the most – though in between I'd been a waitress in several cafés and I'd worked in some other engineering factories. When I was first made redundant the union policy was to put the old ones out of the factory first. Well, that's all right if you give them enough money – because you have more time on your hands so you use more heating and electricity. I thought they should have resisted the redundancies though, but they didn't. At first I didn't know what to do with myself and it probably took about a year to get used to it. I applied for jobs in the beginning – I tried bingo halls, waitressing and things like that, but you never heard a word of a reply. I was pretty active then and I thought I'd get something in a month or two – but of course I didn't, even cleaning jobs, they're very choosy who they have now.

When I was paid off I got £4000, including my pension. So I paid off the car, but then I had to get rid of it because the tax and insurance is too much. I went to see my brother in Ireland because I thought I might never have the chance again, and I took a holiday because I hadn't been able to do that very often before. Even gardening costs you money, you know. Anyway, all that money went and I wasn't able to claim the dole for three months because of it. Now I'm on supplementary benefit and I get a total of £34, of which £13.28 goes on rent and rates. Food is about £12 a week, gas £60 a quarter and £22 electric, so that's between £7 and £8 a week on fuel etc. The phone bill is £25 a quarter. I hang on to that because it would be so expensive to have it put back in. That leaves nothing. So to save on fuel bills I walk around the town, or the park, or take somebody's dog for a walk. I'm in a rambling club but I have to find the money for that, it is £1.60 or £2 a time and food costs a bit because you want something nice in your sandwiches. Evenings? Well, I don't see people, so I knit, or go for a walk. I know various people in the street and I've got very nice neighbours, Indian people, they've lent me a book about their religion actually which I'm just reading. Shopping is done as I need it every day, and since I've had lots of time on my hands I've turned to cooking – I'm quite inclined to make cakes and jam now, which I never had the time for before. And I knit for presents, though that is expensive. But I've got to do all these things to keep myself from going mad. So I'm busy.

A woman in her forties was the third person in her family in Wigan to be made redundant – and it was her second redundancy. Now all six members of her family are unemployed.

I've always worked, since my youngest was eighteen months old and my mother retired and said she'd look after the child. Now, I get up usually about ten o'clock and sit for at least an hour with a coffee and a cigarette. Sometimes I do housework, but my husband won't let me go shopping. We used to do it together but now he won't let me because he says I spend too much. With housework it'll go maybe for a fortnight and I'll not put the vacuum round, but then I'll screech around for two days and when it is all done I'll nag them to keep it clean. Otherwise I spend the day knitting. People get the wool and I knit things on the machine, sometimes for eight hours a day. I wanted shrubs for the garden, but we can't afford them. I don't see any friends – nobody at all except the family, because you can't afford to do things or have people over. I don't go out at all actually, ever. I never go out of this house. In our marriage we've always been all right together but this unemployment puts a strain on marriage. Because he gets bad-tempered and upset about things and I'm not very sympathetic, I want to shake him and say for Christ's sake, stop it. We don't have any proper meal times because you think to yourself, what's the point? There's no regularity in your life. Before we'd all come home and get cracking and have our tea but now there's no set time for anything. We eat messy, in bits and bobs, and I've got no appetite, it's all disorganised. Also, things get to you more, I've said to him often, that woman! [Thatcher] I detest her. They've decimated our lot up here, the government. In the war we kept things going when the Germans tried to bomb our industry, but she's sorted it out in a couple of years. It's personal with me – I detest her.

A skilled telecommunications engineer in Sheffield worked for over twenty years with a group of highly specialised women in her factory. One night on the local television news they heard that they were being closed down. She was made redundant in 1979 after the workers rustled up a last-ditch occupation.

Oh, I loved the work. They were marvellous workers some of them, they could do amazing things. Since the place closed I've been out of work, apart from a few months packing shelves in a supermarket at £7.28 for five hours – that was hard work, I can tell you! Now I don't get any money at all because my husband is working – all those years I paid the full stamp, too! And my husband is on short-time now, one week on and one week off. So we have £122 fortnightly between us. The mortgage is £9.15, gas £75 a quarter, electricity £35, supermarket shopping £10 weekly, and I shop locally three times a week for meat – usually mince, chops and bacon. We share an allotment between three households and that keeps us all in vegetables.

During the day I wander about the town, go to the library – I never had time to read before, so now I read history and murders, anything. And every Tuesday we have a girls' night out. I never get depressed about anything, although I felt I was wasting my time so I went back to school. I'd left at fourteen and didn't feel my education was anywhere near what it should be, so I went to adult education. You can do maths up to TOPS standard but I went just for me. I enjoyed the peace and quiet at home, no more blazing radios like in the factory, and I enjoy doing what I want when I want. I can do my housework when I like and I visit some old ladies every day, and I see my friend – so it's all right.

In Sunderland, I met a tall, dark, handsome woman, with long, red-painted nails, holding a cigarette in one hand and a gin and tonic in the other from the cocktail cabinet in the corner of the living room of the council house she'd bought – the very opposite of the head-scarfed cross between Wilma Flintstone and Flo Capp usually used to portray the working-class woman. She'd worked for thirty-one years as a skilled electrical engineer.

I wouldn't have volunteered for redundancy, because I wanted my job. I loved it. I'd done it for twenty-five years. A couple of years after they'd made me redundant they asked me to go and train people to do that job I'd done all those years. Well, I just about went through the phone.

I got £3,000 redundancy money, for thirty-one years! When I left I was shocked, and I felt very bitter, so mad about the whole thing. For six months, till I got another job, much lower paid, I was crawling up the wall. I wasn't used to being at home, I'd been a career girl, you see. That was my life.

A twenty-five-year-old woman in Barnsley had been made redundant twice, and was about to be again for the third time. She won't appear in the unemployment figures – she explains why:

I'm a secretary. I was first made redundant when the transport firm I worked for merged. I was the only girl working there, and they transferred the administration to the head office. I got £170 redundancy money. Didn't bother us at the time because I was sick of it. My next job, the firm went bust.

For the first few months I threw myself into the house. Then I started crawling up the walls. I'd always go down to the job centre badgering for a job. It's common up here for women not to work. But with us working I'd not been in contact with the community, so I didn't know anybody. My husband was making enough to keep us, but I missed my independence. I was jealous of him having a job. Daft things happened, he'd come in and want to talk, but I'd shout, 'The hoover's broke', and little tiny things become enormous. You take things to heart, you think you're thick and stupid. Then my sister-in-law had a baby. I'd always felt there were enough babies. Then, suddenly I wanted a baby. It was something to do, to plan for, it's a future isn't it? I thought it was great, I was over the moon with myself.

After the baby I resumed work, got a part-time job, the hours were great. My biggest obstacle was my husband. But now he says he can see the change in me, so it's worth it. At least he can come in the door and I'm not waiting to strangle him because I'm so bored and frustrated. Working here in the local community advice centre has shown me I wasn't the only one who couldn't find a job. Actually it's the other way round, it's only the one or two who do. I'd got so depressed, not suicidal or anything, just depressed: hoovering, washing, cleaning, cooking. A friend of mine said let's go over to the advice centre, because there's a mother and toddler group. I took a rent rebate form with me, as an excuse because one part of me didn't want to go, another part did. Anyway, we came over, I had a coffee and it was fine. I'd never been in anything before, and I'd never gone to a meeting of any kind. So then I began to look forward to the meetings because I could spend energy and I learned that there were other women with kids and husband and rows to cope with. I needed that bit of independence, and I really didn't want to be unemployed. I'm not even on the statistics unless I sign on, but it is for nothing. All of a sudden I'm a nothing, I'm not even a statistic. I put a claim in for supplementary benefit after my dole ran out and they sent for me. I had to pay 60p to get there and then they told me I couldn't claim because my husband was earning and anyway if he wasn't he'd have to claim for both of us. So I was paying out money to sign on for money I wasn't getting. How many other mothers don't sign on for the same reason?

Mass unemployment among men evokes a sense of mass martyrdom, a kind of death. Somehow women's mass unemployment seems less of a spectre, and that is not just because there are still some people who believe that women ought to have the public spirit personally to redistribute their jobs. The difference lies in the fact that unemployment for men means their exclusion not only from work but from the environment that makes them men, which is also their route to masculine class consciousness and class strength. While ideas about femininity have been reformed – not without a struggle – so that women are no longer believed to be de-feminised by working for wages, masculinity has remained relatively unreconstructed. Men's tragedy is that unemployment makes them feel unmanned.

Women's Way

The fact that the working class know how to combine and the middle class don't is probably due to their different conceptions of family loyalty ...

George Orwell, *The Road to Wigan Pier*

Amongst working-class women, there is a long tradition of women's institutes, sections, caucuses and clubs attached to the mainstream institutions of the labour movement. One thing unites them above all, a quest for women's place in politics. Men move into politics like learning to walk. The structures are built for them and wives make the space for them. All the women I talk to who are involved in politics have to cope with domestic instability as a result – their politics aren't a natural function of their work, they're experienced as an unnatural response to their station, and it disturbs all aspects of their lives. Especially if it involves kids and work. Some of the old time Labour women's section women had no job, so the ripples were less for them. But women live in the shadow of men's seizure of public life, whether in the public bar or public office. Men's participation in public life involves no threat to their masculine identity. Women's femininity, on the other hand, is anchored in private life. For them going into politics is a gesture of defiance, however timid, against their domestication, although they usually bring with them their experience of domestic responsibility. This is true whether we are talking of the Labour Party women's sections, the contemporary

191

women's liberation movement or campaigns on issues which have been traditionally politicised by women – health, housing and children.

Older women I met said that in their youth the women's sections of the Labour Party provided a corner for women to go unchaperoned into their communities. They were acceptable because they mobilised women for the Labour Party, their legitimacy depended on their role as auxiliaries to the men's party. That's how many of the elderly women who have spent their lives in the women's sections see it – the men's party. As young married women, they were allowed to belong not so much to the community as to the community of women. According to a woman in her seventies, always active in the women's sections and now a prominent member of the regional Labour Party in the Northeast, 'Some women joined the women's section because it was the only way they could get out. I liked the women's movement in the party as opposed to the joint meetings. I like women.'

Today, organisations like tenants' associations or mothers' and toddlers' groups serve a similar function. 'I spent four or five years tied to the house with two kids and my only contact with the outside world was my husband,' said a Sunderland woman in her early thirties who joined a tenants' association on her estate. 'A couple of men wanted a tenants' association because of the problem of stray dogs. I went to the meeting because I saw it as a way of getting out of the house and getting into something, and anyway I said I could type, so I could be useful.' Isolation similarly motivated a group of young mothers in Sunderland to start their own co-op shop, another long working-class tradition. 'We were all going round the bend by being stuck at home all the time. I'd never worked since I was nineteen. My bairns were little and all my friends were in the same boat. I thought, everybody needs food! We thought we'd start a shop and we could have a little room for the kids while one of us watched them.'

These beginnings always involve high diplomacy on the home front. An old-age pensioner in Barnsley who has spent decades in the women's sections of the Labour Party still has to negotiate her right to be somewhere else than home.

If I go to meetings I get back in time to make a supper and look after all his comforts as far as possible. I don't know if it's ruthless or selfish, but they go in for sulks, men. I just ignore it and get on with it. Going to conferences I've sometimes walked out of the door with sullen silences behind me. A lot of us were ordinary working-class women and we've a long way to go before men will let women do as they want.

A woman I met in Sheffield who became a tenants' activist said that it was when the women on the estate started broadening their own horizons that the family problems started.

In our marriage there was no way I was going to be the one who did the housework any more. But it was very difficult for the others. For a start, people can't see friendship between men and women without a sexual context. Women would stop women in the street who they'd met at meetings, but not men. Others would have to beg men to let them go out. It was strangulating at first. It would be rare for a woman not to have a problem with her husband about being involved, you've always got to be aware of the effect involvement will have on women and their families and husbands. A lot dropped out because of the hassles at home. I face problems with my husband, too, and yes, it means you question your marriage, definitely.

The women in the co-op shop find the same problem.

There were hassles with the husbands and a couple of them tried to get their wives to leave, one just wouldn't let his wife out of the house. We were saying we're not content with our lives. My dad blamed it on women's lib, and I said, 'Right, but it's with us and you can't get shot of it.' Without exception, not one of us hasn't experienced difficulty with our marriage. We can talk about it in our group, we can talk about everything, but it's not so easy with the men. Mind you, we did everything to do with the bairns, so the men never had to deal with that.

'The first hurdle you have to get over is your husband,' said a Midlands hospital worker in her forties with a family and a husband who, like all of these women, had to negotiate her right to become a shop steward during the hospital workers' dispute. 'We came out of the dispute much stronger because we went through great turmoils, things like that the house needed cleaning when someone up the road had a house that was spic and span,' said the member of the co-op shop. And for most women, it is they who have to make sure that they'll be able to participate. 'Nobody in my house went without their dinners, I saw to everything,' said a woman in her early thirties living with her husband and two children in a tenement block in Liverpool where the mothers organised first a tenants' group and then their own housing co-op. And another woman said with some bitterness, 'Unlike the men, none of us ever come home and think only about ourselves. That's what drives me batty about trade union men, they don't even *know* they're exploiting their wives.'

Once women have fought the home battle, they come into conflict with men outside about both the form and the content of political representation. A woman I spoke to in a Northeast Labour Party women's section feels that men's resistance and home responsibilities have always stifled women's political aspirations.

Working-class women didn't get into positions. We were always a good pressure group, we did a lot of campaigning work on housing, education, childcare and welfare, but if you are working class and have a family, this is the problem. In those days the women MPs didn't have families. Let's be honest, women in those days had to be ruthless. Miners would no more have thought of putting a woman like me in than fly to the moon. I had the opportunity to go on to a couple of short lists to be a candidate, they were unwinnable seats of course. But I couldn't, though I would have loved it. At the time I just accepted it. I used to think about it though, and I regret it. The branches still have this prejudice against women, they'd rather have a man, they come to meetings saying women should put themselves forward but they never mean in their own seat. That's men all over. In how many families can a woman say, 'I'll go to London and be an MP'?

In the old days, the women's sections of the Labour Party enjoyed substantial support in working-class communities, they weren't regarded as odd or separatist because before the war men and women led separate lives anyway. In the Northeast of England the tradition of community among women survives. It is commonplace for married women to go out with other married women; it's called the 'jolly girls'. And even if they end up the same pub as their husbands they don't team up. The most boisterous 'jolly girls' I met lived on a run-down council estate in Sunderland; they regularly have a night out together at the local pub where they drink half pints in the public bar, challenge the men to pool and organise their own Christmas savings club, £3.50 a week, because they don't have bank accounts. Also, every afternoon several of them meet in one of the flats to knit. If something is made for someone else, they only charge a pound.

The old women's sections were quarantined in their separate sphere to service the party and work among women who had no access to the society of men. Subsequent generations of women were more suspicious of the women's sections. 'I hate the very idea of women's sections,' said a middle-aged woman in Coventry who has worked in the party since the fifties. For many women of her generation, women's sections seem to bear the mark of subservience and subordination; equality with men means being *with* the men. 'To me it's an insult that there's a women's TUC and a women's section of the National Executive of the Labour Party. I'm an equal member of the Labour Party.' In the absence of an independent women's movement, such women refused to see themselves as unequal. But just as they rejected subordination, so they rejected feminism, which carried the contagion of dissidence against the very subordination they denied. With the revival of the women's sections in the eighties, meetings are a miscellany of age, class and culture, with a new mood of militancy expressed in increasingly feminist politics and demands to extend the rights of women in the party. For some time they have been among the most radical sections of the party and their revival is associated with the rise of the Left in the constituencies. Both the feminism and the radicalism of the women's sections draw the fire of men's consolidated power blocs. They are no longer content to be the servants of the party – and that cuts them off from the support, therefore, of men *and* their working-class wives. A Sunderland woman in her mid-thirties, who has been a Labour Party member since the sixties and a feminist since the seventies explains this dilemma this way:

In the old days the women needed a way to meet because they were completely excluded from the men. They did a lot, but the party marginalised them, though because they serviced the lifestyle of the men they were encouraged by the men. Now many of the men who would at one time have encouraged their wives to join women's sections will do the opposite because they're frightened of the feminism, because of course it wouldn't be about the men's lives. They're scared of the women having fun and letting their wives loose among all that. Now feminists are joining the party as feminists, and they're looking for a vehicle that will bring the power for them to implement women's policies. They don't need a legitimate way to meet women, or social reasons, because they've got plenty of those opportunities. They want to come to meetings, get on with the policy and get away. They haven't time for bingo, though with some of the older women the bingo is very important. And there are class differences, age and culture. We still have big arguments about childcare because it became a matter of pride to the older women that they could manage, managing became part of their political creed. At first I couldn't understand why we kept having these arguments, now I think it's because they think it's a weakness if you can't manage, and when they hear women criticising the situations they coped with they feel their own lives are being trashed.

Her colleague, who is in her seventies and sees the revolution within the women's sections with a mixture of empathy and antipathy, confirms this view: 'Family relations between men and women should change. It did in a limited way, but it wasn't something that was talked about, not from a policy point of view. We always thought the first thing you had to do was look after your family. Only this last year or so have we heard of crêches even.' She feels that some of the younger women think 'they've invented the wheel'. 'We were on about some of those things long before. But we did it gradually. These young women are very impatient. It's not that I disagree with them. I've never discriminated against lesbians, and I agree with childcare, but they want crêches at conferences not only during the day, but in the evening too! It's the way they go about things.'

The new-found hostility of men to the women's sections arises from the women wanting to find policies to transform the relationship between men and women. And this veteran's younger ally is afraid that the animus against feminism makes the women's sections -- once a focus for women's politics in the Labour strongholds – a no-go area for the very women who forty years ago would have joined them. 'For working-class women now there is no *obvious* route to politics. That shakes me rigid, it leaves me wondering what is the road forward?'

But in all the towns I visited there was a plethora of women's groups fighting their local authority landlords, fighting for nurseries, for better health care for women, organising mothers' and toddlers' groups, girls' nights in youth clubs and children's playschemes. They are often much less hesitant than some of their feminist sisters about expressing disappointment at men's non-cooperation because they barely expect it to be otherwise, though their criticisms are fortified by the existence of feminism in the culture at large. Women's community politics around housing, health and children – the same preoccupations as united their working-class antecedents throughout the twentieth century – are a continuing indication of women's resilience. So perhaps it would be truer to say there is no obvious route to *party* politics. Men's response to such a suggestion is to throw up their hands in horror: we've never stopped women, they say, it's women who are their own worst enemy. At best they mean individual women, not the collective will of women. No political party in England has yet been transformed into a party for women. Apart from home, there are few places where working-class men and women encounter each other. Politics could be the arena in which their alliance is organised. But the political parties also happen to be the places where women's interests *as women* have been disorganised and defeated.

Women's complaints against the men's movement's ways of doing things are manifest in their local struggles. Housing activists, for example, say that, left to their own devices, women find energy and will, apparently from nowhere, and that they rely on an informality which allows everyone to participate. The men, on the other hand, have to have a committee and rely on formal structures to consolidate their personal power base, which then intimidates people. I spoke to members of a community association that has been set up in Wigan by tenants living on an estate which is, literally, falling apart. After years of campaigning for a community centre to provide a social focus for their desert of semi-detached streets, they have acquired an old school wrecked by arson and vandalism. The association is run by a committee of men and women. Of the members present when I met them, only two were employed, both women. The centre is being rebuilt with their own time, labour, and material cadged from local firms and money raised in weekly fund-raising events which also represent the beginnings of their communal life – bingo, raffles round the local clubs, and children's discos attended by hundreds of children in the neighbourhood every week. Some of the young mothers couldn't get to the evening meetings, so they decided to have a women's section which meets in the afternoon. But that was the source of some aggravation. Here is a discussion between this woman and her husband, a prominent member of the association:

Her: The men wanted it to be like a trade union committee, but my suggestion was that we should have a treasurer and a secretary, yes, and the rest should all be in just one big committee for anybody. Because I know that once people get on the committee they start bossing people about.

Him: We've sorted that out.

Her: I know some of the girls who won't come any more, because people make them feel like 'where have you come from, why are you here?'.

Him: We've sorted that out.

Her: But some of the girls won't come to meetings.

Him: We've sorted it out. You see, in the beginning we said no sex discrimination. But the first thing that happens is some of the women set up a women's committee! The women said they'd had enough of men, they wanted their own meetings because the men have their own nights out.

He explained that the women's section started and involved women who couldn't go to evening meetings.

It's mainly women who have done the discos on Saturday mornings. They've done a lot. Only three men are really active, all the rest are women. They do all the begging for prizes for the bingo round the local shops, and I do the running about negotiating. The women do all the small things, they wouldn't go to the clubs to do the raffles because the husbands wouldn't like some of the places they'd have to go to, they'd object.

As often as not, the issues which divide the men and women rarely come out into the open as the power struggles they actually are. I watched this committee have a bitter argument over admission to the children's Christmas party. What was really at stake was the women's view that since *they* organise the parties and discos, they know all the children, and therefore they should control who was admitted. The men listened politely but thought the women were being unreasonable, bitchy, women being women again. The argument itself seemed almost beside the point – what the women couldn't bear was their feelings being denied.

A Sunderland woman who'd never been involved in any

kind of politics before, joined a tenants' association when her children were quite small. She explains:

It was dominated by men, unusually so, apparently. Women spoke very little. The tenants' association was very formal, constitutions and standing orders. It was our first contact with a meeting-type of organisation and our first step into a committee, so we were awed by it. It included an ex-councillor and a couple of people who'd been active in unions. It was a very vital lesson in how constitutions can become nooses round people's necks. The women let the men get on with it and thought the men knew it all. Then we got involved in a playscheme for the kids during the school holidays. The format wasn't formal, and when the women got together in that it was what *they* knew about. It was very informal but all the business got done. The playscheme gave us the opportunity to talk about ourselves, there was fourteen of us and we could still meet and talk about everything! Such a bond was developed and it was such a support. Women being women, that glowed through it and the relationships developed in that framework. We met in each other's houses and talked about our own kids, too. It was great to be involved in something outside the house, I'd become an imbecile who couldn't talk about anything. I knew no one except family, so I welcomed it with open arms.

One thing I noticed time and again in talking with women was their discovery of the pleasure principle in the political process itself – organising isn't just a boring means to an end, but one of the ends of politics in and for itself. 'I've never been to a good committee,' said a woman organising the unemployed in Rotherham, 'I've never *enjoyed* a committee.' Whether they are organising around housing, health, children or orgasms, they want to *enjoy* it. The fun and companionship is a measure of a project's success. And that produces a sanguine view of the life and death of organisations: 'One of the things I learned working with women is when to let an organisation die – when it stops doing what satisfies people,' said a woman who was active in her tenants' association and in community politics in Sunderland. There's a great difference between this kind of reflection on political experience and the cult of revolutionary defeatism you find among some people on the Left, a cult which separates the majority of the people from the political process by assuming their passivity and apathy, and at the same time shuns responsibility for creating politics that changes life as lived *now*. No less than national political programmes, the politics of everyday life are subject to bitter defeats. For people with little enough to start with, that's hard to take – you can't take too many kicks in the head. While anger may fuel a politics of protest, people can't live too long on rage. Protest has a limited life – it has to ferment into the politics of the possible. That isn't a recipe for 'reformism' or pragmatism so much as a need for creating a new life here and now. So much radical rhetoric gets off on images of the working class as martyrs and is confused by the presence of any pleasure and success in struggle. A community organiser in her early thirties in Sunderland describes the dilemma this way:

A few years ago every bonfire night was a riot in Southwick. It got very bad around the end of the seventies. The police were kept out of the area, but two weeks later they raided the community and it went on for months. A group of parents came in and complained – they were having to put up with screaming headlines in the local papers about Southwick thugs. So we decided to organise something on the next bonfire night. Maggie Thatcher was the guy. The bonfire was guarded and about two or three thousand people turned up. There was no trouble, no arrests, nothing was set on fire except the bonfire. So what have you done? A nice community activity and spectacular fireworks. Everybody had a wonderful time, and we did lots of things like twisting political arms to get first aid provided, things like that. Look at a riot as a political reaction, people so frustrated and desperate they don't care any more as long as there's a way of exploding so people have to take notice of what's going on. If you stop people taking that kind of action, making their point, which can't be made in a cosy way, then what are you doing?

For women, the effort to engage in politics in the first place is often so great that, once committed, they seem fearless. A young mother living in a condemned house in

Liverpool 8, riot city, applied ten years ago to be rehoused in a renovated tenement. 'We thought it would have luxury bathrooms and your own front door. Little did we know that the place would be overrun by rats!' She moved to a flat on the fifth floor when she was pregnant. 'Only then did I realise what we'd let ourselves in for, dragging up all those stairs, with nowhere to play for the children. I used to lie awake writing letters to MPs in my mind saying, "How would you like to bring up kids in this environment?"' Rumour spread that they were to be rehoused by the riverside. 'I thought, thank god.' But the rumour was unfounded.

So we called a meeting and formed a group to question the council. All the women there had babies and pushchairs. Then we saw a thing in the paper about a little boy on the next landing who'd fallen and had a cracked skull. I said, 'That's it.' So about forty of us, with the kids, stormed into the rent office. We'd contacted the local paper and the police were there, too. They said, 'Where are you going, ladies?' so one of the women said, 'We're all in arrears and we've come to pay.' The rent officer said he quite agreed with us but he had no houses – and from there a whole range of things happened, run-of-the-mill pressure, marches through the streets; do you know, women would push their prams through *anything* to get to the town hall. The men were never involved in all this, they thought it was a giggle and we'd never win. Meanwhile, railings were crumbling, concrete supports were shaky and the children's play area was a mess, rats came out at night and sat on the skips, and we had no success after nine months. A lot of people began to feel you just can't win.

Anyway, some of us went to a Labour Party meeting and someone mentioned co-ops. We didn't want to let a day go by and called a meeting immediately and said there's this fella and he mentioned a co-op, and when you're ignorant people say, 'Oh! It'll go wrong.' We didn't understand that it was more than signing a letter. So we contacted the Co-op Development Service and they said if you want it you'll have to fight for it. That aroused our curiosity and the more information we got the more we liked it and the totally new skills we were developing, like learning how you apply for land and get hold of money, hiring architects. Half our lives went on it. We tried to encourage the men but, to be honest, it never entered my head that there weren't any, because the group worked, it wasn't defeatist, and when you live in these places you get a lot of knocks. But then one man turned up and said, why is there no men here? I said why don't you join? He said he was too busy working. Then we started to get trouble when men did start coming. They thought the thing had just happened, they never thought we'd given half our life to it and sat up till four in the morning working on it. There'd been no animosity before, then they moved in and tried to re-organise everything and introduce committees. It happened when the money started coming and things started happening, but I don't know where they were when we were marching. They were like the Three Musketeers, they just brought antagonism with them. All the crises in the co-op stemmed from this. I said to one of them, 'You're ruining this,' and he just said, 'You're arrogant.'

The women who formed the co-op shop in Sunderland also crossed over the boundaries of protest by acting in the working-class tradition of militant self-help. They learned new skills, new control and a new way of life with each other. Now that the shop has closed they still go out with each other and still constitute each other's central reference point in life.

This was the first time we'd organised anything big, we'd all been involved in campaigns over the roads, but nothing like this. We took control of our own lives for the first time. We had everything off great. I did the books at first, it's hard to give away power, I had my hands on the pulse, but we thought nobody should be indispensable so over the three and a half years we did it, everybody did the books for a while. It's important for everyone to know everything so everybody did everything – ordering, cleaning, stocking. Those seven women knew everything. It was great. The lasses still won't go to meetings, but on any level with working-class people we wouldn't feel self-conscious. We really lived our jobs, it was our social life and everything we did stemmed from it. I can remember having people round for supper – that's not done, usually it's men who go out. Social life is outside the home, very little goes on inside the home. If anyone was feeling down or having trouble with fellas we'd talk about it, even if it was only to call them all the names under the sun. The most important thing was the support it's built up over the years. It was important that it was all women because however canny a man is you don't act your natural self with them.

When we had the shop we had a little seat for the old people to sit on when they came in, and the upstairs flat for the children. We'd have three there at any one time, two in the shop and one with the kids. We sold everything, wholefood, tinned food, cooked meat and dairy produce, we liked everything to be clean and fresh. And we had a long bench where people could have a cup of tea and a natter. Old people would come in for a slice of bacon and an egg. We thought that was important. Sweets would be well out of the way. At first we got a few middle-class women supporters, but they didn't last long. The wholefood bit didn't go down too well. We even put recipes on the wall, it was all very bright and cheerful with things clagged on the wall. And a couple of us learned to drive, because we had to collect stock. What freedom! People would come in and say I'll have the sheep's head and have the eyes in, they'll see us through the week.

These struggles were not only about demands upon some external agency to transform their conditions of existence – the housing co-op meant buying land, negotiating grants, hiring architects and together planning the construction of their new homes; the shop involved negotiating with banks, finding premises, stocktaking and establishing themselves as a useful presence in their community. They also enabled the women to become the subjects of political and personal transition, and in their efforts they constituted themselves as subjects in their own right. Women are rarely the subjects, the centre of political change.

These women were changed by their politics, but most of them have nowhere to pursue their own development save through self-improvement – through further education, acquiring skills which they return to their community. I met one woman who was just about to start a community work course having spent several years working part time in a local resource centre with teenagers and running playschemes on her estate. She'd rarely moved away from the estate and suffered from agoraphobia. Another did a similar course after being active in her tenants' association and then got a job servicing several tenants' associations in the town. A woman from the co-op shop became involved with some of her friends in the women's liberation movement and had to cope with middle-class women.

It gets back to that thing about not daring to say things because people will think you are stupid. Education – lack of it more like. I don't know if I'll ever get over it. I was in the B class in junior school and failed the 11-plus. My dad was a bus driver and my mam was a factory worker and I'd have liked to go to college but my mam was short. I only started to get an education when we finished the co-op because I knew I couldn't sit around being a housewife.

So she started an adult education course. 'Going to the refectory and getting something to eat that you hadn't cooked yourself! I still can't get used to that, I'll never take that for granted.' Another woman from the housing co-op went to the university one day a week to do a 'second-chance' course, and then was admitted full time. 'It was a major thing to do to go to university for even one day a week. It was the co-op that built my confidence.'

Their self-improvement puts these women's class belonging in jeopardy, not because they are abandoning their class *allegiance* but because they are rejecting class *subordination.* That happens to men too, but women have their femininity, their very psychology, turning inside out as they become activists. A tenants' activist who became a community worker servicing tenants' associations in Sunderland belongs to a group of women doing similar political work. 'This was a place you could talk openly without reprisals. Women like me, we have to go back to our situation. I used to find some things threatening to my whole life. Being in the tenants' association, where people would go on about it being non-political, made me realise that your whole life is political.' Masculinity has yet to become the subject of such a revolution.

The Unemployed Movement

By far the best work for the unemployed is being done by the NUWM – National Unemployed Workers' Movement. This is a revolutionary organisation intended to hold the unemployed together. ... It is a movement that has been built out of nothing by the pennies and efforts of the unemployed themselves. ... I greatly admire the men, ragged and underfed like the others, who keep the organisation going.

George Orwell, *The Road to Wigan Pier*

A posse of ordinary, poor people walked into the Ritz one day in 1938 and asked to be served tea. It was a stunt organised by the National Unemployed Workers' Movement in the 1930s, a movement able to express demands which united the poor and the proletariat, the rough and the respectable. A self-respecting, self-improving, self-organising proletariat starved of gainful employment couldn't now be distinguished from the poor, the feared, gregarious hordes of the great unwashed whose hand-to-mouth existence had historically separated them from the proletariat.

Now they were all – the poor. A working class without work was an emergency class and the National Unemployed Workers' Movement succeeded in making a movement out of that very neediness. A hungry class was also regarded as a dangerous class, and the NUWM succeeded in taking poverty out of the realms simply of philanthropy and charity and putting it into the centre of class war. The Ritz episode came late in its life, the unemployed movement was already waning in 1938, but it was a striking gesture in its spectacular life. It re-invented protest: in stunts like this, and the Hunger Marches which have become part of working-class folklore, it created its own theatre of politics, bringing the poor and hungry workless into the view of the southern ruling class with its long marches from the distant, distressed areas, isolated colonies living as if they were another country. No doubt this was a function of the movement's isolation from institutional politics – both the institutionalised labour movement and the state machinery of representative democracy.

The thirties, like the eighties, was marked by chronic distress among millions of people and the unheeding resilience of conservative government. The movement was organised by and for the unemployed themselves. Unconstrained by the manners of the institutions, it became an army of insurgents organising against the archaic remnants of the Poor Laws administered by local Boards of Guardians. So the unemployed had a ready-made constituency among those unemployed queuing for their benefits, and harassed by local authorities. The movement was led by unemployed shop stewards with long experience in the labour movement, but it was outside the labour movement, and only by throwing itself into picket lines to support striking and underpaid workers did it overcome the hostility of the employed and the political paranoia of the official trade union movement. Its insurgency was hardened by the birth of the shop stewards' movement during and after the First World War and by the Bolshevik revolution, which galvanised the British socialist movement, primarily among activists in the newly-born Communist Party and the Independent Labour Party. Participants in the NUWM marches took an oath of allegiance against capitalism, and there was then a feeling that the class war could be fought and won. In London, where the movement was led by Communists and ex-shop stewards, they raided public libraries, baths and town halls in the campaign for premises. And the movement organised massive local demonstrations against cuts in relief and for the unemployed's unconditional right to benefit. This was in the face of relentless surveillance by 'narks' of the readiness to work and the imposition of the lowest possible criteria of physical subsistence. It was a heroic movement – but can its nerve and imagination be re-kindled? Is it relevant today?

One of the things which emerges is that not only is there terrible poverty, though on a different scale from that described by Orwell, not as bad in most respects, but what is perhaps worse, political poverty. The fact is that in the 30s people had a political hope invested in Labour. Now there is a terrible atmosphere of political defeat. Not least because Labour has a record to defend, which it didn't then. And also, working-class politics can't survive successive No No Nos. People need a few successes to keep them going and motivated, and up here there aren't any which are within the mainstream of the labour movement.

The movement against unemployment today is in a dilemma: the labour movement in its rhetoric claims a continuity with the hungry thirties: no return to the thirties, says the slogan. But while official unemployment figures match those of the thirties, few of the other conditions of contemporary unemployment do. There is no correlation between the poverty of then and now. The unemployed are not to be found in the streets, hanging around day after day on street corners, queuing for soup or for the dole, they're at home watching television in the middle of the afternoon. You can't picket dole offices today and find captive queues – to address all the claimants in any one unemployment office you'd have to be there every day, all day, for a couple of weeks to catch everyone registered and signing on, an activity which takes only fifteen minutes for each person. 'They'd come out of their foxholes to sign on every couple of weeks and then they disappear,' said an unemployed steel worker active in Rotherham's unemployed centre. Furthermore, 'the unemployed' is a category into which many unemployed people feel they don't fit. Unemployed fitters or electricians may see themselves as fitters and electricians who happen to be out of work – they don't necessarily identify themselves with the bald boys in Doc Marten boots who've never had a job, who have come to symbolise modern unemployment. Women bringing up small children at home don't see themselves as unemployed, they see themselves as mothers. The only thing they share with jobless school leavers is that they don't earn a wage. The equation between unemployment and idleness doesn't apply to them, they are never idle – they're overworked and underpaid.

Unemployment centres have mushroomed during the eighties, often set up with the support of the local trades council or a town's committee with representatives from trade unions, community organisations and political parties, and usually financed with Manpower Services Commission funds to pay full-time staff. Their function is usually to be a drop-in centre somewhere in the middle of town, a place where people can come for advice or just to while away the time. And usually their success or failure is measured in the numbers who drop in. 'It's a matter of pulling in the punters,' said a woman working in a south Yorkshire centre for the unemployed, and a Newcastle organiser among the unemployed pointed out that 'centres tend to feel it's good if they can pull in seventy or a hundred people a week, but that service is only any use for the people who happen to use it, it's no use for all the people who don't.' There are big disagreements among people who run these centres about whether to run social or political centres, about how to draw people in. And since most centres are located two, four or eight miles from the massive housing estates on the edge of the city, participating in an unemployed centre isn't a matter of dropping in, it's the price of a bus fare.

There's an emotional cost, too. When unemployment means idleness it also means depression, self-hatred and pessimism. Contrary to the conventional wisdom that these oppressions produce uprisings, the effect is a kind of sleeping sickness. Participation demands energy, the lethargy of unemployment leads to flight from life. I met a bus driver in the Midlands with seven children. Four of them have left school, and none of them has ever had a job. His house is full of them, big lads, who don't get up till midday and don't do anything all day. Doing things costs money.

If images of hunger were the motif of the thirties, a symbol both of despair and danger, then menacing skinheads have become the modern motif, but they represent danger as much to their own class as to the class enemy; to them the leaders of the working-class movements are only figures of authority, much like school teachers and the police. It isn't that skinheads don't have a sense of class belonging – they do, and theirs is a working-class cult, but it expresses alienation from their parent leaders no less than their parent culture. Conversely, the labour movement itself sees these boys as a problem, a perverse mystery, whose alienation puts them beyond the reach of organisation. For all the butch paraphernalia of these boys – and the problem *is* boys – they talk with a little-boy envy of not only snobs and superiors but Blacks too. Their racism seemed less a theory of Blacks' inferiority, more a feeling of their own. They hate Asians because they're dogged and diligent. The Asians I met were not that white stereotype, smart but soft. Some Asian teenagers educated themselves in the martial arts of self-defence. White boys who've fought Asians *know* they were hard. Black boys might be targets, but they're not victims. They know that the white boys know that the Black boys are big and strong and cool! The form of boys' masculinity constitutes them as folk devils, a 'danger to society'. But for all their aggression, there's an atmosphere of paralytic pessimism about them. They generate a kind of moral panic which is rooted in the crisis of masculinity, symbolised by the social nuisance of big bad boys who bite social workers. The ways they express their racial hatreds are so often in the language of envy: whites see their Black contemporaries, for all their abuse, as cool and hard. That wouldn't be how they see the Asians, in their minds the Asians are quiet and clever. But what they don't calculate for is that the Asian boys may be better fighters than they are. Brute, inebriated hatred is no match for the skilful martial arts of some of the modest brown boys they corner in darkened bus stations and shopping precincts. The girls watch and wish they'd stop – most of the girls I've met don't share the racism of their boy-friends.

Centres for the unemployed provide play facilities to keep them off the streets – pool, table tennis, darts. Or as an organiser in Rotherham put it, 'centres for the unemployed can become glorified youth clubs'. I overheard a conversation in one centre between a 'punter' and a provider, in which the youth threatened lightly to come in and rob the place one of these days. 'Now, why would you want to do something like that? What's your problem, son?' Half an hour later the full-time worker was playing referee in a pool contest between the centre's youth (boys) and a local youth club run for youths on probation (boys). Whatever the pleasure of the occasion for all concerned, the fact was that the worker blatantly enjoyed his power over 'the lads'.

And what does any of this offer to other unemployed people? Some centres try to provide services for women – sewing classes, keep-fit classes, single parents' groups, creche facilities. The Newcastle centre even tried to organise basic manual skills classes, like plumbing and wiring. But none would say that their efforts are successful. Some don't even try and offer facilities for women, and resent feminists' attempts to negotiate time and space for them. Unemployed centres which have made special efforts to recruit girls have found it difficult, though I met three women who run a girls' football club which the girls have all joined. But the girls don't see the centres as something for them, and worse, their access is sometimes blocked by boys. One woman organiser explained that girls were often willing, 'But they'd say things like, "I'd like to go but my boyfriend won't let me".' And underlining the service is the expectation that it is only men who are rendered idle by unemployment, who need some-where to go and something to do.

Neither can the centres provide the educational service they often did in the thirties – not least because that function is better performed elsewhere. The professional-isation of workers' education is one factor, but another is the expansion of education for the unemployed as a veritable growth sector in further education institutions.

The time centres spend servicing coteries of clients may be time not spent putting unemployment on the political agenda. Local activity among the unemployed is barely evident, even in towns where the jobless figures are well over the national average and where campaigns to secure free access to leisure facilities such as cinemas, clubs and public baths and free transport would have both popular, local resonance on the one hand, and local institutions as targets on the other.

In the thirties, local Poor Law Guardians administered unemployment relief, providing a visible and accessible target for protests against cuts in relief. The DHSS is not equivalent to this system. For a start, local DHSS managements are bound by national rules and regulations. Local DHSS staff may be inappropriate objects of attack – many are trade unionists more sympathetic to their claimants than to their employers. In some cities, local DHSS staff collaborated with centres for the unemployed and welfare rights groups to protest against the intrusion of the Special Claims Control investigators. DHSS headquarters in London seem like the head office of a multi-national corporation and, unlike local Boards of Guardians, the government seems distant and immune to political pressure.

The centres' system of funding often puts them in a political cleft stick: many of their workers are funded by the Manpower Services Commission. But the West Midlands MSC board, for example, includes a director from GEC, one of England's most proudly profitable companies which spent 1982–83 negotiating hundreds of redundancies in Coventry to accompany the introduction of new technology. When the 1983 People's March by unemployed people from all over Britain set off for London, the MSC banned the use of MSC-funded centres by marchers. And several centres have had direct warnings from the MSC that their activities are unacceptable.

Some centres have spurned MSC funding for this reason;

many, however, bow to the political prohibition, which is undoubtedly a factor in their de-politicised character. But it isn't the only reason: the differences between the conditions of the thirties and the eighties point to a confusion of purpose in the contemporary unemployed movement. No less important a factor is the relationship between the felt experience of unemployment and the political rhetoric of 'no return to the thirties' and 'full employment'. Many people have no faith that there will ever be a return to full employment, and anyway, do people want the kind of work available to them? While I was in Sheffield the local newspaper carried a story about a local employer's complaint that they were offering work but there were no takers. The story didn't ask why. Nor has the labour movement fully faced the implication of its own relationship to unemployment. Now, as then, the trade union movement is a movement of the employed, not the unemployed. More than that, it is a movement suffering from depression and inertia, it is a movement lying in wait for a spark to ignite its activity.

Many trade unionists I talked to remember the successes of the past, the wave of opposition to anti-union legislation in the late sixties and early seventies and the innovative work-in by the Upper Clyde Shipyard workers. 'That's what we need,' they say. 'There's some action will take place that will galvanise mass action,' said a Sunderland shipbuilder, 'what incident will do it, I don't know.' But the wish is the father of a thoughtless faith that fails to take stock of the movement's inability to move, of the crisis of participation which afflicts the labour movement. Workplace organisation has provided a crucial fund of rank and file activists – but workplace strength only exists when people are *in* work. Local trades councils cross the boundaries of workplace and home, they represent the aggregate industrial strength of a community. 'I see them as button soviets,' said a Sunderland boiler-maker, but he also commented that his own trades council only acts when the movement itself is under attack. 'We support disputes and the rest of the time we are pretty docile. Basically it is there when we have something to defend.' So, often trades councils suffer from the passivity of a defensive rather than offensive disposition.

Now that inertia is compounded by depression. The idea of the 1983 People's March to London at least gave the left in the labour movement something to do. On the other hand, the right on the general council of the Trades Union Congress was content to capitulate to the Labour Party leadership's initial opposition to the march. It became a tussle between the right and the left, with the Labour leadership arguing that the organisation of a march against unemployment – which, together with nuclear war, has been uppermost in the mind of the majority of the population – would get in the way of preparations for a general election. It seems the Labour Party can't organise against unemployment except as a government – it sees itself as a party of government, not a party that organises mass political participation. The hunger marches of the thirties grew out of an integration of thought and feeling – hunger united the mind and body. It was food that represented an irreducible division between rich and poor, an experience of essential deprivation, an emergency of need. But there is as yet no equivalent form of mobilisation that matches the felt experience of unemployment in the eighties.

The relationship between women and the People's March is another exemplar of mismatch. The People's March, some of whose organisers made strenuous efforts to get girls and women on the march, marginalised women. A long march away from home automatically excludes women whose unemployment is a function of having children. Solutions to this problem – a rota of women, a rolling creche – were fought for by feminists, but even among them there was a feeling that this emphasised still further how inappropriate a marathon march is for women. It is yet another mode of politicking to which women have to adapt, instead of one which springs from the conditions of their lives. As a result, there are always a minority of women on these marches, and though women are used to being a minority in politics, the long march involves special stresses. If they get as far as going on the march, the girls have to run the gamut of sexism. A girl veteran of the unemployed marches in the North complained that

you were usually one or two among a dozen or fifteen boys. You just got the boys chasing you all the time and you got very debased. The only solution was that you'd have to get off with one of them, just to hang about with one of them all the time, a kind of safety. You'd be acknowledged then as being somebody else's woman. There was a real pressure in that direction. The alternative was to stay aloof; but then you still came in for it. I felt very exploited by it. It obscured everything I did. I teamed up with one bloke and it was the worst thing I've ever done. It's the whole thing about being a woman in politics.

It is obvious that the marches are a striking and often emotive attempt to make the movement move; they try to bear witness to the tragedy of mass unemployment and to engage the unemployed in action on their own behalf. But, as we have seen, marches are not an action that makes participation possible for most unemployed women. Neither do they help to alert popular consciousness to the conditions which have created unemployment among women. Only a political protest which puts paucity of childcare at the centre of both its propaganda and its practice could achieve that.

All this prompts the question: what and who are the marches for? Are they to be endurance tests for their participants? It is in the nature of the very concept of the long march that it excludes all but a minority of hardy walkers. Part of the problem lies in the very strength and maturity of the labour movement: the extension of representative democracy and the institutionalisation of the movement has encouraged the decline of local spectacle as part of its repertoire, and a widespread feeling among people that politics is something that happens to other people. Another explanation lies in the equation between unemployment and indolence. Searching for an explanation for the extraordinary vitality and popularity of the pre-war movement against unemployment, Peter Kingsford, author of *The Hunger Marchers in*

Britain 1920–1940 (1982), suggests that for some participants 'their decision was a despairing if temporary escape from their homes. Anything was better than vainly waiting about for work. They went because there was nothing else to do. For others it was a rough holiday. For the many who had never been near London, an adventure for the lads, a jaunt.' It should be remembered that according to the 1931 census there were 1,552,000 men classified as 'unoccupied' and 12,055,000 women: there was no 'temporary escape from their homes' for those women. The same applies today – mothers are not rendered idle by 'unemployment', they are only wageless.

If the unemployed movement is to unite men and women it must create itself in the image of the real live unemployed, young and old, fathers and mothers, women and men. And if it is to organise spectacles, ought its campaigning initiatives not maximise, rather than minimise, participation? Why not mass sit-downs in the middle of the High Street in support of free travel, in support of negotiated lobbying between local labour movements and transport authorities, mass watch-ins at local cinemas, dance-ins at local discos, swim-ins at the local baths, eat-ins at local restaurants, or whatever seems to make local sense if these don't.

Finally, there is hunger. Our recognition that unemployment today (like everything else) is not what it used to be seems to have embarrassed us into silence about this single, simple fact of poverty. Many of the people I met living on social security go for days eating chips and bread, biscuits and tea. And there are some days when they don't eat at all. They're hungry, too.

Many of the ideas in this chapter have been developed in conversations with Jimmy Barnes, who has written a pamphlet, 'Unemployed Centres — a Critical View' (Binpress Inc., Newcastle, 1983).

The Road Back to Wigan Pier

Twenty million people are underfed but literally everyone in England has access to a radio. What we have lost in food we have gained in electricity. Whole sections of the working class who have been plundered of all they really need are being compensated in part by cheap luxuries which mitigate the surface of life ...

Economic injustice will stop the moment we want it to stop, and no sooner, and if we genuinely want it to stop the method adopted hardly matters.

George Orwell, *The Road to Wigan Pier*

Now the journey is over and we return to our starting point – George Orwell's book, *The Road to Wigan Pier*. Our journeys share the same themes: the material and emotional economy of poverty among some of the ten million people who are poor in England. Any journey into the landscape of poverty also discloses the drama of social crisis – the poverty of politics. But my journey also had a travelling companion, Orwell's book itself. And just as it always carried the question – how does socialist practice and thought measure up to our economic, emotional and political crisis? – so does that question have to be asked of Orwell's book itself.

What is his contribution to the tradition of English social-ism? The question isn't simply academic – George Orwell is part of our political vocabulary, he changed the very language we speak, and he is a prize in the contest for our culture between the Right and the Left. He is seen by some as somehow speaking with the voice of an authentic English socialism, by others as socialism's executioner. He has a way with words, always beguilingly sensible, and in restating simple commonsense he claims for the Left an English consensus about ourselves. Part of his attraction lies in his affection for somewhere called England. I read Raymond Williams' book, *Orwell* (Fontana, 1979), and he too talks about Orwell's quest for 'an England', a summary, in a phrase, of England. But my experiences tell me there isn't such a community of interest. As Angela Carter says about the feeling she shares with a black girl: 'I was only born here.' Orwell's affection is for the affable, temperate quality of English life, a little sort of life, not to say a suburban life. You can forgive a lot for his few kind words, especially when they are punctuated by his ambitious appeal to the Left to reclaim the principles of patriotism, justice and liberty. 'Those are the words,' he says. And they are the legacy he willed to us in the wake of his odyssey around England. Whenever socialism seems to be on the run, there's a panicky retreat to these evergreen commandments.

However, it is a counsel of despair – when you don't know what to do, you seek solace in the great 'moral virtues'. The beauty of them is that everybody thinks they know what they mean, though they never say what they mean. Orwell moves between these great moral virtues and the private, commonsense morality of decency. He is an anti-intellectual intellectual, a great and popular polemicist who was undoubtedly courageous and innovative in his insistence that the popular culture of commonsense is part of the theatre of politics and not just a subsidiary effect of economic class exploitation. So his mobilisations of decency and patriotism are an important intervention in socialist culture. But Orwell takes commonsense as unified and simple, and it is precisely those virtues that he affirms which have always been kidnapped by the Right, never more effectively than in the eighties, with their rugged renewal by Thatcherism. Can these virtues be recaptured for socialism? And, more pertinent perhaps, should they be?

Orwell's socialist testaments are to be found in *The Road to Wigan Pier* and its sequel, *The Lion and the Unicorn*. His biographer, Bernard Crick, tells us in his elegant introduction to *The Lion and the Unicorn* (Penguin, 1982) that 'Orwell genuinely believed, no mere platitude or rhetoric this, in the innate "decency" (the word he is fond of) of ordinary people.' True values are not to be created nor old values 'transfigured by the revolution, or in a new revolutionary consciousness; they exist already in the decency, fraternity, mutual aid, sociability, tolerance and scepticism towards authority of the working class. ...' He goes on to suggest that 'decency' is not an empty word, but is part of the moral values of socialism which are embedded in working-class culture. 'Decent', 'ordinary' and 'English' become synonymous in Orwell's lexicon. In claiming it for the Left, he seeks to place socialism in the continuum of our culture.

In his own way, Orwell was tussling with one of the great dilemmas of the international socialist movement – how to root collectivism in the commonsense of the common people. So how does Orwell claim consensus for socialism? His quest is for the essence of Englishness, which he finds in the codes of decency and the institution of the family. And he sets these against the interlopers – intellectuals, feminists, naturists and modernists. He appears to propose a politics of everyday life, but in practice he mobilises a conservative commonsense *against* radicalism rooted in commonsense. Liberty, justice and patriotism are key words in his litany of moral virtue, not contradiction, collectivism and cosmopolitanism, not democracy and egalitarianism. His quest for an essential English character stops him prospecting for those creative contradictions which are the watershed of change. He sees a working class excluded and isolated, but he doesn't see a working class clamouring for entry to the political culture. His essentialism produces a working-class scene stripped of the conflicts of interest which have shaped its history as a class in the making – the race, sex and craft chauvinisms which have cauterised the socialist will within the working class.

However, he makes a singular concession to the contradictions in the English character. On the one hand, he evokes the conventional wisdoms about our habits and our habitat – we're a gentle people in a moderate landscape: On the other, we are not puritanical – the English are 'inveterate gamblers, drink as much beer as their wages will permit, are devoted to bawdy jokes and use probably the foulest language in the world.' (He is of course talking about men.) But that apart, he doesn't investigate these contradictions as manifestations of instability in the culture, as a tension between the roughness of the ghettos and the respectability of the well-paid, skilled working class which borrows its domestic ethics, sexual standards and economic aspirations from other classes. For all that he insists on culture as part of the political domain, his anti-intellectualism and disregard of history means he can't account for the cultural revolutions in the history of the working class.

The history of decency and respectability has been the subject of scrutiny among labour historians preoccupied by the ideological contours of class. From their debates it has become clear that decency and respectability were and are part of the ideological material of the upward-striving and self-improvers. They separate them from the raucous street life of their inebriate and indecent inferiors, the casual poor. Respectability and decency are rooted in an ideology of privacy and modesty which has never been universal among the working class but which has been instrumental in dividing strata of the class from each other. Feminist historians have more recently shown how this ideological offensive has been crucial in the control of women, their domestication, dependency and subordination.

Just as Orwell enjoys the term 'decency' uncritically, so he uncritically sentimentalises the institution it defines: the family, plucked from its creation in history, as if it were natural and naturally nice. It is the family of the proletarian man that he particularly loves. In his home

you breathe a warm, decent, deeply human atmosphere which it is not easy to find elsewhere.... His home life seems to fall more naturally into a sane and comely shape. I have often been struck by the peculiar, easy completeness, the perfect symmetry, as it were, of a working-class interior at its best. Especially on winter evenings after tea, when the fire glows in the open range and dances mirrored in the steel fender, when Father, in shirt sleeves, sits in the rocking chair at the side of the fire reading the racing finals, and Mother sits on the other with her sewing, and the children are happy with a pennorth of mint humbugs, and the dog lolls roasting himself on the mat – it is a good place to be in, providing that you can not only be in it but sufficiently of it to be taken for granted.

He moans a little later that it will all change in the utopian future when the 'furniture will be made of rubber and glass and steel' and the birth controllers have had their way.

Orwell compounds his sentimentalisation of the prole-tarian family by drawing on class difference.

A working-class family hangs together as a middle class one does, but the relationship is far less tyrannical. A working man has not that deadly weight of family prestige hanging around his neck like a millstone ... The fact that the working class know how to combine and the middle class don't is probably due to their different con-ceptions of family loyalty. You cannot have an effective trade union of middle class workers, because in times of strikes almost every middle-class wife would be egging her husband on to blackleg and get the other fellow's job.

Note that Orwell makes women the bearer of conservatism within the middle class.

He pursues this metaphor of the family in his quest for the essence of England. England is a family, he says in *The Lion and the Unicorn*, in which 'the young are generally thwarted and most of the power is in the hands of irresponsible uncles and bedridden aunts. Still, it is a family. It has a private language and its common memories, and at the approach of an enemy it closes ranks. A family with the wrong members in control – that, perhaps, is as near as one can come to describing England in a phrase.' Through this family metaphor Orwell evokes an essential unity in England, a shared past, present and future, a sense of belonging. The strength of the metaphor is that it puts private life into the political arena, but Orwell does not use it in order to detonate the silence on the Left about the family and its contradictions, he does not put the family into politics as a *problem*. He does the opposite, and in suggesting national unity through the metaphor he forecloses perhaps the most important conundrum of all in English politics – the relationship between reproduction and class, sex and socialism. Not surprisingly, given the ideological universe he inhabited in interwar England, there is no sense in Orwell of the family as one of the sites of sexual division in the working class, because he takes the standpoint of men, not women. But it is from the standpoint of women that the mythology of working-class unity is most starkly exposed.

We have already heard men and women who were Orwell's contemporaries describe the imprisonment of working-class women in impoverished domestication, of men's detachment from women and children. Old men and women have borne witness to the brutality of that 'comely' place, in which Orwell's 'perfect symmetry' was synonymous with the subordination of women. A more recent cultural historian of the working class, Richard Hoggart, was a bit wiser. Writing in *The Uses of Literacy* (Penguin, 1981) about the inequalities inscribed in the working-class household, where the father is the master, he says: 'This he is by tradition, and neither he nor his wife would want the tradition changed.' Both he and Orwell treat tradition as if it were nature. Neither put themselves in the position of women and thus neither can imagine the political conditions necessary for women to begin to make their own choices. A glance at divorce statistics today shows that once women acquire the minimum means of survival – the right to their home and an income – they begin to be able to turn their back on tradition. In my experience, women both *accept* and *resent* men's domination. Their acquiescence has not a little to do with the men's movement's defeat of women's right to independent economic means – without resources women are in no position to make a run for it – and their right to access to political means within the labour movement. Neither Orwell nor Hoggart ask the question: where does women's subordination and dependence come from?

If the family is the instrument of Orwell's search for an essential, shared Englishness, it also nurtures his longing for continuity, for making the past palpable in the present. For him, the present is drab and the future is dreadful. The national characteristics that he so admires nestle in our domestic past. The problem with socialism, he argues, is that it 'is bound up with the idea of mechanical progress'. He might have said that the characteristic of capitalism is its seizure of control over mechanical progress. But machines don't feature in Orwell's acount of working-class work. Nowhere in *Wigan Pier* is there a sense of the epic struggle between labour and capital, not to mention men and women, to take control over machines, their products and profits. That's because he went to Wigan looking for men and mythologised miners as archetypical proletarian man (he's not alone in doing this). Part of the magnetism of miners was precisely the way in which their work was not mediated by machinery. But there were as many cotton workers in Wigan as miners, many of them women – and their history and the form of their work is shaped by their struggles over the control of machinery. The absence of machinery enables him to equate masculinity, manual labour and elemental man with elemental work. That falsifies *Wigan Pier* as a description of the working class, and it also makes possible his equation between machinery and modernism, and of both with socialism. 'Production suggests socialism, but socialism as a world system implies machine production, because it demands things not compatible with a primitive way of life,' he argues. Mechanical progress makes life safe and soft, it 'frustrates the need for effort and creation,' and worst of all, 'mechanisation leads to the decay of taste, the decay of taste leads to the demand for machine-made articles and hence to more mechanisation, and so a vicious circle is established.'

The 'frightful debauchery' of mechanisation produces a plethora of bad taste. 'In a healthy world there would be no demand for tinned foods, aspirins, gramophones, gas-pipe chairs, machine guns, daily newspapers, telephones, motor cars. ...' So that's the problem: bad taste. He was right, he was a 'revolutionary snob'.

Hoggart ponders the same problematic: working-class taste. 'Can the idea of 'aving a good time while y'can because life is hard open the way to a soft mass-hedonism? Can the sense of the group be turned into an arrogant and slick conformity?' He's worried about traditional values being transformed into self-indulgence. His latter-day apostle, Jeremy Seabrook, pursues a similar theme in his book *Unemployment* (Quartet, 1982):

What has been happening to the function – and hence the sense of identity – of the working class has been even more deeply submerged by the noise and display emanating from the market place in recent years. The exaltation of material concessions yielded by capitalism has meant that those improvements have been used, not primarily as a relief from that older poverty, but as a means of creating a different kind of subordination of the working class ... Among those losses, apart from the damaged sense of function, have been some of the humanising responses to that older poverty, the solidarity and sharing ... – dignity, frugality, stoicism – which offered an alternative to the brutalising destructive values of capitalism. This has been the greatest loss of all.

According to Seabrook, this loss has occurred because 'the option of that alternative as something that could have grown organically out of the way people lived their lives has been crushed.' Seabrook admits that 'one thing is sure: we shan't build socialism out of those values now, out of that endurance and frugality, out of that pride and solidarity. The moment has passed.' But he is sorely tempted: 'Because the old working class expressed something lasting and profound about the nature of human life this response must be rediscovered.'

All these statements lament the degeneracy of modern life

and conjure up older solidarities without asking the question: whose work was it that kept the neighbourhoods alive? A devastating critique can be made of the destruction of working-class communities by housing policies and the police in the postwar period. But that same critique often washes over a crucial transition in the work of women in those communities. Senile old ladies and gentlemen were once cared for in overcrowded slums, tended by their exhausted daughters. Now their daughters might be home helps, psychiatric nurses, secretaries, school dinner ladies – all paid for their time and their labour. And because their labour is not assumed, wrenched from them by the individual and arbitrary ties of kinship, the conditions are created in which they can, at last, care collectively, and, because it is social, the *conditions* of their care become our collective, political responsibility.

Looking at it from a feminist perspective, many of those good old values rested on the weary labours of women whose economic, social, sexual, cultural and political interests are yet to be given any political primacy by any political party. A renaissance of those old virtues is precisely impossible because the working class has changed: as Seabrook says, it is no longer the heroic men who work in coal, steel, construction and fishing. He reminds us that only a fraction of the workforce 'can still call on the epic associations of their past. This is essentially true of the miners who, with their heroic past and elemental work, are the subject of working-class folklore.' Yes, but did these men collaborate in creating a folklore that expressed the interests of women? No. And are not the clerks and cleaners and caterers of the health service the contemporary heroines of the workers' movement? The gushing pessimism of Seabrook's thesis leaves no room for the evidence of new forces within popular politics and new forms of political struggle. The changing profile of work and workers demands a leap of the political imagination, the making of alliances between producers and consumers of which no amount of epic nostalgia can conceive.

His pessimism also colours his picture of working-class

consumers as passive victims of a cruel con trick, consumers of a culture in which they never *intervene.* The degeneracy of working-class politics, the decline of what he calls 'dignity, frugality and stoicism' characterises for the working class yet another defeat. These qualities have been stolen, he says, by our collective subordination to the laws of the market place, and bonds of kinship, good neighbourliness and workplace solidarity have been destroyed. He paints a picture of the working class as still life, inert, dependent on the shoddy goods and cheap thrills of cynical consumerism. He sets up the working class as victims, and then blames them. It's as if he feels we've betrayed him; the working class has gone AWOL from its heroic mission.

Seabrook buys the myth of postwar affluence, workers rolling around in second-hand Jaguars, stupefied on 'Coronation Street', drinking Cinzano and eating beans from the tin and fidgeting listlessly on its squeaky vinyl three-piece suites. It's all a scream against the *materialism* of the working class. It has its precedent in Orwell's embarrassing critique of the consequences of mechanisation. What do the working class need of wirelesses? wails Orwell. And tinned food. And gas-pipe furniture! What next?

While Orwell was wondering why people need wirelesses and newspapers, the working class itself, particularly women, were finding that through mass communications they had access to the national culture. The complaint from the moral school of socialism against material goods is always about the working class having them. Presumably if they were going to the opera on HP instead of buying automatic washing machines, there wouldn't be a problem. Orwell anticipates and Seabrook accepts the great myth about the *effects* of affluence in the fifties. Of course, what they aren't concerned with is that most of the domestic durables associated with affluence are machines worked by women, often acquired by the wages of women. 'As far as I'm concerned, the invention of the front-loading automatic washing machine is more important for women than the landing on the moon,' said a woman in her forties, who brings up children and holds down the job that bought the washing machine.

All this anti-consumerist talk is so anti-mass pleasure; it makes my spine shiver with the fear that Big Brother Orwell is going to take away my fridge and hi-fi, that he'll melt down the Beach Boys and the Supremes, Blondie and Bob Marley, and there will be no more discos, no more late-night movies on TV, no more Fred Astaire and Ginger Rogers, no more 'Soap'; he won't allow us our pleasures.

However, Orwell does make a concession, albeit an avuncular, disengaged concession, to the primacy of pleasure in working-class culture.

Life [on the dole] is still fairly normal, more normal than one really has the right to expect. Families are impoverished, but the family system has not broken up ... in a decade of unparalleled depression, the consumption of all cheap luxuries has increased. The two things that have made the greatest difference of all are the movies and the mass production of cheap smart clothes since the war. ... You may have three-halfpence in your pocket and not a prospect in the world ... but in your new clothes you can stand on the street corner, indulging in a private day dream of yourself as Clark Gable or Greta Garbo.

But the avuncularity turns to acid.

Of course the postwar development of cheap luxuries has been a very fortunate thing for our rulers. It is quite likely that fish and chips, art silk stockings, tinned salmon, cut-price chocolate (five two-ounce bars for sixpence), the movies, the radio, strong tea and the football pools have between them averted revolution. Therefore we are sometimes told that the whole thing is an astute manoeuvre by the governing class ... the thing happened, but by an unconsciousness process – the quite natural interaction between the manufacturer's need for a market and the need of half-starved people for cheap palliatives.

These writers' critique of consumerism falls into the Left's lacuna about the prospects for socialism in a class which isn't poor. The lessons of the sixties have shown, however, that socialism thrives on plenty and pleasure, too. Sacrifice and suffering are not necessarily the midwife of socialism. So now we can add to our earlier conundrum the relationship between poverty and politics, and pleasure and politics. Which takes us back to the question, where does socialism come from?

Bernard Crick and others have shown that Orwell's affirmation of ordinary values, the people's commonsense culture, as part of the vocabulary of politics forms a crucial element of his critique of economic determinism – the reduction of the culture we inhabit to a function of economic relations of exploitation. In *Wigan Pier* the economic myopia of the working class is explained by two things: 'The English working class do not show much capacity for leadership, but they have a wonderful talent for organisation. The whole trade union movement testifies to this; so do the excellent working men's clubs – really a sort of glorified co-operative pub, and splendidly organised – which are so common in Yorkshire.' At the same time he offers a benign criticism of these very characteristics among the uneducated working-class activists he met on his journey – 'the warm-hearted, unthinking socialist, the typical working-class socialist' – whose vision of the future 'is of present-day society with the worst abuses left out, and with interest centering on the same things as present – family life, the pub, football and local politics'.

Again, Orwell is talking about working-class *men*, and a masculine labour movement. The men's movement has produced a minimalist socialism that was never so much socialism as social welfare. The history of trade unionism, in practice, is rooted in men's beliefs about the nature of decent respectable life – they believed their wives should stay at home and look after children, so no need for nurseries; they believed – and many still believe – in their own rights as breadwinners, which gave them the power to distribute their earnings within the family – they even initially resisted the introduction of a social contribution to the cost of children, the family allowance. Since the family allowance was established, there has been no commitment within the trade union movement to make it commensurate with the actual costs of childcare, for that would remove one of the last bastions of privilege in the patriarchal pay packet. If the actual cost of children were met by a social benefit, men's preferential treatment in pay would have no foundation. They have built a movement based on differentials, on unequal access to skill, and so have always maintained an ambiguity about the labour movement's rhetoric of collectivism and egalitarianism – they haven't created it in their organisations, so why should it feature in their future? As one feminist trade unionist put it at a meeting during the 1982 Trades Union Congress, 'We need to put the collective back into collective bargaining.'

Socialism in England is equated with the welfare state, which is paid for less through the contributions of capital than the contributions of workers themselves to collective services. And yet it was precisely the escalation of the workers' contribution during the period of the social contract in the seventies that caused an important sector of the working class, white skilled manual men, to cut adrift from their historic allegiance to the Labour Party. Their own economic individualism subsequently found an authentic expression in the new Right, Thatcherism. That re-alignment of the historic core of the working class wasn't because they were daft, blinded by Thatcher's domestic economics. Nor was it because they were decent chaps with a flair for pigeon fancying, trade union organisation and drinking, with never a thought to higher things. Nor was it that Labour was bad at propaganda (though it's true, it is). It was that the men's movement's relationship to women and children, the political settlement between men and women, produced a historic compromise with capital which closed their socialist imagination. Having reached that historic compromise, they created a people's movement in their own image – an image Orwell and Seabrook seek to reincarnate.

Orwell shares with his decent chaps a toxic scorn for precisely those socialist milieux concerned with making concrete their critique of the quality of life in capitalism, however shaky and tentative, those elements of the socialist tradition so glibly dubbed utopian. He compares unfavourably with his decent, uneducated chaps, 'the intellectual, book-trained Socialist, who understands that it is necessary to throw our present civilisation down the sink ... and this type is drawn, to begin with, entirely from the middle class, and a rootless town-bred middle class at that.' So Orwell mobilises his own utopianism to blast the utopians. I wonder what he would have made of the young, working-class punks who populate Wigan's buoyant and boisterous Youth Campaign for Nuclear Disarmament, who draw smiles from blue-rinses ladies at the bus stops as they stride by with their pink and green hair, wearing makeshift ensembles that mix combat jackets with fifties frocks, mini-skirts and dyed denims, whose clothes don't mimic their elders and betters so much as mock them, who don't eat meat, who take the Pill for granted and who feel disowned by the patriarchs of the labour movement because they don't seem to want to change anything, and who disown the competitive individualism that happens in most of the meetings they've ever been to except their own?

Just as the middle class has been both proletarianised and radicalised, so have many sectors of the working class itself discarded the slough of respectability. The sons and daughters and wives of the respectable working man who represented the class have rebelled against his moral virtues. The wives work and the sons and daughters have 'illegitimate' children. It is they who are on the move, changing themselves and changing the character of their class. But whatever is afoot has little expression in the institutions of politics. Orwell's own prejudice against 'high-minded women and sandal wearers and bearded fruit juice drinkers ... escaped Quakers, birth control fanatics' was and is, of course, simply prejudice, but it finds echoes today in some quarters of the labour movement which have set their face against the interlopers of 1968, the generation that created radicalism not out of unendurable poverty but for precisely the cultural revolution 'to throw our present civilisation down the sink', which Orwell affirms – and then disowns. Like the soft centre in politics, he makes his definition of virtue the imperative of cultural revolution. The idea of 'decency' has *displaced* socialism in that vocabulary. I heard a Labour councillor greet the 1983 People's Marchers in his town with a speech which claimed the march for the Labour Party (which had initially tried to persuade the TUC not to support it) and then rambled on about 'our shared concern, employed and unemployed, with the creation of a decent society'. The word socialism didn't pass his lips.

It is the kind of retreat from radicalism which has made elements of the Labour Party and the Left seek to manage consensus rather than change it, constantly capitulating to its conservatism. Housing is a case in point – the municipal godfathers buckled under a combination of central government financial pressure, on the one hand, and an ideology of modernism in mass housing, on the other. Modernism in housing may indeed prove Orwell's point about the elision between socialism and mechanisation, but not because the modernists were the incubators of a socialist form of housing. Rather Le Corbusier *et al.* were the architects of a quint-essentially bourgeois housing form. Homes are machines for living in, said Le Corbusier. Who needs windows, they're just holes in the walls, he said. Who needs messy decoration? Bric-à-brac is an affront to efficiency. Le Corbusier is Dickens' Gradgrind of modern housing.

You must discard the word fancy altogether. You have nothing to do with it. You are not to have, in any object of use or ornament what would be a contradiction in fact. You don't walk upon flowers in fact; you cannot be allowed to walk upon flowers in carpets. You don't find that foreign birds and butterflies come and perch upon your crockery. You never meet with quadrupeds going up and down walls; you must not have quadrupeds represented upon walls. You must use,' said the gentleman, 'for all these purposes, combinations and modifications (in primary colours) of mathematical figures which are susceptible of proof and demonstration. This is the new discovery. This is fact. This is taste. (Charles Dickens, *Hard Times*)

The municipal merchants of mass housing for the people planned homes *for* the people, not *with* them, they forced high-rise blocks, for example, on reluctant inhabitants. They knew people didn't like them, but they built them nonetheless.

The same assumption of the people's passivity shapes the way the revolutionary sects create a hierarchy of representation in their theory of the revolutionary party. At the top of the pyramid is a commando corps of leaders, clever young men born to rule. According to the Euro ultra-Leftist, Ernest Mandel, this Praetorian Guard has its relationship to the masses mediated by a middle strata of activists, those working-class militants who are the NCOs of the class war. And buried underneath are the slumbering masses who have a tendency, he says, to retreat into the long sleep of private life (no politics happens there!), waiting to be awakened, like Sleeping Beauty, by the handsome Prince, with a kiss of life to send them into heroic assaults on the enemy's fortifications. It is a structure that leaves no room for ordinary people who don't get their O levels, parents, people with period pains, bad backs and depression. It assumes the absence of the people from politics, it assumes that they are, to borrow Thomas Carlyle's words, a 'dull compendious mass'. This approach tends to reduce politics to propaganda, and its adherents are to be found hovering around the sacred ground of factory gates handing out tracts designed to cast the scales from the eyes of the stupified multitude by their Damascan revelations. It also takes its commandos as the models of humanity to which we should aspire. A contemporary of mine once said, self-critically, 'I used to think that what I was fighting was for people to have access to a good education, good housing, good books, to be fearless, to be like me, actually.'

In Britain, the ultra-Left has been demobilised, a victim of its courtship of the militant factory workers, and its ambition to woo them from the influence of the Communist Party in industry. Interestingly enough, their infatuation with the sacred bulls of the working class hastened their rejection of feminism. Then, in the late seventies and early eighties, many activists moved from the ultra-Left to the Labour Party, chastened by their experiences on the margins of Left life, and, no doubt, the Realpolitik of institutionalised politics. The state isn't like Buckingham Palace, after all, 'seizing state power' isn't just a matter of going over the wall. In the context of Thatcher's return in the election of 1983, it is clear that it is precisely among state employees and some councillors representing the local state that some of the effective opposition to the Right is to be found. One of the most arresting symbols of the transformation of the state that I have seen happened the last time I was unemployed – my case was courteously administered by a young black woman, the counter clerk in the dole office, who had a copy of her union journal *Red Tape* beside my claim form.

Whatever their differences, what unites most parties on the Left is their sense of themselves as fully completed subjects. Left parties still conduct politics *for* the party, they rarely see themselves as being transformed by the people with whom they struggle or by struggle itself. They see themselves as agents of change, not subjects of change. Consequently they are isolated from the working class, which is itself in the process of transformation. At best, they ratify the experience of protagonists outside the parties. The movements which have disrupted consensus in British politics during the eighties have not been the political parties, and the mainstream political institutions still fail either to represent those movements or to learn from their inventiveness. They still too often seek to mend their bridges with the Right.

Most importantly, the radicals within the working class I met were mostly women; they were the most reflective and imaginative, it was they who affirmed democratic ways of working, it was they who affirmed egalitarianism, it is they who are on the move, and it is they who are being transformed by their own experience of change. The men's movement seems not to have noticed. Orwell's socialism comes out of a tradition that hasn't and won't represent women. If the men's movement is to cooperate with these women, then it must look to itself and put the reform of men on its political agenda. That is the condition of women's creative cooperation with the men's movement.